MW01611461

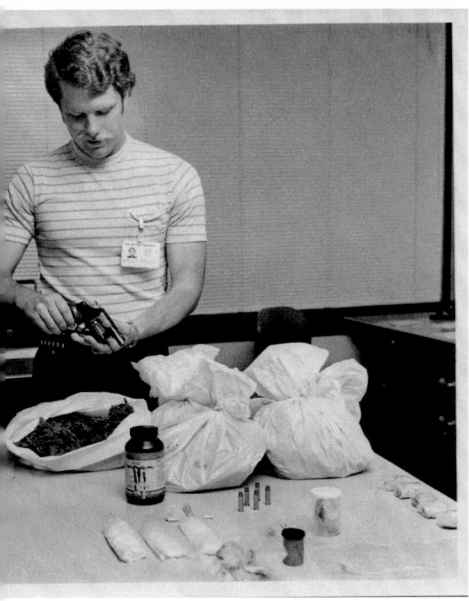

Young officer Ted Sumner with evidence from a narcotics bust.

Under cover officer Sumner (third from left) following a narcotics take down.

nder cover officer Sumner (right) with fellow officer who is reading a spect his rights following a narcotics arrest.

Selling At High Schools

DRUG RAIDS IN S.J.

SAN JOSE NEWS

Vol. 104, No. 115, 92nd Year   San Jose, Calif., Wed., June 4, 1975   128 Pages   ★   15 Cents

Classified — 289-7515   CIRCULATION — 289-9220   Other Depts. — 289-XXXX

24 Suspected Pushers Arrested

By MARK JOHNSON
Staff Writer

San Jose police conducted a series of simultaneous raids on residences throughout the city this morning, arresting at least 24 persons suspected of selling hard drugs and marijuana at local high schools.

The raids climaxed an intensive 2½ month undercover investigation into the high school drug scene which narcotics bureau Lt. Arnold Bertotti called "the first of its kind in this area."

Some 32 plainclothes officers in eight teams began the series of raids at 6 a.m., and planned to have everyone on the list of suspected pushers in jail by this afternoon.

Bertotti said the total num-

drugs, not just one or two types.

"The most common drugs are cocaine, PCP (crystal) and LSD," he said. "We found a couple of heroin pushers but on the basis of our experience so far I would say that the heroin problem in the high schools is relatively insignificant."

Bertotti said his agents spent most of their time on the high school campuses but did not enroll in any classes.

School officials were not notified that the officers were on campus and the officers also observed how

(Back of Section, Col. 1)

CIA Is Charged In Slaying Plots

By AL EISELE

WASHINGTON —The chairman of a Senate com-

ment in those assassination attempts.

"I have been concerned about the apparent attempt

tee on governmental intelligence gathering activities, said that both his committee and the commission headed

The high school drug raids begin to make headlines

DR. LEON FOX, chairman of Valley Medical Center's department of obstetrics and gynecology since 1959, is the hospital's "Man of the Century."   Page 7A

WITH 6,500 VOLUNTEER HOURS logged already, 78-year-old Ettel Kessler still is going strong, coddling and comforting the children confined to Alexian Brothers Hospital.   Page 1B

Sports

AS SUNS STAR KEITH ERICKSON put it, the Warriors played like a team picked to finish last and Phoenix played like champions. That was the story Sunday as the Suns beat the Warriors 94-86 to win the seventh and final game of the NBA West playoffs.   Page 1D

THE SAN JOSE EARTHQUAKES defeated the Vancouver Whitecaps 2-0 behind the outstanding play of George Sorgis, who scored both of the Quakes' goals. San Jose now owns a 4-3 record with 36 points, just four behind Southern Division leader Dallas.   Page 1D

REX BEAUCHAMP SLIPPED BY TEENAGER Jay Springsteen on the last lap to win Sunday's ninth running of the $21,000 San Jose Mile championship 25-mile final at the County Fairgrounds.   Page 3D

Section A	Section B	Section C
NEWS	LIVING	TODAY

Section D
SPORTS

JOE WEATHERMAN
WEATHER REPORT
FAIR AND WARMER

"Dr. John Bunzel, president of San Jose State University, is going to be the commencement speaker at the University of Santa Clara," Joe Weatherman said to Mrs. W. today. "The Spartans and Broncos have been unusual rivals, so that's kind of unusual."

"Well, who is going to act Christian if not the padres at Santa Clara?" the missus asked.

"I suppose you have something there," said Joe. "Anyway, Doc Bunzel is a good talker. He will give them a humdinger of a

Jose State's commencement," said Mrs. W.

"Maybe State is waiting for Santa Clara to get a woman president," said Joe. "Then if it asks her it will prove State is really broad-minded."

He wondered if that was too subtle for Mrs. W. as he added: "Santa Clara Valley: Fair and warmer through Tuesday with highs in the 70s and 80s; lows tonight in the upper 40s and low 50s; northerly winds to 20 miles per hour.

The Tass news agency said "prompt measures are being taken to eliminate the aftermath of the quake and to give relief to the quake victims."

The jolt had a force of 9 on the 12-point Soviet Medvedev scale.

In Washington, the U.S. Geological Survey reported the tremor reached 7.2 on the open-ended Richter scale, which would be "several times bigger than the Italian earthquake in terms of energy." A quake with a reading of 7

(Back of Section, Col. 1)

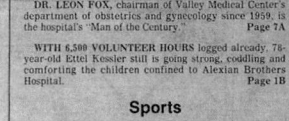

DENNY MATASCI and E. Davey Croackett flanked by wife BARBARA and children MUNDI and MIKE

Valley team vaults to frog title

By JIM DICKEY
Staff Writer

Santa Clara Valley's winningest frog jumping team has done it again.

It came home Sunday from the Calaveras County Jumping Frog Jubilee as sort of a triple crown winner of the "ribbit" realm.

E. Davey Croakett, entered by Denny Matasci, a 37-year-old dry wall installer of 1009 Blackfield Way, Mountain View, took the top

prize in the celebrated contest.

Davey set a world record in doing it. It leaped 20 feet, three inches and won $1,200 for the team.

Matasci is part of an 11-member team consisting of three families — The Matascis of Mountain View, the Guruleses of Santa Clara and the Gindtieses of Los Altos.

E. Davey Croakett was one of nine frogs that beat the 10-year-old record of 19 feet 3½ inches in

three consecutive leaps.

Matasci and his partners have been jumping frogs for about 10 years and call themselves the Eastridge Frog Jumping Team, named after the shopping center.

Matasci won the contest in 1972 with a female frog named Turly Locs, and another member of the team, Kaye Guzules, captured the prize in 1974 with E. Dynamic Denny.

Matasci said the team, which

consists of the three couples and their children, captures the frogs in the same place every year, a secret location in the San Joaquin Valley.

They return the jumpers to the same spot every year.

Asked if E. Davey Croakett, E. Dynamic Denny and Turly Locs might all be one and the same, Matasci said he was assured they

(Back of Section, Col. 1)

Kissinger 'prefers' to quit

United Press International

On the eve of the Michigan and Maryland primaries, Secretary of State Henry Kissinger said he would "prefer to leave" office in January even if President Ford is elected.

And Democratic front-runner Jimmy Carter won the endorsement of Jesse Unruh, the treasurer of California, whose governor was based at the Santa Clara Valley Methadone clinic on Bascom avenue, according to narcotics unit Lt. Arnold Bertotti.

Kissinger, interviewed on NBC's Today program, went further than ever before in stating his desire to finish out the year and leave his controversial post. While not absolutely ruling out service beyond the next inaugural, Kissinger said, "on the whole I would prefer to leave."

39 seized in S.J.'s biggest roundup of heroin dealers

By MALINE HAZLE
Staff Writer

San Jose Police have arrested 39 persons and are seeking 29 more in what the head of the narcotics unit has called the largest roundup of suspected heroin dealers in San Jose history.

A six-month undercover investigation which led to 68 Grand Jury indictments also has indicated that one group of suspected dealers was based at the Santa Clara Valley Methadone clinic on Bascom avenue, according to narcotics unit Lt. Arnold Bertotti.

Those arrested in widespread raids this morning and last week, Bertotti said, belonged to two loosely-knit heroin dealing networks concentrated in the east and west sides of the city.

The westside group, Bertotti said, was based at the Bascom av-

purchases made by undercover officers at the clinic and several others resulted from contacts made at the clinic. Bertotti said.

The arrests this morning and last week and those yet to be made all resulted from Grand Jury indictments. Sixty-two were for suspicion of sale of heroin, five for suspicion of sale of cocaine and one for suspicion of sale of PCP.

Although no large seizures of heroin were made in the raids, Bertotti said, many of those arrested allegedly were dealing several ounces of heroin a week. Heroin sells for approximately $450 an ounce, Bertotti said.

Twenty-one persons were arrested this morning in raids that began at 4 a.m. in 50 different places around the Valley. Bertotti said.

dercover agents were involved in the raids.

Warrants issued with the indictments were served on 18 persons last week, including 11 who al-

(Back of Section, Col. 2)

As the arrests grow, so does the press coverage

Dope Jettisoned in Wild S.J. Chase

'STREETS OF HEROIN'

Girl, 13, In Hell 181 Days

San Jose Mercury

More Than a Century of Service—1851-1976

FINAL

MAIN NUMBER 289-5000
CIRCULATION 289-5222

SAN JOSE, CALIFORNIA, WEDNESDAY MORNING, SEPTEMBER 8, 1976 ★ 15 cents

PORT MOODY, Canada (AP) — A Port Moody man was charged in British Columbia Provincial Court on Tuesday with kidnaping a 13-year-old girl, raping her and holding her captive in an underground bomb shelter for 181 days.

Charges of kidnaping, rape, gross indecency and abduction with intent to have sexual relations were filed against Donald Alexander Hay, 43.

Authorities said the girl, Abby Drover, was found Monday night, thinner by 10 to 15 pounds and dehydrated but otherwise in good condition. She was 12 years old at the time of her disappearance last March 10.

"She is having a tough time walking without assistance," the child's mother, Ruth Drover, said Tuesday. "Abby's going to need a lot of tender loving care right now."

Constable Wayne Smith of this (Back of Section, Col. 6)

Heroin Litters

Wife's Lover Guilty

Killing-for-Hire Verdict in S.J.

By JOE FREIN
Staff Writer

Richard Thomas "Bud" Zurcher, lover of the widow of slain San Jose realtor Floyd Argo, was found guilty Tuesday of first degree murder and conspiracy charges in the alleged hired kill...

Sumner's under cover work sends shock waves through San Jose, CA

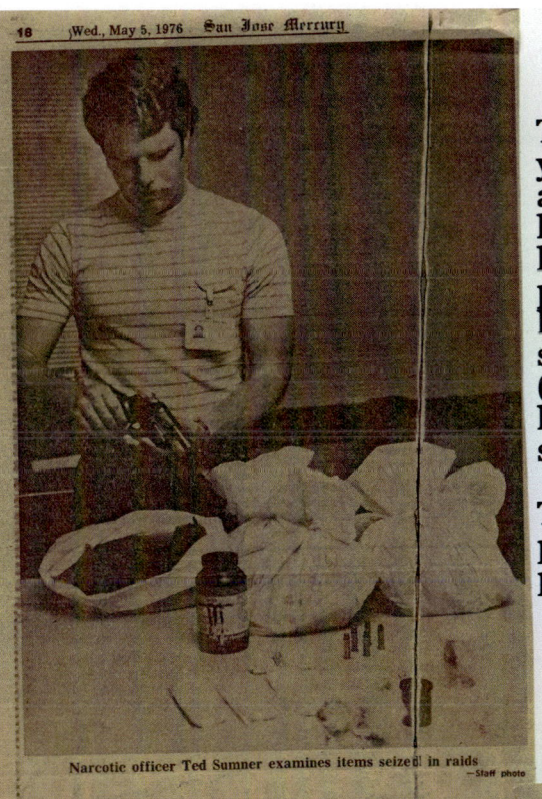

18 | Wed., May 5, 1976 | San Jose Mercury

Narcotic officer Ted Sumner examines items seized in raids
—Staff photo

Ted Sumner was young, fearless, and and accomplished a level of success that had never before been possible. The longer he worked, the more successful he became (and the longer his hair grew and the scruffier he looked).

The orriginal of this picture is shown on a previous page.

'Major Valley Drug Ring Broken'

Above: from Left to Right, Tim Bersick, Pat Coffey, A very young Kenpo Instructer Ted Sumner, Bill Yazel. Everyone is toasting Pat Coffey for his successful Shodan test.

In Later years:Prof. Kufferaths 8oth birthday Luau party. Pictured Above:ack Row L-R Joe Halbuna , Bob Maschmeier , Hans Ingrebresen, Sig Kufferath , Dale Kahone ,(Unknown) .
Bottom Row L-R **Ted Sumner**, Richard Bunch , Russ Rhodes

Photo from Prof. Kufferaths 8oth birthday. Pictured (from Left to Right) James Moro (8th Dan Goshin Chow Hoon Kenpo Jujitsu) , Sig Kufferath (10th Dan Dan Zan Ryu Jujitsu) , **Ted Sumner (8th Dan Tracys Kenpo)**

Current Picture: L- Ted Sumner 9th Degree Black Belt R- Jeff Speakman Head of Kenpo 5.0 System

Ted with the love of his life, his wife Suzanne, on a Carribean cruis

Young officer Sumner's son Geoff standing in front of Him. Ted's sister's son Tim, and Ted Sumner's mother. Look closely you can see the splint and bangage on Ted's right hand. This was where he was wounded in a shoot out with a mob hit man early in his career. This was shortly before he was asked to go undercover.

A young officer Sumner with his children

Ted and Suzanne on their wedding day, with Ted's daughter Alanna and son Geoff.

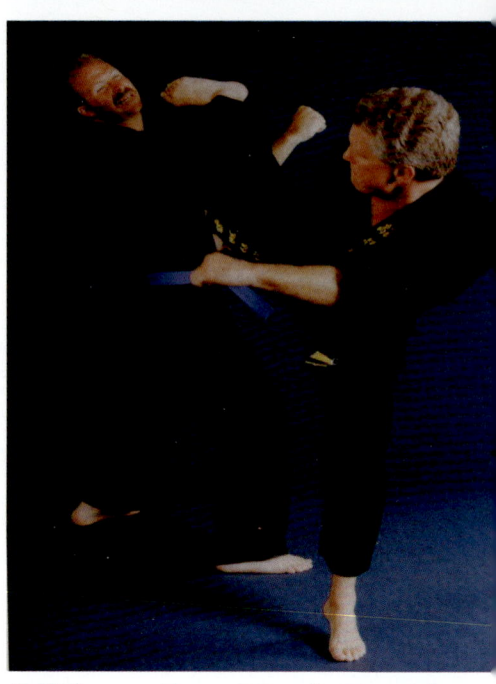

Taking our wedding vows before the Police Chaplin.

With student Mark Huggins.

Taken at Heminway's House on Key West. Ted and his bride taking a bit of inspiration from his favorite author.

DEEP COVER COP

DEEP COVER COP

TED SUMNER &
MILLS CRENSHAW

Limited First Edition

INTRODUCTION

S an Jose is a city located in Northern California fifty miles south of San Francisco. While San Jose is often regarded as a "bedroom community" it has grown from a farming environment to become the heart of the high tech "Silicon Valley." The metropolitan "Bay Area" is a homogenous metropolis of approximately ten million souls. The Bay Area is comprised of the North Bay, the East Bay, South Bay and the Peninsula with a large body of water, the San Francisco Bay directly in the middle. San Jose lies at the hub of this urban center connecting the South Bay to the peninsula and East Bay—a teeming multicultural melting pot with close economic, cultural and kindred ties to both the Orient and Latin America.

In the South Bay, San Jose's posh, urbane modernity comes to an abrupt end at the redwood forest separating her from the Pacific coast. Within the dense primeval woods between San Jose and ocean is a wilderness of giant woodlands and lush undergrowth teeming with wildlife, antediluvian flora and dopers. Hidden in the forest's remote density, away from the watchful eyes of the San Jose Police Department, drug users, suppliers and manufacturers thrive in an environment of virtual nihilistic lawlessness.

Because of its location and diverse denizens San Jose has become the gateway for the distribution of the illicit heroin and cocaine from Mexico and South America, for the opiates and hashish from the Orient and for the hallucinogenics and stimulants produced by the local chemists who populate the secluded forests of the coast mountain range.

It was into this invisible underworld of iniquitous depraved criminality that a young San Jose Police Officer was immersed in a first ever attempt to identify, infiltrate and build prosecutable criminal cases against the facilitators and promoters of the industry of illegal drug distribution. Sumner looked like a naive, fresh faced kid; a fact that aided his descent into the Northern California high school drug culture. Unlike Audie Murphy who lied about his age and subsequently became a warrior, Sumner was a battle-hardened veteran, much older and wiser than his very youthful appearance.

It was during these investigations that undercover officer Ted Sumner walked through the dark, demonic world of outlaw drug addicts and pushers, befriending and trafficking with criminals from the street level dealer to the kingpins of syndicates with international connections. Working alone and unaided in a capacity of deep undercover, Sumner faded into the shadowy purgatory of drugs and crime, meticulously building case after case that brought to justice hundreds of dealers and wrecked and dismantled dozens of narcotic distribution organizations.

It has been stated that police work is comprised of days and months of tedious routine interspersed with moments of stark terror. Sumner's career was anything but routine. Real life police work is sometimes messy and often repetitive. There are no neat story lines that lead from episode to episode. There are only the realities of dealing with the never ending challenges presented by that most dangerous of predators, the human criminal.

Everything you are about to read is factual. Only the names have been changed to protect those who might be compromised or endangered by such disclosure. It really happened in just this way.

BOOK I

THE ROAD TO UNDER COVER

CHAPTER 1

Sumner woke up feeling groggy and a little thick headed. He had been in court the previous two days and was functioning on three hours of sleep a night. After getting off swing shift at 3:00 AM, he had to be in court at 9:00 AM. He would rather have stayed in bed to log a little more sack time, but he had already missed one workout this week and did not want to skip another. He dressed in his workout gear and headed for the Fitness Center Health Club. It was Thursday, and that meant all the competitive body builders would be in for their workout. *Training around those guys,* Ted observed, *is always great motivation.* The core of the bodybuilders' population was a group of garbage men— sanitation engineers whose lives revolved around training and competing in body building contests.

§

"Hey, Sumner, can I ask you a question?" The question came from Ed "Candy Ass" Candeleria, a mountain of a man who looked to be chiseled out of stone.

"Let me see," Sumner pondered looking at the ceiling knowing full well that it would be a smart ass question …"Sure."

"How come you and Doc train harder than anyone else around here and after years of work you still look the same?" Doc was a dentist and

Sumner's regular workout partner. Candeleria wasn't curious; it was just his lame attempt to needle Sumner. The fact that Sumner and Doc did not engage in the use of steroids, coupled with their strict cardio regimen that centered on running, resulted in both of them developing long, lean, tough muscle that contributed to martial arts effectiveness and not the extreme bulk sought by most of the serious lifters at the Fitness Center. A result they were only able to achieve with the aid of anabolic steroids.

"Well, it all has to do with the fact that being real men, Sumner sneered, we do not possess the homosexual hormones that all of you do in such abundance." Doc snorted in his attempt to stifle a laugh. "That and the fact that we do not engage in the gay life style that you so embrace." Candy ass stared blankly at Sumner and nodded his head ever so slightly. *He has no idea what I just said.*

"So what's been happening out on the streets?" ask Eddie Alvarez, a sanitation engineer with a physique like Hercules.

"Stopped a car loaded with six teenaged kids last night," Sumner explained. "A fifteen-year-old in the backseat started eating all the marijuana in the car and wound up choking to death." Sumner picked up the ninety pound dumbbells and climbed onto the inclined bench.

"Yeah, when I was a kid and cops pulled us over, we used to eat everything in the car," announced Candy ass.

"But all you ever had in the car was pussy," Doc offered quietly. Sumner struggled to control his laughter and the dumbbells, but finally dropped the weights on the pads next to the bench as he and everyone else in the weight room erupted in laughter.

They completed their workout at 1:30 PM on the dot, as Doc announced, "I got one in the chair," referring to his dental practice.

"See you Saturday," Doc called to Sumner as they crossed the parking lot.

§

"Sumner," called out the watch commander conducting roll call for the swing shift.

"Here, sir."

"6102," he announced indicating that Sumner would be the swing car in District 1, downtown, working beat 2, which was the west side of central downtown. The district Sumner normally worked was on an overlap with the other district team and it was Sumner's teams turn to work "in the hole." "In the hole" indicates that rather than working their regular assigned beat, those officers would be dispersed throughout the city to fill beats left empty due to officer illness, vacation, and military leave. Sumner had worked Beat 2 on midnight shift several years before and was familiar with the "hot" spots, the most troublesome of which was a stretch of Buena Vista Blvd south of West San Carlos Street. South Buena Vista Blvd was lined with clusters of small bungalows owned by the State and used to house ex-convicts recently released from prison during their rehabilitation back into society. The problem is that many of them came out of prison more violent and less civilized than they were when they entered. *It's a cool evening. Maybe everyone will stay inside tonight.*

§

Floyd Cominsky boarded the flight to San Jose at 9:05 AM Thursday morning. His American Airlines flight would take him from Detroit to Dallas and then on to San Jose. He had sent his "tool kit" ahead by UPS listing it as "machine parts." It was to be delivered by 10:00 AM to Giacoloni's Auto Body shop on Sunol Ave where it would be delivered into the custody of Tony Giacoloni until it would be retrieved by Floyd, sometime around 5:00 PM. His tool of choice was a Ruger .22 Caliber semiautomatic pistol that fired full jacketed long rifle rounds. Floyd's business was death, and he was on his way to San Jose to perform a job for which he had been hired by local "businessmen"...mobsters engaged in what could only be characterized as a "hostile takeover" of certain business concerns.

CHAPTER 2

Sumner, along with the rest of the swing shift officers, exited the basement door of the Police Administration Building, where the Patrol Division was housed, and stepped into the cool misty November evening air. They headed across the parking lot toward the police garage to claim their assigned vehicle for the evenings work. Each officer would then drive around the garage to the locker room where they would gather their gear.

Sumner placed his duffle bag, containing extra handcuffs, ammunition, 42 inch "boken" (wooden, Japanese practice sword), blankets, and other possible necessities, in the trunk of the police vehicle. He then removed five 12 gauge double 00 buck shotgun rounds and loaded his police Winchester pump shotgun. Locking it into the gun rack in the front seat of his vehicle, he proceeded to conduct the required vehicle safety inspection of his patrol car before proceeding to his beat.

"Where you working?" called Roy Barlow as he walked his K-9, a 110 lb. German Shepherd named Roscoe, into the backseat of his vehicle.

"2," Sumner replied.

"Let's get together for a cup later."

"Sounds good."

Sumner started his vehicle and proceeded out onto the street. "6102, 10-8," Sumner spoke into his microphone.

"6102…10-4," spoke the dispatcher haltingly. *Rookie dispatcher on district one, Sumner noted.*

§

Floyd Cominsky stepped off the plane and proceeded to the car rental area at the San Jose International Airport. He chose Avis Car Rental and stepped up to the counter. Cominsky requested a compact vehicle and produced cash and an Illinois driver's license that identified him as Thomas McMahon, a resident of Chicago. Cominsky signed the rental agreement initialing each of the boxes requesting additional insurance. "You can't be too careful," he said to the smiling clerk.

Cominsky was directed to the parking lot containing the rental cars where he took possession of a two-year-old Ford Maverick. He checked his map and determined his route. He would take the back streets around the airport and down Coleman Ave to where Sunol Ave. crosses Auzerais and where Giacoloni Auto Body is located.

Upon arrival at the body shop, Cominsky proceeded to the counter where he handed a business card to the middle aged woman talking on the phone. She glanced down at the card as she continued talking. "Mazetti World Wide Shipping," she froze for a moment. "I'll have to call you back," she hung up the phone and hurried to the shop where she handed the card to Tony Giacoloni. Although she didn't know exactly what the card meant, she'd been working with Mr. Giacoloni long enough to know not to ask any questions.

Giacoloni walked to a locked cabinet and spun the combination lock. He removed a plain brown paper wrapped package from the top shelf and proceeded into the office. "Mr. Haskell?" asked Giacoloni.

"No, no," corrected Cominsky. "Mr. Osborne."

Giacoloni smiled and handed over the package. The correct response had been given and returned. His involvement in this matter, whatever the matter might be, was concluded.

Cominsky returned to his vehicle and drove to the parking lot of Angelo's Restaurant on The Alameda at Race St. He was now just down the street from his target location. There he opened the package and removed his "tool kit". The corners of his mouth twitched upward in a grimace that no rational person could interpret as a smile. He was anticipating the kill.

CHAPTER 3

Sumner cruised along West San Carlos Street approaching Meridian Ave. On the left was Sears, the earlier site of the Old O'Conner Hospital where he had been born in 1950. Crossing Meridian on the right, kitty corner from Sears was The Tracy's Kenpo Karate School, where Sumner had studied and taught the martial art of Kenpo for many years. *A lot of scars and bruises were received over the years at that school,* he thought…but *oh, the great memories. OK Sumner, FOCUS! Enough with the stroll down memory lane, time to get to work.*

He continued westbound on West San Carlos St. and headed toward South Buena Vista Ave. *Better get a good look at that place before it gets too dark.*

He turned left onto Buena Vista and made mental notes of the vehicles parked on the street and in the driveways as well as the disposition of the residences, trees, and assorted paraphernalia strewn about the landscape of the dilapidating bungalows. A tall skinny WMA (white male adult) covered with prison tattoos stood on the sidewalk, glaring menacingly at the passing police car.

Sumner suddenly applied the brakes bringing the vehicle to an abrupt halt. He was out the door as the police car skidded to a stop. He grabbed his nightstick as he started toward the tattooed subject, who quickly turned on his heels and headed for the door of the nearest bungalow.

"Hey, Holmes," Sumner called. "Hold up there."

"Me, what for?" asked the incredulous man. "I ain't done shit." He continued toward the door.

"Because I said so, asshole," boomed Sumner's stentorian baritone voice. Polite behavior and proper public relations has no effect on ex-convicts.

The subject stopped and turned to face the smiling Officer Sumner. "You live here?" Sumner asked.

"Yeah, I live here," replied the man.

"What's your name?"

"Robert Jones," came the snide reply.

"You got some ID that verifies all that?"

"No, man, I lost my wallet."

"Put your hands behind your head and interlace your fingers," Sumner ordered.

"What for, man?!"

"Because I said so," replied Sumner, tapping the man's left arm with his nightstick.

The subject complied, and Sumner proceeded to conduct a pat down search of the man's person.

"Hey, I found your wallet," Sumner joked, as he removed the wallet from the subject's back pocket. He then opened the wallet and removed the man's identification. *California ID card. No driver's license. Must have a problem with alcohol or drugs or both.*

"How long you been out?" Sumner asked.

"I'm no con," the reply was indignant.

"Your name's not Robert Jones either—Jesse James Black."

"Two weeks."

"What were you in for?"

"Non support." The sarcastic reply was a stock answer given by most ex-cons.

"Let's go take a look at your room," ordered Sumner.

"What for man?"

"So I can report to your PO that you are behaving yourself and cooperating with the police." Sumner took Black by the arm and headed to the front door of the bungalow that he had indicated to be his residence.

"All right, all right," protested Jesse James. "I don't live there. I live at the Terry Hotel." The Terry Hotel, two miles further east on San Carlos Street, was also used by the State to house parolees.

Sumner removed his handcuffs and placed them on Black.

"Whoa, what the hell is going on here?" Black said.

Sumner then proceeded to conduct a thorough search of Jesse's person. In the sock of his right leg, Sumner retrieved two bindles of white powder. From the looks of Jesses James Black, Sumner guessed it was probably meth-amphetamine, speed.

"So, Jesse…you here selling or buying?"

"I don't know what you're talking about, man. I don't know where that shit came from."

Sumner placed Black in the backseat of his patrol car and proceeded to PAB prisoner processing where he made positive identification of Jesse James Black, as well as the name of his Parole Officer, who was contacted by phone. He requested that Sumner book the subject on the appropriate charges and asked that he inform the Deputies working the Main Jail that Snyder would be placing a parole hold on Black and that he would not be eligible for bail.

Sumner booked the evidence and placed it in the locker for substances that required analysis by the County Crime Lab. He then walked Black over the Main Jail Booking area where he was to be processed.

§

Back on patrol Sumner called in to let dispatch know he was in service. All and all it was a good start for the night. When Sumner came on the San Jose Police Department as a rookie, the Chief of the Uniformed Division, one E. Dale McKay, had a standing policy for the officers under his command that began when McKay was a mere Patrol Sergeant. McKay wanted two, two, and two from each officer on each and every shift. That is two felony arrests, two misdemeanor arrests, and two moving violations cited. Though it was unrealistic to expect that of each officer on every shift, it became, nonetheless, the yardstick by which excellent police work was measured at the San Jose PD. Sumner had already made two felony arrests that evening…technically. The one bust had yielded a felony possession of a controlled substance arrest, as well as the arrest of a parole violator. Though E. Dale McKay would never have acknowledged arrest of a parole violator as a true felony arrest, it was still a felony to be in violation of one's parole. Now he was watching for the moving violations and possible misdemeanors. Yes, not a bad start at all.

§

Cominsky parked his rented vehicle on the dark street several blocks behind the Auto Dealership. He then placed his "tool" under his jacket and walked over to the dealership showroom. As he walked across the lot full of new cars, he noted the area designated for employee parking and made special note of one particular vehicle.

Cominsky was a killer, predator. He was a master at hiding in plain sight. He was average height, no distinguishing features, his "working" clothing were off the rack, J C Penny's Middle America. The kidskin driving gloves he wore were flesh toned; and even the colors of the clothes he chose were nondescript. In a crowd, he was the invisible man.

A salesman approached and proceeded to fire questions asking Cominsky about his particular vehicular wants, needs, and desires. Cominsky was polite, but not engaging. He strolled around the showroom looking at the various new cars on display; but at the same time he kept an attentive eye on the executive offices.

At a little after 6:30 PM, the object of Cominsky's interest ambled down the hallway from the executive offices past the sales staff offices where he slowed to greet and offer words of encouragement to several of the young sales people who would be working the evening shift. A fit and always nattily attired man in his mid-thirties, the general manager of the dealership was an astute businessman and marketing expert who was popular with his employees as well as with the owners of the business. Since his taking the helm of this dealership, it had set sales records that were the envy of the industry. He headed out the showroom door toward the employee parking lot…followed stealthily by Cominsky.

CHAPTER 4

The GM reached his vehicle and unlocked the door. He climbed into the driver's seat, placed the key into the ignition and started the car. He reached for the gear shift to put vehicle into reverse as the driver door opened suddenly. Before the GM could unravel his confusion, Floyd Cominsky, with lightning precision placed the barrel of his "tool," the .22 caliber pistol, behind the GM's ear and pulled the trigger, discharging one round. The .22 long rifle bullet crashed through the handsome young GM's skull and tore into his brain killing him instantly. Cominsky felt no anger, no remorse; just pride in his skill.

Cominsky, with cool professionalism, quickly pushed the body onto the passenger side floorboard and climbed into the driver seat. He checked all points of the compass and then drove off the lot onto the Boulevard in a westbound direction. Two blocks down the street, he made a right turn and drove another two blocks where he made another right turn onto a darkened side street where he pulled up and stopped directly behind his parked rental car. He exited the vehicle, carefully locked the doors, and then flung the keys onto the roof of the abandon building in front of which he was parked. He checked his watch. 6:42 PM, plenty of time to make his 7:40 flight home. *I'll be half way to Denver before cops ever find this stiff.* He started his rental car and drove eastbound another two blocks to where he turned right and then right again onto the Boulevard where he proceeded to drive at a leisurely pace past the car dealership. He simply could not resist returning to the scene of the crime. As he rolled past the front of the dealership, he detected no unusual activity. *Business as usual… damn, I really am the best.*

Cominsky continued to watch the comings and goings occurring at the dealership as he proceeded well past the location, nearly straying out of his lane and into a parked vehicle. Startled by the near collision, he settled into the task of navigating his way back to the air port.

At the intersection with Race St. where the broad avenues of The Alameda turn to the north, he became somewhat disoriented. He had turned onto backstreets and they did not look familiar. *Need to get back to Auzerais and Sunol.* He turned left onto Race St. and proceeded south. At Park Ave. he turned left. *This is beginning to look familiar.* When he reached Bird Ave. he turned south but quickly realized he had made a mistake. He immediately executed a U-turn and proceeded north on Bird to where it splits into north and southbound one way streets, the northbound becoming Autumn Ave. Suddenly the red lights of a police car filled his vehicle. He looked into his rearview mirror and saw the patrol car directly behind him. There was no mistaking the situation, the officer intended to stop him. "Damn," he hissed at himself as he pulled to the right side of the street and stopped. There was no fear, just annoyance. After all, he was a pro—a master of life and death. He knew he was in control of the situation, so he made a decision to just play it cool.

§

Whoaaa! Sumner swerved to the right to avoid collision with the tan Ford Maverick conducting a wild, and illegal, U-turn across Bird Ave. *Got my two felonies, looks like I get my first mover,* he automatically tallied his night's work.

Now Sumner was about to write his first moving violation of the evening in his neverending effort to live up to the expectations of his former commander.

Sumner slipped in behind the Maverick as he noticed the Avis Rental Car sticker on the bumper as well as the Avis license plate frame. *Some out of Towner probably lost or disoriented. Time to get my public relations work out of the way for the evening.* Sumner keyed his mic "6102, 1195."

"6102...10-4," it was the halting voice of the rookie dispatcher. "1020?" Meaning what is your location.

"Autumn and Park," replied Sumner as he engaged his forward red lights and flashed his spotlight across the vehicle.

"Autumn and Park, 10-4."

As the Maverick slowed to a stop at the curb on Autumn Ave. just south of the intersection with Park Ave., Sumner pulled up behind and put his police vehicle into park. His "potential threat level" evaluation was low and he was feeling gratified that he would be able to assist a citizen in need, possibly someone from out of town. He had been trained to understand that in a contact such as this he would be representing the entire City of San Jose. As he exited the police vehicle, he did not bother to remove his nightstick from its holder on the door of the car. After all, he was anticipating an amicable and brief encounter. He stepped out to greet the "Citizen."

§

Cominsky watched in his rearview mirror, as the cop exited his patrol car. *Hell, he's just a kid,* he thought, *and look at that shinny new star on his chest.* He automatically shifted into predator mode. He glanced around the area looking for witnesses—none. He went through his own risk profile thought process, *what if he radioed my license plate? ...Rented with phony I.D.—no risk. OK, I'm going to end this right now and have a little fun with this bumpkin.* Then he slid his hand across the seat and grabbed his "tool kit."

§

As the door to Sumner's patrol car closed, Sumner noticed that the door to the Maverick had opened slightly. The driver was shining something at Sumner but he could not determine precisely what. He briefly registered a small pin point or dot of red light. Sumner unconsciously noticed that it was shining on his badge. *Something's not right.*

CRACK, the driver's pistol erupted sending lead, flame, and smoke from the barrel of his gun. Sumner detected the muzzle flash at the same instant the bullet struck his badge followed by the eardrum crushing explosion. The impact sent him reeling, and he fell on his back, facing his assailant. Dazed, he reached for his service revolver just as another explosion burst from the shooter's pistol, this time striking Sumner just below the middle knuckle of his right index finger. *My trigger finger…damn that hurts.* With the shock and pain, the world seemed to shift into slow motion. As Sumner cleared the holster with his Colt Python 357 Mangum, the assailant's weapon fired once more sending a bullet that struck the forward site of Sumner's pistol just as it cleared the holster. *It's now or I'm dead,* Sumner realized as he finally became operational. His Magnum answered the attack with a massive explosion that bespoke the power of the weapon. But the shot was high, wide, and to the assailant's right. *Damn, he's going to fire again,* Sumner raged as he struggled against the molasses of time. He moved with all the speed he could muster to get off another round. Though everything seemed to be happening in slow motion, Sumner was moving with incredible speed. His Magnum roared again and this round found its mark striking his tormentor in the right shoulder. *He's down, but not out,* Sumner realized, as the injured predator staggered but kept his feet as he brought his weapon to bear yet again. But it was too late for this would-be cop killer. Sumner had found the mark. Four more shots in rapid succession ripped from the barrel of the 357. All four struck the attacker in the abdomen. The hollow point bullets entered his intestinal track where the soft lead exploded and the copper jacket contorted into lethal shrapnel, ripping his stomach and innards into a mangled coagulation of obliterated flesh, blood, and feces. The assailant staggered forward two steps, and then fell to the ground face down.

Sumner staggered to his feet and moved quickly forward, turning the suspect onto his back and grabbed the pistol from the hand of his would be killer. The assailant's eyes demonstrated that he was still alive. *Not taking any chances with this guy.* Sumner rolled him back onto his stomach and cuffed his hands behind his back. He then patted the suspect down, removing his wallet. He checked the wallet for any form of identification— Thomas *McMahon from Chicago. I wonder what his beef with me was all about?*

Sumner left McMahon/Cominsky lying in the street between the two cars as he walked shakily, back to his patrol vehicle. "Control, 6102."

"6102 go ahead."

"Control, dispatch an ambulance code three to my 1020, suspect down with multiple gunshot wounds," Sumner advised.

"6102, affirmative," the quick, sharp voice in response was suddenly a much more efficient dispatcher.

"6102, do you require assistance?" the senior dispatcher asked, taking charge of the situation.

"Affirmative," Sumner responded. "Please dispatch 6100 (the district sergeant) to my 20. And notify the night dicks of an officer involved shooting."

"10-4," replied the senior dispatcher.

"6100 in route, code three. "

"6100 thirty seconds away…hang on buddy," came the concerned and reassuring voice of the senior dispatcher Weird Ralph, a veteran dispatcher for the SJPD and a personal friend of Sumner's.

"It's code 4 (situation under control) at the scene," Sumner advised. "Have 6100 reduce response to code 2." *It won't help to have the district sergeant stack up his car on the way.*

"10-4, 6100?"

"6100, 10-4," The ever calm and always in control voice of Sergeant Dominic Dayton. Sergeant Dayton was a Viet Nam veteran and had served as a Los Angeles City Police Officer during the 1962 Watts riots. Sgt. Dayton had figured prominently in Robert E. Conot's bestselling book recounting the riots, titled *Rivers of Blood, Years of Darkness* in which Conot identified Dayton as having personally dispatched several rioters with his service revolver. Dayton had subsequently been acquitted of any wrong doing in the incident by both an LAPD Shooting Board the Inspector General of the California National Guard.

6105 skidded to a stop in the lane next to Sumner's patrol car. Spotting the body lying in the lane between the two vehicles, Officer Frank Santos positioned his cruiser to block traffic in that lane and engaged his flashing lights to warn oncoming traffic. He ran to Sumner who was standing on the sidewalk.

"What the hell happened, any other suspects, is everything secure?!"

"Everything is secure," Sumner replied. "I'm just trying to figure out why the hell this all happened."

6100 arrived just as the ambulance was pulling up. Santos directed the ambulance in behind his vehicle and advised the EMTs that they had a gunshot wound and a badly bleeding subject. The EMTs immediately went to work with an efficiency and professionalism that belied the slight regard with which they were held in the medical community.

Sergeant Dayton stepped up on the curb looking at Sumner with smirk on his face that could only be appreciated by other men who have looked into the face of death with its sinister smile…and answered back with the correct response. There was something about merely being in the presence of a man like Sergeant Dayton that made one want to be their best. To be accepted as an equal by Dayton always made Sumner feel like a man with whom to be reckoned.

"That hand looks nasty," Dayton said, calmly jutting his chin at Sumner's right hand.

"That'll keep for the moment," Sumner replied.

Dayton smiled broadly. "How does it feel?"

"It feels like I don't know what the hell just happened," Sumner replied. "He had some sort of red light on his gun; it was weird— like a small dot. What the hell do you think that was all about?"

"Where's the gun?"

Sumner handed the suspect's pistol to the Sergeant. Dayton inspected the weapon meticulously. "I'll be damned."

"What? What the hell is it?"

"He has a laser mounted on the barrel," Dayton instructed. "Apparently he was using it to sight the weapon. Wherever the red dot shines is where the bullet strikes."

"I've never heard of any shit like that."

"The military has been working on it for years," Dayton explained. "But this is the first time I've ever heard of any civilian having something like this."

"I just stopped him for making and illegal U-turn that nearly slammed into me," Sumner explained. "I saw the rental car stickers and figured he was lost tourist. I was just going to give him directions when he opened up on me."

Dayton stood silent in deep contemplation for several moments. "There's a hell of a lot more to this than appears on the surface."

"What are you thinking?"

"I'm thinking that we need to black this thing out as best we can until the dick bureau can unravel the whole thing." Sergeant Dayton looked over at the suspect who had been deposited onto a gurney and was being loaded into the ambulance and with all the sensitivity of a Mafia hit man, he yelled, "Don't you die, asshole. We need to have a talk with you."

"You want a ride to the hospital in the ambulance?" Dayton asked.

"No, I'll drive myself."

"Like hell you will. Your vehicle is part of the crime scene and I'm obligated under departmental regulations to take possession of your firearm," he advised. "And like it or not you are going to receive medical treatment. Dammit, you have a gunshot wound!"

"Yeah, OK. If I am going to be unarmed, send someone else to guard this prick. You can drive me to the hospital."

§

The Crime Scene Unit arrived and immediately began taping off the area. Sergeant James Guido stepped up to Sumner holding open a clear plastic bag. "Drop it in," he ordered Sumner who dutifully placed his service revolver in the evidence bag. "How many shots discharged by you?"

"Six."

"Six?! Are they all accounted for?"

"Five are still in his body; my first shot went high and wide to the left."

Sumner proceed to explain how the situation had unfolded, step by step meticulously walking through the entire incident, demonstrating where he had been and what he did the while likewise explaining the actions of the suspect.

"That hand looks nasty," observed Guido. "You better get some medical attention."

"That can wait for right now, you need this information if you're going to be able to reconstruct this thing."

"How many did he fire?"

"Three…they all hit me."

"I see your hand. Was that the first shot?"

"The first shot hit my badge."

"The hell you say! Let me see," ordered Guido igniting his flashlight. Guido looked closely at the crumpled badge, then shined the flashlight at an angle. "It looks like the round careened off your badge, broke up and several pieces penetrated your clothing." "Unbutton your shirt and let's have a look."

Sumner unbuttoned his uniform shirt and pulled it open. Sergeant Guido stared in dismay. He then turned to Sergeant Dayton. "This man's injured. You better get him to the hospital."

"OK, that's it, let's go," ordered Sergeant Dayton, his patience with Sumner at an end.

"You got everything you need here?" Sumner asked.

"We're set," replied Guido looking up from where he was huddled with the Crime Scene Unit and Night Detectives.

CHAPTER 5

Sergeant Dayton drove Sumner to the Santa Clara Valley Medical Center where Sumner received treatment from the emergency room physician on duty. "You're lucky to still have that finger. It got hit hard," advised the doctor. "It's going to be really sore for a while."

Officer Pete Kendall entered the emergency room stall where Sumner lay squirming in discomfort as his wounded right hand wound was being irrigated with a saline solution. Kendall had taken custody of the suspect at the scene and ridden to the hospital with him in the ambulance.

"Your buddy is in surgery," advised Kendall. "The Deputies in charge of the patient prisoners have taken custody of him. Here are your handcuffs. They're holding him as a John Doe". "We need to make ID as soon as possible, and I need your booking sheet to take over to the jail so they can complete the processing. Sergeant Burroughs from Homicide is sending over an affidavit for setting of bail."

Sumner and Dayton looked at each other quizzically. *Why the hell would Homicide be requesting setting of bail? This is getting more interesting by the moment.*

"Dom, what do you think is going on?" Sumner inquired in curious bewilderment.

"I don't know; let me make a few phone calls."

Sumner flinched as the physician began picking tiny pieces of bullet fragment from beneath the skin on his chest. "There, the rest will work their way to the surface over time," he advised, placing band aids over the half dozen wound sites. He then proceeded to stitch and bandage Sumner's right hand.

Sergeant Dayton reentered the treatment room and stood by silently until the attending physician finished his treatment of Sumner. Dayton sat down on the gurney as the doctor departed and moved in close, speaking in hushed tones.

"They found a body over on Julian Street, looks like the same caliber, maybe the same weapon used by your suspect. Burroughs has taken over the investigation and ordered complete news blackout until we get things sorted out. If reporters show up here, you do not say a thing."

Sergeant Burroughs— a brilliant homicide detective. I played football with his son in high school— a bruiser, just like his father. "The news people have to know something happened, they monitor our radios all the time."

"Yeah, the dicks have got a big mess over at your crime scene with reporters all over the place. But they don't know the details and Homicide doesn't want them, or anybody else without a need to know to be told anything, anything at all."

"Do they have my name?" Sumner was suddenly concerned that his wife might hear something before he could talk to her.

"I don't think so," advised Dayton rather unreassuringly.

"I've finished my notes," advised Sumner. "I'm going to dictate this report; I don't think I'm up to writing it."

He got dressed and preceded to the pay phone in the lobby of the emergency room. He phoned home where his wife answered. She had been dosing on the sofa in front of the television after putting the children to bed. He explained that he had been involved in an arrest and had sustained a slight injury to his right hand and was at the hospital. He said that he was done at the hospital and would be returning to PAB to complete his reports and would then be heading home and might be a little late.

"Let's go," called Dayton, grabbing Sumner by the arm as he exited the phone booth. They proceeded to PAB where Sumner used the phone in the Patrol Division Report writing room and called up to transcribing.

"Wanda Brookes, please," Sumner asked politely. Wanda had been Sumner's neighbor when he was growing up. Her son and daughter had attended high school with him.

"Wanda Brookes," her cheerful voice answered on the other end of the line.

"Wanda? Ted."

"Ted! Are you all right?! I heard about the shooting!" She was frantic and began to sob.

"Hey, I'm fine," Sumner assured. "This is important. I'm going to dictate the report right now and I need you to transcribe it for me."

"Yes, yes of course, no problem." She was still unnerved.

"Wanda, you can't let anyone see this report and you can't talk to anyone about what's in it."

"No, no problem, I'll take care of it."

"Wanda, this is important, you need to personally deliver the report to Sergeant Burroughs. He's in charge of this investigation. Can you do this for me?"

"Yes, yes, oh my god I'm so glad you're all right." She began to weep openly.

Recalling that Wanda's husband had been killed in an industrial accident several years earlier, Sumner was sympathetic to her emotional response.

"Wanda, I'm ok. I'll come by tomorrow and we can have coffee and I'll tell you all about it, but I need you to promise me you will not let this report out of your hands until it gets to Burroughs."

"I understand," she assured, her voice still quivering. "I understand."

He hung up, then called into the transcription center and dictated his report. The Novocain was wearing off and his right hand was beginning to throb. He walked down the hall to the elevator and rode up to the third floor where the Detective Bureau was housed. He entered the Homicide which was now a buzz with activity. He found Sergeant Burroughs who was engaged in collaboration with several other detectives.

Burroughs looked up and spotted Sumner. A broad smile crossed his face as he stepped forward. "How you doing—are you all right?" He took

Sumner by the arm and led him into the Lieutenant's office. Though he was not the commander of the Homicide Unit, his stature as the most successful homicide detective in SJPD history and the solver of several of the most high profile murders in America, afforded him certain status. "You really stirred up a hornet's nest here."

"I dictated my report, Sumner explained. "Wanda Brookes will transcribe it and she has strict orders to bring the original directly to you."

"Excellent; thanks, kid."

"So what the hell is going on with all this?" Sumner asked.

"We believe that the murder of the general manager of the car dealership and this assault on you are related," Burroughs explained. "We are still trying to get a positive ID on this guy but this looks like mob activity."

"Mob activity?! I was just trying to help a motorist who looked lost."

"All indications are that the trigger man was brought in from out of town to do this hit…you just stumbled across him as he was making his get away."

"Getaway?"

"He had a ticket for a 7:40 flight to Detroit via Denver. We are not sure which, or if either, was his final destination. When we know that we will have a much better shot at getting him ID'd and then we can start to fully unravel this thing."

"Shit, this is getting interesting," Sumner acknowledged.

"You look a little beat. Why don't go home and get some rest."

"Yeah, you want me back here tomorrow?"

"Well, technically you are on admin leave, but I would sure like to have you here to assist with anything that might pop up about which you might unique knowledge."

"What time?"

"Make it easy on yourself. Sometime after lunch."

CHAPTER 6

Sumner arrived home just before dawn. His right hand was throbbing and there was a pinching pain deep in his chest. He entered his house through the garage and headed upstairs where he checked on his sleeping children. He next checked on his wife who was sleeping soundly. His hand throbbed so he decided to go back downstairs. On autopilot, he poured a shot of Wild Turkey Kentucky Whiskey and then proceeded outside to wait for the paperboy.

The paperboy arrived just before 6:00 AM. Sumner was standing in the driveway and received the newspaper in a football style handoff from the kid, who did not slow his bicycle as he moved on to the next house. Sumner went back into the house and placed the newspaper beneath the sink in the downstairs bathroom cabinet. *I'll check that in the morning.* He then went up to bed where his pillow beckoned irresistibly.

§

He rolled over and pulled the pillow over his head as the telephone continued to ring and ring and ring. *Dammit. Doesn't anyone have any respect for a day sleeper?* He checked the alarm clock…8:10 AM. He slowly picked up the phone. "WHAT?" he shouted into the mouthpiece.

"Officer Sumner, please," the caller cleared his throat. "This is Deputy Chief Rodgers speaking." *Oh, hell, I just yelled at the Chief of the Uniformed Division.*

"One moment, please," Sumner stalled. He got out of bed and walked to the hallway where he hollered into the stairwell "Te-e-d-d, telephone," his voice echoing up into the bedroom. He then ran downstairs and picked up the phone in the kitchen.

"I got it," Sumner called.

"Sumner, this is Chief Rodgers."

"Sir," Sumner snapped. "Excuse me one moment." He partially covered the mouthpiece as he called "I've got it, hang up. One moment, sir." He raced upstairs and hung up the extension in the bedroom, then shot back down to the kitchen. "Sorry, sir, we have a houseguest and he's a late sleeper." *Damn, I'm lame.*

"Sumner, I wanted to check and see how you're feeling. You had quite an evening."

"I'm fine, sir, a little sore but I'll be OK."

"I know things got a little hectic last night, but you failed to submit to interrogation by Internal Affairs," the Chief pointed out, "and that interview is required under Departmental Administrative Orders."

"Sorry, sir, I expected them to show up at the hospital as it was unknown if I was going to be admitted or released," Sumner explained. "I returned to PAB around 11:30 PM, submitted my report and then reported to IA, but nobody was in," Sumner fibbed. "I was feeling a bit woozy from the medication, so I headed home to get some rest. I was extensively questioned by Sergeant Burroughs last night though."

"That investigation is an entirely different matter," the Chief admonished. "It is absolutely mandatory that you submit to interrogation by Internal Affairs and that you answer all questions completely honestly."

"I apologize, sir. Like I said, I did look for them but they weren't around."

"Sergeant Garringer from IA was here this morning and he believes you have been evading him."

"Sir, that is simply not true," Sumner pleaded. "I'll be there in an hour and will report directly to Internal Affairs."

"That will be fine. I'll let Garringer know," the Chief relented. "You did a hell of a job out there last night, young man, we're all glad you are safe."

"Thank you, sir."

"Oh, uh, and you are aware there is a complete news blackout concerning everything related to this case."

"Yes, sir."

"And that includes talking about this with your buddies over a beer."

"Sir."

Sumner poured a cup of coffee and took two Tylenol for the throbbing pain in his hand. It was clear that the injury was significant. He still had an uncomfortable pinch in his chest. He slowly removed the bandage from his right hand. Blood and metabolic fluids had dried on the gauze during his two hours of sleep. He cracked the bandage loose from the wound and inspected his swollen mangled index finger. *Ouch.* He showered, shaved and dressed, then proceeded to PAB.

§

First things first. He headed up to Homicide where he found Sergeant Burroughs still at work. Though he had worked through the entire night, he still looked fresh and alert, as if energized by being on a challenging new case.

"You back already?" Burroughs looked up from his desk smiling broadly at Sumner.

"Deputy Chief called to remind me that I have to talk to IA."

"Yeah, that blood sucker Garringer was up here looking for you a couple of hours ago." "Don't screw around with this. You have no choice, you must tell IA everything."

"I don't know everything," Sumner shrugged.

"This is not optional," Burroughs was suddenly dead serious as he expressed his concern for the young officer. "You are under total obligation to submit to questioning by them and you better get to it right now."

"Yes, sir, anything you need from me before I'm fed to the sharks?"

Burroughs stifled a laugh. "Just go get that done, then report back here. I have some information that you may find interesting."

Sumner walked down the hall to the Office of the Chief of Police. He entered the foyer and turned left entering the Office of Internal Affairs.

"May I help you?" asked the middle aged receptionist.

"I'm Officer Sumner. I'm here for an interview."

"Sumner...we've been looking for you."

Sergeant Garringer and Sergeant Donald bolted from their officers into the reception area like a couple of hungry lions at feeding time.

"Sumner, where the hell have you been?" demanded Garringer.

"I've been looking for you in order to submit to the departmentally mandated post shooting interview," Sumner explained smugly. "I couldn't find you at the hospital last night and there was nobody around early this morning when I submitted my report."

"You're not supposed to submit any reports on this matter without our approval," Garringer chastised.

You blood sucking sack of shit. "I'm sorry, but I couldn't find any of you anywhere and we have a rapidly developing murder case for which Sergeant Burroughs was in need of all available information." Invoking Burroughs name brushed them back a bit. That is one man these predatory lackeys do not want to cross. "It is only with the timely acquisition of the information in my report that Bobby was able to piece this case together." Both investigators raised an eyebrow at Sumner's familiar use of Sergeant Burroughs first name. Sumner looked back and forth at the surprised faces of the investigators. *Time to twist the knife a little.* "Oh, sorry, Bobby Jr. and I went to school together."

"All right, my office," order Garringer gesturing to the door. Sumner entered and sat down as Sergeant Donald took a seat behind the end of the desk and Garringer seated himself regally in his wingback swivel chair across from Sumner. Donald removed a tape recorder from the drawer of Garringer's desk and set it up between them and Sumner. "This interrogation will be recorded."

"Do I need my attorney?" asked Sumner, knowing the answer.

"You are not entitled to representation by counsel at this proceeding," instructed Garringer. "You are required by Departmental Order to answer all questions honestly and completely."

"Of course, why would I do anything else?"

"What the hell happened?"

Sumner proceeded to explain in precise and exacting detail each and every action that had transpired. The investigators grilled him relentlessly as to the disposition of his shot that had gone wide, missing the target. Did he know where it went, did he know if it hit anything and what precisely? Why did he miss, was he current on his pistol range qualification? Did he do anything to provoke the suspect?

"Provoke him? Hell, sir, I didn't so much as speak a word to him. I stepped out of my patrol car and the son of a bitch shot me in the badge!"

"Watch your language, officer; this is an official police investigation."

"Sir."

Sumner looked at his watch. *Almost lunch time. I can't believe this. The entire incident took less that five seconds and these assholes have been grilling me for over two hours.*

Once the investigators had satisfied themselves that Sumner had not done anything for which the City or Department might be held liable and that he had conducted himself in a manner that would not bring any embarrassment to the Chief they concluded the interview. "You can go, officer. But do not discuss the details of this matter with anyone," said Sergeant Garringer.

"We may have more questions later," warned Sergeant Donald.

"Call me anytime," offered Sumner. "We'll do lunch," he mocked.

§

Sumner hurried back up to Homicide, but Sergeant Burroughs and several of the detectives had stepped out for a quick lunch. *He's sure entitled.* Sumner then proceeded down to Admin and the Records Division where he found Wanda Brookes.

"Wanda, got time for lunch?"

She looked up startled, sat down the pile of reports she was holding and walked over to him wrapping her arms around his torso and placing her head against his chest. *Ouch, that really hurts.* But he was not about to say anything to his friend. The diminutive woman sobbed quietly for half a minute as she held onto Sumner while he gently stroked her hair.

"I don't think I would have been able to go on if anything happened to you," she sobbed. "First Jeff, (her husband who had died five years before) and then Rich (Officer Richard Huerta who had been shot and killed during a routine traffic stop two years before), if you…; I don't think I could go on working here."

"Look, Wanda, everything's OK. Come on, let's grab some lunch."

"I'm the supervisor on duty. I can't leave; and your hand looks like they strapped the kitchen sink to it."

"It's still oozing a bit, so they got drainage bandages on it," he explained. "I'll go over to Pete's Steak House and get us a couple rib eye sandwiches."

"That would be very nice," she patted his shoulder with motherly affection.

He fetched the sandwiches and returned to PAB meeting up with Wanda in the Records Division employee lunch room. He enjoyed a jovial and pleasant lunch with Wanda reminiscing about the old neighborhood and all people who were their neighbors and friends on East Alta Vista Drive in the picturesque east foothills of the Valley above the San Jose Country Club. She reminded him of the 1950 Dodge he had purchased for fifteen dollars when he was thirteen years old and which he and his friends spent hours driving up and down the private road on which they lived. She reminded him of the stormy night his family's horses had escaped and of Sumner and his brother running through the field next to Wanda's home in their pajamas and slippers trying to corral their three Arabians. It was a pleasurable hour and, he could see, quite cathartic for her. She appeared calm and refreshed at the completion of their meal.

He walked her to her desk with his arm around her shoulders in a reassuring embrace. "Don't worry about me," Sumner reassured. "If there is anyone I'm looking out for, it's me."

"Be sure you do," she smiled as she brushed her fist across Sumner's chin.

CHAPTER 7

When Sumner returned to Homicide he found all the detectives back at work. "Anything new?" he asked Sergeant Burroughs.

Burroughs looked up from his desk. "Sumner, sit down." He then looked around pensively. "Wait, come in here." Sumner followed Burroughs into a soundproof interrogation room. "We have some new information…" Sumner could have cut the tension in the air with a knife as he waited. "The FBI has identified your attacker as one Floyd Cominsky from Detroit."

"Detroit? What the hell was he doing here?"

"Let me finish," said Burroughs. "He is a free lance hit man; he does a lot of work for local mobsters but will occasionally pick up a contract for the Mafia."

"And this ties in with the body found on Julian …?"

"We think so. The hospital just called and said he is now conscious. I sent Adams and Kowalski over to interrogate him; we'll see what they come up with."

"Do you think he'll talk to them?"

"He might as well, the doctors have little hope that he'll make it," explained Burroughs. "Your hollow points apparently made his insides look like Swiss cheese. Good shooting, by the way."

"You should hear IA tell it," Sumner bemoaned. "They're trying to paint it like I just incompetently sprayed shots into the air just for fun. They can't accept that I do not know precisely where my first shot went."

"We'll account for that round," reassured Burroughs. "The Tech Team has been out there since dawn. And don't worry about IA. This is the cleanest shooting I've seen in my career."

§

Sumner drove home where he lay down on the sofa in his family room and turned on the television. *Captains from Castile" starring Tyrone Power*, he noted with some satisfaction, Good *historical piece.* He drifted off to sleep, exhausted by his injuries and the events of the past few days.

He awoke just after 5:00 PM. His head was foggy and he was slightly nauseous. *The pain meds are wearing off and the pain is catching up.* He got up and staggered into the kitchen where he poured a glass of milk. *Wife will be home soon. Better get started on dinner.* He pulled a pound of ground beef from the freezer and placed it in a pan of water to defrost. He then picked up the telephone and called the Detective Bureau. "Homicide Division, please," he asked politely.

"Homicide Unit, how can I help you?"

"Dolores, this is Sumner."

"Officer Sumner, how are you feeling?"

"A little rough. May I speak to Burroughs, please?"

"I'm sorry, Officer, but he left. He went over to VMC I believe."

"Do you know what for?"

"I'm afraid not. Is it important?"

"Come on, Dolores, everything pertaining to this case is important. Are either Adams or Kowalski in?"

"They have not been back since this morning," she replied. "Can I take a message?"

"No, that's fine…thanks."

He hung up and then proceeded to prepare dinner for his family. It was a dish his mother used to make; but the recipe had been provided to his mother by his third grade school teacher. The concoction had subsequently come to be affectionately referred to as "teachers favorite." It was simple to prepare. First he placed one quarter cup of chopped red onion in a frying pan, followed by one crushed garlic clove. The hamburger was then added and browned. When it was fully cooked, the grease was drained off. He then added one can of Campbell's condensed Cream of Mushroom soup and half pint of sour cream. It was then left on very low heat for one half hour. It would ultimately be served over white rice with a side of mixed vegetables. The house soon became inundated with the ambrosial odors of the simmering meal.

Sumner's wife arrived home with the children at 5:45 PM. Though agitated by the stress of the day, she was nonetheless pacified by the savory smells of the dinner preparation. He greeted her with a kiss and took his son in his arms.

"Dad-de-e-e," his son, Geoff, screamed with delight.

"How was your day, dear?" he asked.

"The day from hell. Would you change her diaper," she asked handing his infant daughter into his arms.

"No problem," he assured her.

He proceeded upstairs where he changed his daughter's soiled diaper, then proceeded to his son's room to change him into play clothes. "I want to go outside and play with Matt," his son demanded.

"OK," his father replied, tying his son's shoes.

Outside, his son Geoff climbed onto his "Hot wheels" super tricycle and took off toward the closed end of the cul de sac in close pursuit of the next door neighbor, his best friend Matt. Matt's father stepped across the walkway between their respective homes and handed Sumner a bottle of beer.

"How are things?" asked Dennis, toasting with a tap of the long neck beer on Sumner's bottle. Dennis Tognetti had been a promising baseball player in high school and college. He had been an all conference catcher at the University of Santa Clara and had been extensively scouted by several major league teams and subsequently drafted by the Pittsburg Pirates. But Uncle Sam had a draft of his own at that time. Dennis wound up in the United States Army serving with the 1st Air Cavalry Division. During his tour in Viet Nam Dennis had been badly wounded while conducting rescue operations to extract a reconnaissance team that had become trapped and surrounded in enemy territory when the soldier behind him had tripped a land mine. The shrapnel had maimed Dennis' left leg leaving him a gimp and ending all his hopes of a career in professional baseball.

"Good, how are things at PG&E?" Dennis was a line manager at the Pacific Gas and Electric Company.

"A slave mine— like always."

They both laughed. They discussed the San Francisco 49ers chances of making the playoffs and football in general while their sons raced around the cul de sac on their "Hot wheels." "Well, time to feed the family. Thanks for the beer."

§

After dinner, Sumner cleared the table then rinsed the dishes and placed them in the dishwasher while his wife bathed and readied the children for bed. As he was finishing cleaning the kitchen, his son raced down the stairs in his pajamas and jumped onto the sofa ready to watch television with his father.

"No, it's time for you to go to bed," called his mother in hot pursuit of Geoffrey. Geoffrey screamed his defiance.

"Oh let him watch a little TV," Sumner intervened.

"OK , but you're getting him up and taking him to preschool tomorrow morning."

"That's fine."

Sumner tuned in his son's favorite show "Starsky and Hutch" and they sat down to watch together. When the show ended, Sumner picked his son up off the sofa and placed him up on his shoulders. He then marched down the hall to the living room, through the living room and dining room into the kitchen and back into the family room as Geoff squealed and laughed. Sumner then proceeded upstairs, deposited his son into bed and tucked him in for the evening. He then went in and checked on his infant daughter who was sleeping soundly.

When he got back down to the family room, his wife was finally relaxing on the sofa watching the television. "Is everything all right?" she asked.

"Yeah, why?"

"It just seems like there is something funny going on."

"Like what?"

"I don't know. Is everything all right at work?"

"Yeah, fine."

"Something's just not right, and I don't think you're being completely honest with me."

"Everything's fine," he assured her.

She shook her head and sat pensively in front of the television not watching at all. *Damn that women's intuition.*

§

Sumner dropped his son off at Green Valley Preschool just down the street from the Fitness Center where he trained. He then proceeded home where he poured a cup of coffee while he dialed the number to the police department. "Homicide Unit, please."

"Homicide," the voice was far too cheerful for this time of the morning.

"Dolores, it's Sumner. Is Burroughs in?"

"Yes, he is. Please hold on."

"Burroughs."

"It's Sumner. What do you know?"

There was a pause. "You better come in; I don't think we should discuss this over the phone."

Sumner was intrigued. "When?"

"Come in about 11:00, then we'll grab some lunch."

"See you then."

§

Sumner arrived at PAB at 10:40 AM. He stopped at the Bureau of Field Operations office where he encountered Sergeant Bill Pierce who had been one of Sumner's training sergeants while he was undergoing field training as a rookie.

"Hey, how you doing?" asked Pierce.

"Good."

"You feeling all right? O'Day says you put that crook down like a rabid dog."

"Well, it didn't go down quite that smoothly," Sumner explained. "There were a few rough spots."

"Sumner, can I have a word with you?" called Deputy Chief Rodgers.

"I was just coming to see you, sir."

Sumner entered the Chief's office where he took a seat next to Captain Sherman who was already seated. The Chief took his seat behind his spacious walnut desk. "Sumner, I'm a little concerned," the Chief explained. "Sergeant Garringer has indicated that he feels you haven't been completely honest and forthcoming with Internal Affairs regarding the incidents of this shooting."

Sumner's stomach roiled in frustrated disgust. *The only thing that will make that son of a bitch happy is if I confess to some heinous wrongdoing that will end my career, absolve the department of any liability and somehow make him look like the heroic and pristine conscious of the San Jose Police Department who is courageous enough to give up a dirty cop. Asshole!*

"Chief, the entire incident took less than five seconds. How much is there that can be fabricated? The physical evidence is all there. What? Does he think that I shot this innocent citizen then shot myself to cover it up?"

"No need to get testy," calmed the Chief. "Maybe it would be good ideas if you went up and talked to him...you know, allay any concerns that may be nagging him."

"Whatever you say, Chief." It was all Sumner could do not to scream out in frustration and anger.

Sumner headed to Homicide where he found Sergeant Burroughs in Lieutenant Hettinger's office. Hettinger was the commander of the Homicide Unit and had been Burroughs first partner, and the man who taught him all the ropes, when he was initially assigned to the unit eighteen years ago.

"Sumner, how are you?" asked Hettinger extending his right hand to shake. Sumner held up his bandaged right hand and then took the Lieutenants right hand in his left. Sergeant Burroughs closed the office door. "Sit down," "Hett" gestured toward the chair in front of his desk. Sergeant Burroughs tossed one leg up on the corner of the LT's desk and looked at Sumner sternly.

"Your suspect has been very forthcoming with information," Burroughs explained. "We talked for several hours before they took him back into surgery. He's well aware of his eminent demise, in spite of the fact that the doctor's are doing everything in their power to save him."

"What's his problem?"

"They can't find all the holes your hollow points punched in his intestine," Burroughs explained. "He's developed a severe infection that has progressed into peritonitis. If they can't patch him up, he is going to die an agonizing death."

"You're breaking my heart," replied Sumner sarcastically.

A stifled laugh erupted from Burroughs. "He said you would probably say something like that. His only condition for talking to us was that you not be allowed to visit him."

"Me?!"

"Yeah, his exact words were 'I don't want that punk cop who shot me coming around.' He's quite disgusted with himself for letting you get it over on him."

"So I don't get it. He had me dead to rights. Why didn't he just shoot me between the eyes and have an end to it?" Sumner pondered his fate.

"He said he had intended to play it cool and take the ticket," Burroughs explained. "But then he saw your face in his rearview mirror and was surprised by how young you were—punk kid, he said. He thought you must be a cadet or maybe a reserve. That's when he decided he would allow himself a little recreation and kill you. His plan was to disable you with a shot through your shiny new badge. Once you were down, he planned to execute you with a single shot between the eyes. He drew a bead on your badge and fired...but then things went wrong for him."

"I know what happened next, but please, fill me in. What happened to this plan of his?"

"First, he had somehow gotten the idea that our badges are made of tin. The sterling silver your badge is made of, is a tough metal that broke up his bullet. You weren't disabled by his first shot, only shaken up. When he saw you make your move, he was surprised, but still thought you were just a kid and held your attempts to defend yourself in contempt, so he decided to cripple you with a shot to your gun hand. Once you were disabled he intended to finish his execution in a leisurely manner."

"So far his plan was working well," Sumner acknowledged.

"He fired hitting your right index finger, but you just kept up your effort to defend yourself. He became frustrated with you, he fired another shot at your hand, this one hitting the front sight of your revolver. He couldn't believe you were still fighting back after being hit three times, and he was determined to finish off this 'child,' as he referred to you."

"Then?"

"Then you unleashed your first shot," Burroughs explained. "He admits he was startled by the power of your magnum. He decided that that powerful a weapon made you a big man, and he decided to change his plan and finish you with his next shot. But he took just a little bit too long drawing his sight picture and your next shot hit him in the shoulder. He was hurt but still game and determined to finish you off when your next four shots tore his innards apart."

"Well..." Sumner contemplated what he had just been told. "He's quite the sportsman."

"He still can't believe you took him down," Burroughs explained. "According to him, he's the best there is."

"We'll have that engraved on his tombstone," Sumner replied sarcastically.

"You did a hell of job," composed Lt. Hettinger. "That was the most courageous defense I ever heard of, but if it had not been for his arrogant determination to stage your 'execution,' you would be dead right now."

"Let's drink a drink to arrogance," replied Sumner, now thoroughly unnerved by the revelation of what his assailant had intended.

"Why don't you head home and get some rest," said Burroughs.

"Chief Rodgers wants me to go talk to Garringer in IA; it seems he does not believe my statement."

"What's not to believe?!" roared Burroughs. "That sleazy piece of dog shit, I'm going to kick that little son of a bitch right in the balls!"

"Thanks, Bobby," said Sumner in true appreciation of his friend's protective response. "But I don't want you taking any shit over this; I'll just go talk to them again."

Burroughs shook his head in disgust. "By the way, the Crime Scene Unit found your errant round. It was lodged in the wall of that travel agency down the street from the scene."

"That's a relief," Sumner sighed. "At least I didn't shoot some innocent bystander."

CHAPTER 8

Sumner reported to the Office of Internal Affairs. Sergeant Donald was out of the office, but Garringer greeted him in the reception area. Sergeant Garringer seemed almost reluctant to speak with Sumner. *What's his problem?* Diffidently, he led Sumner into his office. This time he kept the door open.

"So, what brings you up here?"

"Chief Rodgers says that you're not satisfied with my statement."

"Well, that's a little overblown. We're very concerned about the disposition of your first shot and why you missed so wildly."

"The fact that I had absorbed three shots from the suspect before I finally was able to return fire might have had something to do with my initial poor aim. But missed wildly is a bit of an exaggeration. If you check with the Crime Scene Unit, they deduce that the trajectory of my round missed the suspect by less than three inches."

"Then they've accounted for that round?"

"Yes, it lodged harmlessly in the wall of the Atlantic Pacific Travel Agency."

"Oh, well, that is good new. Thank you for that information."

What's wrong with this guy? Without his sidekick, he's a real milk toast.

"Well, that's all, Officer. Thank you for stopping in."

"That's it?"

"For now, yes."
This was a total waste of time. What an insipid asshole.

§

Sumner returned home where he began preparing dinner for the family; His grandmother's recipe for homemade macaroni and cheese. His wife arrived home at around 5:45 PM. He dutifully took the children off her hands.

"How was your day?" he asked.

"Fine." She was short and curt. *Uh oh, something is very wrong here.*

Sumner headed upstairs where he changed his daughter's diaper while his son changed into his play clothes. He then made a discreet exit to the front yard where the children could play.

"So how you doing?" came the jovial voice of his next door neighbor Dennis.

"Well, I think all right," Sumner was hesitant. "I'll let you know for sure tomorrow."

"Job or home?"

"A little bit of both I think."

"Uh oh." He then called to his son. "Matt, go get daddy two beers."

His son dutifully returned with two Budweiser long neck bottles of cold beer. Dennis handed one to Sumner.

"Thanks," said Sumner, as he took a long pull on the beer. "I may need several of these."

"If you're going to have 'a talk,' you better keep it at one," Dennis admonished. "Never have 'a talk' with the wife when you've been drinking."

"You're right. Thanks."

As darkness began to fall, Sumner and his neighbor gathered their offspring and headed indoors for dinner. Sumner sat out the plates and utensils then gathered the family to the dinner table. His son wolfed down two large helpings of macaroni and cheese. After the meal, Sumner cleared the table and washed the dishes as his wife took the children upstairs where she bathed them and prepared them for bed.

"The kids are ready for you to tuck them in," she called as she proceeded into the family room where she sat on the sofa in front of the television.

When Sumner returned to the family room after tucking his children into bed, his wife was absorbed in rumination. He sat and began to watch "Dallas." *Old JR is in some hot water...and so am I it appears.*

"What was that shooting about the other night?" she asked pointedly.

"I don't know. Some motorist got pulled over for a traffic violation and decided to take a shot at the officer."

"And you had nothing to do with it?"

"No. Why do you ask?"

"Well I think it's just strange that you wind up with an injured hand that same night, you've been very evasive about work and I found this under the sink in the guest bathroom." She produced the newspaper that Sumner had hid the morning after the shooting. He had never even looked to see if there was anything in the paper about the incident. "It's from the morning after that shooting," she accused. "Several people brought the paper into work and asked me if you were involved. I figured you would have told me if you had been, then I find this hidden under the sink...the same edition newspaper...what are keeping form me?" She was becoming teary eyed.

"Everything is all right. I'm OK."

"You're not being truthful with me," she was lachrymose and becoming almost desperate as she implored pitcously. *This charade is over! Time to come clean.*

"I'm sorry. I should have been honest with you, but I did not want to worry you."

"You were involved in the shooting?"

"Yes, I was the officer involved."

"And your hand, that's where you were shot?" she was now frantic.

"Yes, but it was no big deal."

She burst into tears and cried unreservedly. "My god, my god, what the hell happened...and why weren't you honest with me? You lied to me; why did you lie to me?"

"Karen, I couldn't talk to anyone about this—orders; there's a complete news blackout." *That at least is true.*

"I don't think they expected you to lie to your wife. You should have been honest with me." Her tears were flowing freely. "Why did he shoot at you?"

"I don't know. He shot and I shot back."

"Did you kill him?"

"No, he's still alive."

"Are we in any danger? What if he comes looking for you? What about the children?"

"We're not in any danger. The children will be fine."

She held her head in her hands as she bawled like a hurt child. "I can't take this anymore," she sobbed. "I can't take it; I don't want to live like this. Why can't you get a normal job with normal hours?"

Not this again. "Karen, this is what I do—this is my job. You knew I was going to do this before you married me."

"I had no idea. I thought I could take it but I can't, I just can't, I want out of this." She wept profusely. Sumner attempted to comfort her, but to no avail. He tried to put his arms around her, but she pushed him away. "I can't take this, I just can't take this!" She ran upstairs.

Shit! That went well. He poured himself a shot of Wild Turkey and sat down to watch the evening news. *Damn, damn, damn, damn, damn! Why do I feel like a criminal? I didn't do anything wrong and yet between Internal Affairs and my wife I feel like the perpetrator of some horrible crime.* He poured another drink and sat down to watch Johnny Carson's monologue on "The Tonight Show."

CHAPTER 9

Sumner woke up with a slight headache. He got up and put on a pair of sweats then woke his children, dressed them and fed them breakfast while they watched "Sesame Street." He then dropped his daughter at the babysitters and took his son to preschool. When he arrived home, he removed his sweats, put on his shorts and running shoes and took off for a run along the Guadalupe River. A five mile run knocked the fogginess out of his head.

He returned home and showered and dressed, then drove to the PAB.

§

At the Administration Building, he found Sergeant Burroughs in the Homicide Unit. "Sumner, come with me, I've got some information for you." They entered the Lieutenant's office and closed the door. "Your buddy has been useful source of information on organized crime activities, both here and in Detroit."

"Great, anything I should know?"

"What I am going to tell you must be kept in the strictest confidence," he warned. "Intelligence as well as the FBI are processing the information he has been providing. This entire matter will soon be taken over by the FBI and will entirely cease to exist as an SJPD case. They want this kept confidential…top secret, he is beginning to give information on some Mafia figures and the feds don't want any word of it getting out. Do you understand?"

"OK."

"It seems that a certain criminal organization has been trying to take control of all the distribution and dealerships for the Japanese automotive industry in the western U.S. They've been muscling the competition out by selling cars from their dealerships at below cost. This has been drying up business for the other dealerships, which they then buy for a song."

"That would explain some of the sweetheart deals a lot of the officers have gotten on new cars," Sumner mused.

"This activity has had a very damaging effect on American car dealers in this area as well and has hurt the UAW in Detroit. The bosses sent word for this process to cease, but was apparently ignored by the west coast bosses."

"So they sent Floyd Cominsky out here to deliver a stronger message by making an example of someone," Sumner reasoned.

"Correct. They didn't dare harm any of the family, so they made an example of the general manager, who had no criminal ties to anyone."

"So that poor dumb son of bitch just got caught in the middle?"

"That's it. He chose to work for the wrong people and got caught in the crossfire."

"Bobby, my wife freaked out last night," Sumner confided. "She brow beat a confession out of me about what happened. She got hysterical and went on about our family and children being in danger…what do you think?"

"Not a chance," he assured the young officer. "Cominsky is free lance, no family ties, and the information he is giving us only goes up so high. He won't inform on any mafia people."

"So where does that leave me?"

"Floyd is going to die in the next few days. The doctors all agree that there's no way he can survive his wounds. They've done all they can. And that will be the end of your involvement in this matter. Our Intelligence, the State Bureau of Investigation, and the FBI will take it as far as the information he provided will allow."

"Maybe I should stop by, say hi and thank him," Sumner wisecracked.

"He makes it very clear each time we talk to him that he does not want you anywhere around him."

"So that's that?"

"That's that. Why don't you go home and take it easy?"

"It's difficult to relax when IA is trying to end my career on the one hand and my wife wants to divorce me on the other."

"Sure makes you wonder why anyone would choose a career as a police officer, doesn't it?"

"Yeah, it sure does. Please keep me informed if anything else develops."

"Of course," Burroughs assured him.

Sumner headed downstairs to the Bureau of Field Operations Office where he found Deputy Chief Rodgers at his desk in his office.

"You back again?" asked the Chief. "Why don't you go home and get some rest?" "You're on admin leave and you're injured."

"Yeah, well, I need to get back to work. When is the shooting board?"

"Next week, but you're not going back out on the street until you get a medical clearance."

"Yeah, OK. Please keep me informed on the shooting board."

"Sure will, now go get some rest."

Dammit, I can't sleep, they won't let me work, my wife hates me, and I am forbidden to talk to anyone about the cause of all this hullabaloo. Sumner felt lower than he had ever experienced. As he was considering going home and getting drunk, an inspiration hit him…*Father Barta.* Father Barta had been Sumner's Company Chaplin while Sumner was in the army. Barta was an Anglican Priest who held a PhD in history from Oxford University. He was related to just about every royal family in Europe, and his family were the first Europeans to colonize the Caribbean island of St. Croix. He and Sumner had become fast friends while in the service and had spent many memorable evenings sitting up late into the night drinking port and pontificating on the many obscure machinations of European history. Father Barta had recently separated from the service and was now the Vicar of St. Andrews Episcopal Church in Monterey, California.

Sumner turned his vehicle southbound on Highway 17 and headed for Monterey an hour away.

CHAPTER 10

Sumner arrived at St. Andrews just before noon. Father Barta greeted him at the door to the rectory. "Ted, how are you, this is a surprise."

"I hope this is not a bad time, but I was wondering if you had a few minutes to talk."

"Of course," he assured. "This is actually fortuitous. I just had an appointment cancel and I am free for the next two hours."

They entered the church office where Sumner took a seat while Father Barta prepared tea. Barta handed Sumner his tea with a lemon wedge, which he remembered is the way Sumner takes it, and then took his seat and looked over at Sumner offering his complete and undivided attention.

Sumner began haltingly, describing in detail the events of the evening of the shooting and all the subsequent drama. Father Barta listened intently. He had the gift of making Sumner feel he was the most important person on Earth. Through most of the recitation, Barta remained expressionless and unemotional, though he did wince noticeably as Sumner described the bullets striking his badge and hand. As he unburdened himself, Sumner began feeling better. As his chosen clergyman, Barta was sworn to confidentiality and Sumner began to feel increasingly relieved as he poured out his soul to his friend. He spoke without stopping for nearly thirty minutes, about his deteriorating marriage, how fed up he was at being treated like a 'kid' by his fellow officers, because of his youthful appearance, even though many were not much older than he; and then he stopped stopped abruptly, completely exhausted.

Father Barta sat for several moments in silent contemplation. He processed and filed all the information he had been given into that magnificently perfect mind of his. He then looked sympathetically at Sumner. "Well, everything is going to be all right with the police department. You're just going to have to endure their processes. That's just part of being a police officer. But it is this situation with your wife about which I am concerned."

"But there is no middle ground for me," Sumner explained. "She does not want to hear anything about my work, but then when something happens and she hears about it from someone else or reads about it in the paper, she attacks me for not being honest with her."

"She is your chosen wife, joined to you in holy matrimony by a minister of God, in the Church," he explained. She deserves your complete confidence and trust."

"What do I do when she says she doesn't want to hear about my work?"

"You don't need to trouble her with the day to day routines, but when something of this magnitude occurs, you need to explain that it is important and that you must take her as a partner in the matter. It is the way God intends for married couples to live. Hiding the newspaper and concealing the cause of your wounds is toxic to a healthy marriage."

I guess that was pretty childish.

"And you need to learn to face up to what you have done and take total responsibility for all your actions," Barta admonished. "To attempt to fool the Chief into believing that it was a houseguest who had yelled into the phone was behavior unworthy of a man who just hours before had faced a cold blooded killer in mortal combat and prevailed over him."

"Yeah, I do feel like an ass over that one."

"You are a fine man, a brilliant man, and faithful servant of God," Father Barta encouraged. "But you must trust your judgment to do the right thing and then not be afraid to fess up and take responsibility when you fall short."

"Yeah, you're right, as usual. Thank you for taking the time to listen."

"The pleasure was mine. It's not every day I get to be part of excitement of that sort. My pulse is still racing."

"I just finished Lord Kinross' *History of the Ottoman Empire*," Sumner offered. That did it. The two men spent the next hour and a half in contemplative and sometimes heated discussion over the impact of the spread of the Ottomans and Islam through the Mediterranean and the southern continent on the military-political developments of medieval and renaissance Europe. It was just the intellectual medicine Sumner needed to pull him out of his funk. By taking his mind off his own domestic problems for that brief period, he felt refreshed, clear headed and more able to cope with the problems that still confronted him.

Father Barta walked Sumner out to his vehicle at 2:15 PM. He patted Sumner on the back with reassurance and waved goodbye as Sumner drove off.

CHAPTER 11

The telephone rang and rang and rang. *Dammit go away.* Sumner pulled the pillow over his head, but the phone kept ringing. Finally he fumbled for the receiver knocking it from the cradle onto the floor. *Great.* He rolled over and looked at the clock...7:15 AM. "Hello."

"Sumner, Bobby Burroughs."

"Yeah, what's up, Sergeant?"

"Floyd Cominsky died this morning."

"When?"

"About 5:00 AM. I waited to call you. Sorry to wake you up so early. I know you're back on swing shift."

"That's all right. I appreciate your letting me know."

"No problem."

"So...where does that leave me in all this?"

"It's all over. The FBI wants it all kept confidential until they have made use of all the information he provided. Cause of death will be listed as accidental gunfire. You're finished with it."

"No trial, no hearing, no nothing?"

"No, the coroner is closing the case. The FBI is picking up all files and reports regarding the matter. It's theirs now. And as you know the shooting board cleared you of any wrong doing."

"Thanks, Bobby. I couldn't have gotten through all this without your help."

"Forget it, kid. You did a great job."

Sumner hung up the phone. *Over huh?* — *except when I close my eyes to go to sleep.*

§

That incident was closed, but not forgotten. The stress of that event had lasting repercussions on the Sumner family. Eventually Karen could no longer deal with life as the wife of a police officer. As happens with far too many law enforcement families, their marriage ended in divorce.

This was a harrowing event; but a much more dangerous part of his career was about to begin.

CHAPTER 12

The phone began to ring continuously, with a sharp, insistent clamor. *Dammit, just stop ringing.* The phone refused to cease its' torment of the desperately sleep deprived Officer Sumner. Working the midnight shift always made it difficult to get a "good days sleep" and, as a result, graveyard officers tended to be chronically sleepy. But when the phone kept ringing it became impossible to get enough rest. Sumner had become convinced that there was a conspiracy to deprive midnight shift officers of their needed sleep. Typically, midnight officers ended up being scheduled for court during the afternoon sessions. As a result, their slumbers were often interrupted midsleep, in order to make their appearance to testify. And the Detectives, anxious to make progress on their caseload, would invariably telephone the midnight officers throughout the day, in a thoughtless effort to obtain pertinent information relative to the officers' reports. It was common knowledge that to work the midnight shift was to be chronically fatigued.

The phone stopped to catch its breath, and then started demanding attention all over again. *Dammit, that phone is just not going to go away.* Sumner reached for the receiver. "Hello! what?"

"Sumner? This is Sgt Dreyer from Narcotics."

"I didn't do it," Sumner joked his way through his irritation.

"I'm calling because we have an opening in the Unit and you had indicated a desire to work Narcotics on your last "Assignment Preference Report"."

"No I didn't," Sumner replied.

"Uh, well, uh, are you saying you don't want to work Narcotics?"

"No, I'm just saying that I never listed Narcotics as an interest on my "Assignment Preference Report"."

"OK, look, Lt Bertotti would like you to come in for an interview this afternoon."

"An interview? I never requested assignment to Narcotics."

"Look, would you just be at the Narcotic Unit at 4:00 PM?" Dreyer's patience was wearing thin.

"Yeah, I'll be there," Sumner replied. *Might as well find out what the hell this is all about.* Sumner rolled over pulling the pillow over his face and fell into a light, fitful sleep. He was unable to achieve that deep refreshing slumber that night sleepers are able to enjoy.

§

"I have an appointment with Sgt Dreyer and Lt. Bertotti," Sumner reported to the Narcotic Unit secretary, a pleasant looking young woman wearing glasses with her hair done up like a school marm.

"Please have a seat, I'll let him know."

Lt Bertotti entered the outer office carrying a clip board followed by Sgt Dreyer. "Let's go down to the conference room," Bertotti suggested.

Sumner followed the Lt and Sgt to one of the smaller conference rooms located at the end of the hall next to the Chief's spacious conference room. Bertotti took a seat across the table as Dreyer closed the door and then slid into the chair next to his Lieutenant. Sumner sat down across the table, placing his hands, fingers interlocked, on the table.

"So you want to be a Narc?" asked Bertotti.

"No."

"Then why are you here?" asked an incredulous Bertotti.

"Sgt Dreyer said you wanted to talk to me."

Bertotti looked at Dreyer as they stared blankly at each other for several seconds. Finally Dreyer shrugged his shoulders. "Fill him in," advised Dreyer.

Bertotti drew a long breath as he stared Sumner down. "We have a major problem that is increasingly growing into a political hot potato," he began slowly. "We're getting tremendous pressure from the Mayor, City

Council and City Manager to do something about it." Bertotti brought his gaze to bear on Sumner. They sat in silence for several seconds. Sumner shrugged his shoulders as if to ask "how does this involve me".

"The volume of illicit drugs that are making their way into our high schools is reaching epidemic proportions and parents, homeowner groups and PTA's are letting the City know that they demand something done about it."

Sumner nodded in agreement.

Bertotti looked toward Dreyer. Dreyer nodded. Bertotti sighed. "The Chief has authorized us to insert two undercover operatives into the high school culture," he explained. "Their job will be to gather detailed information as to the sources and types of drugs being supplied as well as the methods of distribution." "In addition they will be authorized to make contact with such suppliers as they are able with the purpose of making covert purchases of illicit drugs." "This operation has been authorized for six months, then the officers will be returned to Patrol duties." "The entire project is scheduled to be completed one week before high school graduation." "The Chief intends to make a major round up of all the suspects at that time in a high profile dragnet to be covered extensively by the press and television." "He wants to put the fear of god into the dealers and dopers." "Anyway, you were recommended as a possible candidate for this assignment."

"By who," inquired Sumner?

Bertotti and Dreyer looked at each other in exasperation. "You're not going to make this easy are you."

"I'm just wondering why you want me for this assignment and who it is that thinks I would be well suited to it," Sumner explained.

Bertotti shook his head. "This will be a deep undercover operation, nothing like this has ever been done by this department," he explained. "The operatives will be working alone, completely isolated from any form of supervision or assistance. The dangers and pressures, both physical and psychological will be tremendous."

"So— why me?"

"We need officers who look young, enough to pass as high school students. We conducted an exhaustive search of all personnel records and came up with about a dozen candidates."

"So— why me?" Sumner repeated.

"Dr Robb, the Police Psychiatrist, reviewed the files of each of the candidates and determined that you were best suited emotionally and intellectually to handle this assignment."

"Why the hell is that?"

"Like I said, there will be dangers both psychological and physical," Bertotti explained. "You are a Black Belt in Karate, we feel that minimizes your vulnerability to physical danger, you have a MENSA IQ which Dr. Robb feels equips you to better handle the emotional pressures of isolation as well as enables you to more easily assimilate into an alien environment. And on top of all that you minored in English in college and, frankly, you write top notch reports."

"So you want me for this assignment?"

"Yes, we do," Bertotti finally admitted.

"Six months, right?"

"That's all we are authorized for," Dreyer explained.

Sumner pondered the ramifications of the assignment. *Hell, I don't know anything about narcotics and I don't really know anything about how those types of people conduct themselves. I could fall flat on my face on this job.* But Sumner had been extremely uneasy in his work as a patrol officer since the hit man Floyd Cominsky incident. He was continually on edge and saw every encounter on the street as a possible threat. He moved in quickly in almost every encounter with the public and conducted a pat search for weapons on most subjects, even little old ladies during routine traffic stops. He had been the subject of several Internal Affairs investigations since the shoot out with Cominsky, where citizens complained that his conduct with them had been high handed and, what police officers refer to as "badge heavy". He was definitely in need of a change in environment...*this might be it* he thought.

"All right, I'll do it." *Damn, I hope I'm doing the right thing.*

The men stood and shook hands. "Monday morning 8:00 AM," Bertotti advised. "We're going to put you through a week of intensive training and then turn you loose."

CHAPTER 13

S umner pulled into the student parking lot at Pioneer High School on San Jose's south side. He parked his Volkswagen beetle on the west side of the lot near the fence and sat back in the seat waiting for class to let out. It was his first day on the job as an undercover narcotics operative after being abruptly transferred from Uniformed Patrol Division and receiving five days of intensive training on the habits, mannerisms and vernacular of the high school drug culture. He was nervous and unsure. While his training officers, Sergeants Dreyer and Brown had been confident that they were equipping him with the information necessary to effectively conduct undercover operations in high schools, Sumner was unconvinced. After all, when being interviewed for this assignment he was informed by the command staff that one of the major purposes of the operation was to identify the types of drugs being purchased by high school students as well as the avenues of supply. His training officers had informed him that he would be buying mostly marijuana, and possibly some LSD but nothing heavier. *If they knew that for sure they would not have brought me in...looks like there is going to be steep learning curve and a lot of OJT.*

A few young people, presumably students wandered through the parking lot, giving little notice to Sumner. The bell rang at 12:00 PM and the entire school became a veritable beehive of activity. Though ignored by most of the students, a few of the rougher looking kids congregated together taking a keen interest in the outsider sitting in the parked Volkswagen. A young girl about fifteen years old entered their group for a moment, and then approached the driver's side of Sumner's vehicle.

"Excuse me." Sumner turned to face the girl standing by his window. "Are you a Nark?" she asked.

Shit, they made me, Sumner was nearly panicked. *How the hell did they know?*

"No," Sumner replied haltingly. "Are you?"

"Then what are you doing here?"

What the hell am I doing here??? Oh yeah. "I'm meeting someone. I think he goes to school here."

"What's his name?"

"None of your business. Why are you so nosey?"

"Well those guys over there think you're a Nark," she replied gesturing to the five young men fifty feet away.

"Well those guys don't know shit," Sumner replied with feigned indignance.

"Karl is a mechanic at the Police garage and he works on all the Nark's cars. He knows who all the Narks are and he says this is one of their cars," she claimed gesturing to the Volkswagen.

Dammit...of all the luck. This is just not working out. Time to bob and weave. "Karl is full of kha kha. There are probably thousands of Volkswagens just like this around town."

The girl shrugged and turned to walk away.

"Hey which one is Karl?"

The girl pointed to a tall skinny guy with long brown hair standing in the center of the group of toughs.

What the hell, Sumner thought; *they're paying me to engage so I might as well engage. If the jig is up, I'll know in a minute.*

Sumner walked rapidly past the girl and approached the group. They turned toward Sumner assuming a hostile profile but began to shuffle uncomfortably as he got closer.

"Hey Karl," Sumner called from ten feet away as he approached. "Why are you trying to hang a jacket on me? I don't even know you man.

That's not cool, not cool at all." Sumner stepped up looking Karl straight in the eye. Karl met his gaze, and then looked away. *Well I'll be...he's a bull shitter and got called on it.* Sumner decided to press his advantage. "So, is that what you do, go around hanging Nark jackets on people? You'll get yourself shanked pulling that kind of shit in County." (Meaning the County Jail).

Karl regained some of his composure as his associates moved to surround them both and other kids moved closer to hear what was transpiring. "What the fuck are you doing here man? You don't go to Pioneer," he accused indignantly.

"I'm meeting someone here if it's any of your business," Sumner snapped back.

Sumner noticed a bulge on Karl's belt. *He's packing heat. Something's not right here. Better play this out.* "And what the fuck is it to you? You don't go to school here either."

Karl was now quite unnerved. "Well I used to go here," he stammered.

Ah ha, not a student. This is getting more interesting.

"So what the hell are you doing here?" Sumner demanded. "You don't have any more right to be here than I do."

"Hey he used to go here until he dropped out," offered one of the toughs in Karl's group.

"Shut up punk," Sumner snapped. "Unless you're going to take care of business for me I suggest you mind you own business." Sumner turned and walked back to his vehicle where he lit a cigarette.

The bell rang and the crowd began to disperse. A few minutes later Karl ambled over to Sumner's vehicle.

"I didn't mean anything man," Karl explained. "We just get a little edgy when a stranger suddenly appears."

"Yeah, that's cool," Sumner relented. "So, why you packing heat?"

Karl reeled in astonishment. "How the hell did you know!?"

"Don't worry, it's not that obvious. But why do you need heat?"

"To protect my stash. I don't want to hurt anyone, I just need to protect my stash."

"That's cool. Well, it looks like my man is a no show."

"What are you looking for?" Karl asked.

"Anything to get high. I'm completely dry."

"Well…" Karl leaned closer in feigned nonchalance. "Would you be interested in scoring a couple lids of primo pot."

"That should do it," Sumner replied. *I'll be damned. A minute ago he was accusing me of being a Nark, and now he's apologizing and offering to sell me drugs. I've got to settle down and not be so jumpy.*

"You drive," instructed Karl climbing into the passenger seat of Sumner's vehicle.

Sumner drove to an apartment complex off Cherry Ave as directed by Karl. "Who lives here?" inquired Sumner.

"Me and my old lady. Wait here."

Karl returned several minutes later and reentered the vehicle. From beneath his shirt he produced two plastic bags filled with marijuana. "Twenty bucks each."

Sumner handed him two twenty dollar bills and received the merchandise. "Thanks, what else can you do?"

"I can get you pretty much whatever you want."

"Cool, I was looking to score some acid, but this will do for now. I'll catch up with you later."

"Yeah, sure. Hey can you give me a ride?"

"Where to?"

"I'm going to trade school to be a mechanic and I've got to get to class by 3:00."

"So you're not a mechanic at the police garage?"

"No, but those poop butts at the high school don't need to know that."

"Naw," Sumner agreed.

Sumner drove to the Adult Education Center on Hillsdale Ave where he dropped Karl. "How you getting home?"

"I'll have to hitch."

"Shit, what time are you done? I'll pick you up."

"8:00 PM. Thanks man…thanks a lot."

Sumner drove to a secluded spot along the Los Gatos Creek and parked off the road where his vehicle could not be seen by passersby.

There he completed his report and marked the evidence with his initials and badge number and placed it in a plain brown envelope. He then drove to the gas station at Camden and Kosher Avenues where he used the pay phone to call his handler, Sgt Dreyer.

"Almaden Fashion Plaza, behind the Emporium, twenty minutes," Dreyer instructed. Sumner hung up the phone.

CHAPTER 14

After turning over his report and evidence to Dreyer, Sumner decided to check activity at Leland High School. Leland is located in the upscale Almaden Country Club Area of San Jose and is attended by an affluent student body. Kids with plenty of money to spend on whatever diversions they might choose to amuse themselves… including drugs. The school is located on the west side of Camden Ave with a jogging trail and the Coyote Creek on the east. The parking lot and football field are located on the south side of the campus along Reykjavik Ave. There are no residences facing Reykjavik, only the sides of homes located on the streets that insect, therefore creating a remotes location free from the prying eyes of residents.

Sumner noticed three lowered vehicles parked along the south side of Reykjavik. These were the type of vehicles typically found in the largely Hispanic neighborhoods of the city's east side. Sumner parked his vehicle and got out. He pulled out a cigarette, placing it in his mouth and leaned against the fence. The sound of the school bell wafted through the air from the across the football field. Soon a dozen or so students from the high school ambled across the street to the parked vehicles where, through the passenger side window they exchanged cash for items contained in small plastic bags. Sumner watched for ten or fifteen minutes as transaction after transaction took place. *This is a veritable flea market.*

When the traffic thinned out, Sumner walked over to a cobalt blue lowered Chevrolet Impala. He stood several feet from the window with an unlit cigarette in his mouth. Without taking his gaze off the school parking lot Sumner asked the young Hispanic man in the drivers seat "You got a light?"

Without looking toward Sumner the man handed his burning cigarette out the window. Sumner took it and lit his cigarette, then handed it back. "You holding?" he asked.

"What are you looking for?"

Sumner thought for a moment. *Better get this right. Small plastic bags, probably speed or LSD. Maybe cocaine, these are rich kids. Naw, these Mexicans are selling speed or acid.*

"Whites," Sumner said indicating the small white "x" scored tablets of amphetamine so popular with students.

The passenger turned and spoke in Spanish to the driver. After several seconds he turned to Sumner. "How much?"

"A dime," answered Sumner indicating a $10 bag of tablets.

The passenger took a deep breath and sat silently. Sumner stood quietly in the awkward silence for half a minute before he realized the man was holding a small clear plastic bag of white tablets in his right hand. Sumner made a mental note of the tattoo of a serpent wrapped around a woman on his right forearm. Reaching quickly into his pocket for money Sumner fumbled a roll of bills dropping them on the sidewalk. He groped clumsily picking up the money.

"Hey Holmes, be cool," replied the passenger as he closed his hand to conceal the contents of the bag.

"Yeah, sorry," said Sumner as he handed the money over. Taking the merchandise he made his farewells. "See you next week man."

"Pendaho," muttered passenger as the driver started the vehicle and drove off. Sumner made a mental note of the license number.

Sumner drove to the parking lot behind the public library on Pearl Ave. *Unlikely to have any dopers at the library.* There he took a blank police report and evidence bag from beneath the spare tire compartment of his vehicle. Upon completing his report and marking the evidence he then drove to Der Weiner Schnitzel where he called in to his handler and then dined on two hot dogs with sauerkraut and a soda. After finishing his meal and reading the newspaper he headed to pick up his new friend Karl.

Sumner pulled into the parking lot of the Adult Education Center just after dark. Karl climbed quickly into the vehicle and frantically directed, "Go, go."

"What's up," asked Sumner as he pulled away.

"Some stereos got stolen out of some of the guy's cars," he explained. "I thought it might be you."

"Well, car stereos are definitely my forte, but it was not me this time."

"Let's get out of here anyway. I'm hungry. Would you stop at Jack in the Box?"

Sumner drove to the Jack in the Box located at Branham Lane and Almaden Expressway and as he turned in three young men in various states of intoxication blocked the driveway. When they did not move Sumner tooted the horn. A young man, short and stocky with curly light brown hair turned and began pounding his open hand on the hood of the car and yelling obscenities. Karl alighted from the passenger side and, producing a pistol from his waist band grabbed the young provocateur sticking the barrel of the pistol under his chin.

"Why are you pounding on my friend's ride asshole?"

"Hey let him go man," pleaded the other two inebriates.

"Shut the fuck up or you're all gonna get your fucking heads blown off," Karl warned pushing the barrel harder against the toughs chin as the two moved back. People began to exit the establishment as Sumner moved up quickly behind Karl placing his right hand on Karl's shoulder.

"Be cool man," Sumner muttered to Karl. "It's OK," Sumner announced raising his hands and facing the growing group of onlookers. "It's all cool. He's just a Viet Nam vet who got a little jumpy. Never make loud noises around a vet." Sumner turned to Karl. "Let's get the fuck out of here!"

"What was that all about," inquired Sumner as he accelerated out of the parking lot.

"That guy was a douche bag. He needs to learn some manners."

"Yeah well, pulling a rod in public could get you shot. Did you even look to make sure there weren't any bulls around?" (Bulls are how the criminal *element* refer to uniformed police officers).

"Fuck'em…they're all a bunch of pussies."

"OK, well McDonald's will have to do. I'm afraid our behavior at Jack in the Box was somewhat less cordial than they require of their patrons."

Karl stared blankly at Sumner for a moment. "What the fuck did you just say?"

Sumner looked back at Karl. After several seconds they both burst out in laughter. "You're a good partner," Karl said. "I appreciate you taking care of me tonight and I didn't like that little prick screwing with you."

"I'm cool with it," Sumner replied. *Partner? This morning he was trying to give me up as a Narc and tonight I'm his partner. This assignment is going to be one hell of a roller coaster ride.*

CHAPTER 15

"Karl Koningsburg. He did eighteen months in CYA for assault and battery. It seems he has a bit of a temper," Dreyer advised as he received Sumner's report and evidence through the car window.

"Yeah, I got a little demonstration last night. He pulled his gat on some drunk dumb ass who wouldn't get out of the driveway at Jack in the Box. It could have gotten messy."

"Based on the other information in your Daily Report the registered owner of the car at Leland High is Reuben Gonzales. He was probably the driver. Small time dealer. Speed and grass. From your description of the tattoo on the passenger's right forearm we believe him to be Roberto Pagan, Gonzales cousin. Goes by the nickname of Snake. He's a little heavier operator. Did some time at Folsom for auto theft and possession for sales. He's on parole."

"What the hell are parolees doing hanging around a high school?" Sumner marveled.

"This is why we brought you up, to find all that out."

"Dandy, just dandy. So much for the low risk operation."

"Are you going armed?"

"I haven't been. That revolver is a little bulky and hard to conceal."

"The Boss is going to get departmental clearance for you to carry an automatic for this assignment." San Jose Police Department had a strict policy of officers carrying only revolvers. "What do you think you want?"

"A Walther PPK," Sumner said without hesitation. "Double action on the first shot, small and easy to conceal."

"Not a lot of hitting power," Dreyer cautioned.

"Well, it will all be at close range if comes to that." Sumner put his Volkswagen into gear and headed out of the underground parking lot. "See ya."

§

Sumner drove to Lynnbrook High School on the west side of town. There he engaged a group of students in the park across the street. After some inconsequential conversation Sumner directed his comment to one particularly talkative young man.

"So who's got the bag?"

All went silent and uncomfortable as the students made their way back to campus. The young man held out his hand. "I'm Wade."

"Les," Sumner shook hands.

"The only way you score here is through Jesse," Wade informed.

"Who the hell is Jesse?"

"The school hired him as a security guard this year. He's some kind of police school student, but he's taken over all the dope on campus. He's even got girls he works out of his van." *Prostitutes at a high school?*

"Can you duke me in?" Sumner asked.

"I guess, come with me."

Wade was an awkward kid. Never really part of the in crowd, but because he was harmless he was tolerated. Wade was desperate to have a friend of some consequence, as this would, of course, define him as a person of greater distinction. Wade attached himself almost desperately to Sumner.

As they approached a grey van in the far corner of the parking lot a large black man stepped from behind the vehicle wearing dark blue wool slacks and a light blue shirt. *Dressed like a security guard.* "What are you doing?" he demanded. "Who's this?"

"This is my cousin from Utah," explained Wade. "He needs something."

"What?"

Hell I don't even know what this guy peddles. I'll have to make an educated guess.

"I'm looking for some acid," Sumner replied.

"How much?"

"A quantity if you can do it." A quantity is 100 doses.

"You got any money?"

Sumner produced a roll of $100 bills.

"Yeah, I can do that. But then you get the fuck out of here. You ain't gonna be cutting in on my action around here."

"Not a problem," said Sumner as he peeled off two $100 bills and received a clear plastic bag containing purple tablets. "Purple haze... cool."

Jesse laughed. "Hey, a good looking kid like you should have a date."

"A date?"

"Yeah, I got a couple girls. One right here in the van who would love to party with good looking white boy like you."

Amazing, the guy is supposed to be providing security and he's selling drugs and hookers right on campus. Well, I guess the administration can't complain. After all, he did get rid of all the other drug dealers.

"No thanks, but I will get back to you next week. What else can you do?"

"Anything you want man. You know you really need a date."

"Yeah, see ya."

"Hey, how long you going to be in town," asked Jesse, now growing cautiously suspicious.

"Just till summer, then I go into the Army."

"The Army?!"

"Yeah, I'm on the college plan. Catch you later."

"Are you really going into the Army," asked Wade as they walked toward Sumner's vehicle.

"Yeah, why not?"

"That's cool."

"Hey let me give you a ride home," offered Sumner as the bell rang signaling the end of the school day. "So what's the deal with this Jesse guy?" asked Sumner as Wade guided him through the affluent Westside neighborhood toward his parents home.

"The school was having a lot of trouble with dealers selling dope in the parking lot. The police department said they didn't have enough officers to watch it all the time and suggested that the school hire off duty police to work security, like what they do on the eastside. But the Principal didn't want armed police officers on campus so they went through some police school where guys go to learn how to be cops and hired this guy."

"Don't you think it's a little strange that the guy who is supposed to be keeping the place drug free is the one selling the drugs?"

"Yeah, but everybody is too afraid of him to say anything."

This shit is going to have to come to an end, Sumner thought. "Hey I've got a date tonight. Do you know where I can get some coke?"

"Yeah, the PK...turn here," Wade directed.

PK? Wade guided Sumner back to a residence around the corner from the high school.

"Tommy Samuelson. He used to sell a lot of dope at school, but Jesse chased him off, along with everyone else who was peddling."

"Why do you call him the PK?"

"His dad is Reverend Samuelson at the New Life Church. So Tommy is the Pastor's Kid." *Clever.*

When they arrived at the two story residence Wade rang the doorbell , which was answered by a disheveled, sandy haired young man wearing nothing but his boxer shorts. "Hey, Wade. What's the haps?"

"Tommy, this is my old neighbor Les. His family moved to Indiana and they're out here visiting. He has a date tonight and she likes coke." *Damn, for a nice, clean cut kid this guy is a pathological liar. He makes up believable whoppers on the fly.*

"A coke whore, huh?" Tommy smiled and extended his hand to Sumner.

"She's not a whore," said Sumner with some indignance. "But she does like coke."

"Sorry, I didn't mean any offense." *Good, he's contrite.*

"Hey no offense taken," said Sumner shaking his hand. "Can you do a gram or two?"

"Come on upstairs." Sumner and Wade followed Tommy to his bedroom on the second floor. As they reached his bedroom the door bell rang again. "I'll be right back."

Tommy returned a moment later with two attractive blond haired girls in their late teens.

"This is Lucy and this is Ashley," said Tommy gesturing to the girls. "This is Les from Indiana. He's a friend of Wade's." Sumner greeted the girls with a bow of his head.

"Is this a bad time?" asked Ashley obviously uncomfortable with the presence of a stranger.

"No, he's cool. What do you need?" Tommy announced.

"We just want to each do a line," she replied coyly.

Sumner silently mouthed the words "Coke whores." Tommy suppressed a chuckle then nodded affirmatively.

"No problem," replied Tommy pulling a 6 x6 inch mirror from the bottom drawer of his night stand. He then proceeded to pour some cocaine from a bindle folded from the page of a magazine. Tommy chopped up the white powder with a razor blade and arranged the substance into two three inch lines. He then handed Ashley a short section of a drinking straw and the mirror. She looked at Sumner somewhat self consciously and then quickly drew half the line of cocaine through the straw into one nostril and then switching drew the rest into the other side of her nose. The process was repeated with the other line by Lucy.

"Aaahhh," said Lucy rubbing the side of her nose. "Good stuff." She then ran her finger across the mirror picking up the residue left on the glass and stuck her finger into her mouth rubbing the powder onto her upper gum.

Sumner produced two $100 bills and handed them to Tommy.

"You want to try this?" asked Tommy holding up the mirror that Lucy had returned to him. *Shit, how am I going to get out of this?*

Sumner looked at Lucy and Ashley for a moment. Turning to Tommy he shook his head. "Naw, I gotta stay straight until tonight. Besides this is a pretty good endorsement of the quality of your blow," he said gesturing to the girls. Tommy smiled broadly and handed Sumner two bindles.

"So what's the story with this Jesse dude?" Sumner asked.

"Ewwwweee. He is so creepy," groused Ashley.

"They hired him to keep the drug dealers off campus, but now he's selling all the drugs," alleged Lucy. "He has a car full of Black Panthers driving around all the time and if anyone fucks with him he calls them for help on his radio. I heard they killed a cop at Prospect High." *Oh my god how rumors roll.*

"He's bad news," advised Tommy. "Stay away from him."

"We gotta go," said Sumner waving to Wade.

"Can you give us a ride?" asked Ashley.

"Sure, where to?"

"Westgate mall."

"Hey, I'll see you two in Sunday school?" Tommy called to the girls.

"Of course," they chirped sweetly.

Sumner drove to the Westgate Shopping Mall where he dropped the girls.

"I need a smoke, I'll be right back," said Sumner. Exiting the car he called to Ashley who was walking through the entrance of the Mall.

"I'll be right there," she called to Lucy. "Yeeesss," she sang to Sumner.

"Hey I'm going be here for a couple of months until I go into the Army. I need a solid connection. Do you know someone who can handle a little larger volume than Tommy?"

"You just want to get hooked up with a connection? Awwhh, I thought you wanted to ask me out." *Oh hell, how do I get out of this?*

"Ashley, I'm just a Midwest boy from the farm country. You are just w-a-ay too much woman for me."

Ashley smiled seductively. "Are you sure?"

"Do you have a connection?"

She moved alluringly placing her mouth almost against Sumner's right ear and breathed hotly as she ordered him "Pick me up after school tomorrow…at the park across the street."

Sumner turned to face her, his mouth less than an inch from her lush lips. "After school it is," he answered as he turned sharply and walked off. *I don't know. I just don't know about this.*

"Did you get a date with Ashley?" Wade asked as Sumner climbed into the car.

"Yeah, yeah I got a date."

"She's the hottest girl in school. You're a lucky guy, you just got here."

"Yeah, I'm real lucky all right."

Sumner drove Wade home. They exchanged phone numbers. "I got some things going tomorrow. I'll see you on Friday," Sumner advised.

"There's a party on Friday night. Some kid from Saratoga High is throwing it. Ashley could get us in."

"I'll ask her."

"Yeah," replied Wade knowingly as he winked and closed the car door.

§

"Christian Book Store…fifteen minutes," Dreyer stated.

Sumner hung up the phone and retrieved his reports and evidence from the gun locker located in the clothes closet of his bedroom. When he arrived at the store the parking lot was full. *No crooks anywhere near the Christian Book Store.*

As he passed the evidence envelopes and reports through the window to his handler Dreyer looked dour. "When are you meeting this Ashley girl?"

"This afternoon at 3:00."

"Be very careful with this. She's a minor. Take someone with you."

"All right, I'll get that kid Wade to come with us."

"Your subject Jesse has several aliases…Jesse Black, Jesse Driscol, and Jesse Johnson. A pretty lengthy rap sheet. Done time for rape, assault and battery, pimping. A bad boy."

"He's supposed to be a student at some police school. Were you able to find anything out?"

"He's a student at San Jose City College, majoring in their Law Enforcement Program. That's how he got this gig. Someone recommended him to the principal at Lynbrook."

"How the hell does an ex con get into the Law Enforcement program at City College?" Sumner was perplexed. "His operation needs to come to an end today."

"I talked to the Boss. We do nothing until this investigation is concluded."

"Jeez Sergeant. This guy is selling drugs, running hookers and generally terrorizing the kids at that school."

"The Boss is adamant that this operation will not be compromised. He goes down with everyone else when you and Beckworth have completed your investigations. The only kids that are terrorized are the drug dealers he's chased off. The dopers buying drugs from him would be getting their dope from somebody. The Boss wants you to concentrate on what you're doing and don't worry about making any arrests."

"What about Tommy Samuelson?"

"Clean as a whistle. No priors, nothing."

"We may find a lot of that with these more affluent kids."

"Then find out who is supplying them. That's what we need to know. That's why we brought you into Narco."

"I'm on it. See you later."

CHAPTER 16

A knock at the door. *Dammit, who now?* The young undercover officer squirmed with discomfort at the thought of more unknown criminal drug addicts arriving. *They're going to be paranoid as hell about me...anything could happen.* There were already four "hypes" present in the "shooting gallery" and they were all highly suspicious of the newcomer. John Fisher cracked the door and peered out.

"What?" asked Fisher abruptly.

"You holding?" came the almost desperate plea.

"Goddammit, I told you to always call first. And who the fuck is that?"

"My partner Rickie, he's cool."

"I'll decide who's cool, asshole," Fisher admonished harshly. "Now get him the fuck out of here."

"Can I just score two bags? We're really hurtin'."

"Come back alone and we'll talk." Fisher slammed the door.

"Now who the fuck did you say you are?" Fisher turned to the inexperienced young narcotic operative with demanding resolution. "And who sent you here?"

Sumner's hands were beginning to sweat and his pulse was racing. *Damn, my face is flushing bright red* just like it always does when he became nervous or frightened. This was his first "cold shot" as an undercover operative. Unlike his rather easy foray onto the high school scene, Ted Sumner was attempting to insert himself into the drug culture of well-known addict and heroin dealer John Fisher, without an introduction by any trusted acquaintance of Fisher's. And, though he had allowed the unknown individual into his "crib," Fisher was growing ever more suspicious of the identity and motives of his visitor.

"You're the one who told me to come here dumbass," Sumner answered, mustering what little gumption he still possessed.

"I did?!"

"You told me over at Mike Boyles, while you were packing your nose with about a quarter ounce of the coke I had just copped for my old lady, that if I ever needed anything to come to you."

"I did?"

"You did."

"Ooooh-h...I don't remember."

"How convenient," Sumner challenged with growing confidence.

Fisher looked around the room pensively. The others were waiting anxiously for his direction. Three of them were entering the first stages of heroin addiction withdrawal and were in need of a fix, but the slightly overweight 20 year old blond girl appeared healthy.

"OK, we're going to need to see you shoot the dope," Fisher ordered the officer.

Sumner was on the spot. He was not an addict and an intravenous injection of this type might end his life, not to mention his professional career as a police officer. *Time to dance.*

"Look man, I thought it was going to be just you and me. I don't know these people. Someone could be a narc."

"I can vouch for everyone here except you," Fisher stated with rising incredulity.

"I'm just a little nervous with people I don't know in the room." The officer was being methodically boxed in and his inexperience left him running out of options.

"Well I came here to do this and I don't care, I'm ready," announced the young blond girl.

Fisher eyed the young undercover as the black haired hype prepared the solution. He first emptied the contents of two rolled balloons into a filthy soot covered kitchen spoon on which the handle had been bent back in order that it might stand on it's own without spilling the contents. He then emptied water drawn into a hypodermic syringe into the spoon. The girl wrapped a piece of rubber surgical tubing around her upper left arm and began patting the inside of her left elbow in order to draw up a vein, as her associated lit two matches and held them under the spoon, bringing the contents to a boil. Next, he rolled up a small piece of cotton that he tore from a filthy ball lying amongst his paraphernalia and dropped it into the boiling solution. Finally, he placed the point of the needle of the syringe into the cotton ball, in order to filter any impurities that had failed to dissolve, and drew the solution into the needle.

Officer Sumner grew squeamish as he was about to observed for the first time, a drug addict "mainlining" heroin. The black haired hype turned to the girl to administer the injection, but she took the syringe from him his hand holding out her left arm. "I'll do it honey, you tie me off."

The needle pushed against the raised vein but did not puncture the skin. *Dull from overuse* Sumner surmised. Her companion then took the syringe gently from her and pushed the needle against the vein as he tapped on the backend with his index finger. The needle tore through the skin plunging into the vein as blood formed around the ragged injection site. The officer watched with rapt fascination as the hypodermic slowly emptied into the young girls arm.

Her companion removed the needle and rubbed the injection site for a moment, then removed from her arm the surgical tubing that he had used to tie her off. She sat back on the dilapidated sofa with an expression of dreamy contentment as the black haired hype drew water from a glass into the syringe and squirted it out in order to "clean the rig".

"You're right, this is better than any orgasm," she purred softly as her eyelids slowly lowered to half mast.

Fisher turned aggressively to the undercover. "It's showtime."

Suddenly the young girl jerked uncontrollably, then began to convulse violently.

"What the fuck?" Fisher howled.

"She's ODing," her companion shot back.

"How could she be ODing? You said she gets down with you all the time."

"She just chips, this is the first time she's ever mainlined. What the fuck do we do?" the hype pleaded

"Shoot her up with milk...I heard that works," Fisher offered.

"You're going to have to call an ambulance," Sumner insisted. "She's dying."

The girl convulsed violently, and then slipped into unconsciousness.

"No ambulance," Fisher stated firmly. "You're going to have to get her the fuck out of here."

"Where am I supposed to take her?" the hype objected.

"I don't know, just get here the fuck out of here," Fisher demanded. "How could you swack her up with two bags when she's never mainlined?"

"I wanted her to have a good rush...I didn't think your shit was that potent."

The girl gave one last shudder as her breathing came to a stop.

Sumner looked on helplessly as the young girl took her last breath. Fisher and her friend continued to argue as the other two hypes quickly departed the apartment.

Sumner turned to Fisher handing him thirty dollars. "Give me two bags, I'm getting out of here."

"You gotta help us get rid of this body."

"Screw you, this is your problem."

Fisher handed Sumner two rolled balloons each containing one quarter teaspoon of Heroin. "I still don't trust you."

"You got bigger problems than me," Sumner replied. "See you later."

When he got his undercover vehicle Sumner drove four blocks to the Boots and Saddles Saloon. There he used the public telephone to call SJPD Communications and advised of the recent overdose and dead body that would soon be disposed. Shaken and angry, Sumner then drove back to the scene and parked his undercover vehicle in the guest parking lot of the apartments across the street and sat silently in the dark watching and waiting.

Approximately twenty minutes later he observed Fisher and the dark haired hype coming down the stairs carrying a rolled up blanket, quite obviously containing the girl's body. They walked through the carport area and across the parking lot of the adjacent apartment building where they deposited the body in the garbage dumpster. Furious that his call to communications had not been responded to by the Patrol Division, and disgusted with the waste of a human life, Sumner shook his head in bewildered anguish. *If I had known what this was going to be like I would never have taken this assignment* he thought to himself.

CHAPTER 17

Sumner sat in his parked vehicle surveying the parking lot in search of Wade. At 3:00 PM the bell rang signaling the end of the school day and people began to file out of the buildings. Then he spotted her approaching. *My god. Could that skirt be any shorter or those heels any higher.* Ashley crossed the street wearing the shortest mini skirt Sumner had ever seen and at least five inch high heels. She climbed into the passenger seat and leaned in toward Sumner's face in an attempt to kiss him. Sumner turned his face forward and started the car. "Where to?"

"Willow Glen High. Come in on Cherry Ave. My friend is usually out behind the football grandstand," she directed.

When they arrived there were four cars parked on Cherry Ave directly behind the grandstand, which conveniently shielded them from view from the school. There were several dozen young people milling around. Ashley approached a tall, skinny, greasy haired man in his early twenties with a swarthy complexion and a pitted face. As he turned to greet Ashley he placed his right hand on the back of her neck, grabbing the nap of her hair he placed his open mouth on hers and began plunging his tongue into her mouth. *Whoa, that sleaz looks like he might have syphilis.* Ashley tried to pull away but he placed his other hand on her buttocks and pulled her tighter. After several seconds Ashley was able to discretely extricate herself from his grip. After a short conversation she gestured toward the car. The man looked toward Sumner. *Oh hell, Frank Pimentel. And he does have syphilis.* Sumner had arrested Pimentel three years earlier for Burglary. *He must have just gotten out of prison recently. If he recognizes me this operation is finished.* As they approached the vehicle Pimentel again grabbed Ashley behind the neck and stuck his tongue into her mouth. Ashley pulled away and gestured toward Sumner.

"Frank, this is Les. He wants to do some business."

Pimentel opened the door and sat down in the passenger seat. He stared contemptuously at Sumner for a moment. "Don't I know you?" he asked with latent suspicion.

"Maybe. I've been living in Chicago the last ten years. You ever make it out that way?"

Pimentel continued to examine Sumner for several seconds. "I don't know man, you look familiar."

"Yeah, well, I have that kind of face. Can you do a quarter ounce?"

"A quarter ounce?! That's a lot of blow."

"Girls like Ashley are expensive."

Pimentel cautiously looked Sumner over once again, then reached into his waistband and produced a paper bag from which he removed a rolled plastic bag containing white powder. "Five big ones," he ordered holding out his right hand.

Sumner pulled a roll of bills from his pocket and peeled off five $100 bills. The transaction complete Pimentel exited the vehicle. As he attempted to grab Ashley once again she adroitly ducked under his reach and entered the vehicle.

"Go," she ordered. Sumner made a large u turn across the middle of the street and headed toward Curtner Ave. Ashley appeared visibly perturbed and was not talkative as Sumner headed back toward her home. Finally she spoke, "You know that guy is not my boyfriend."

She's going to want to party and this is a perfect pretense to get rid of her.

"You could have fooled me," Sumner feigned jealousy.

"I didn't want him to kiss me," she protested.

"You probably didn't want to open your mouth so he could stick his tongue in either."

"Oh yuk. Just the thought makes me want to throw up." She softened her countenance. "Let's go to my house and party before my parents get home," she cooed.

"I don't think so."

"Why not? Are you mad?" She placed her hand on Sumner's leg. *This ain't good.*

"I don't know. I feel a little weird." *I've got to disengage. I can't supply her with cocaine.*

"Well let me make you feel better," she leaned over and began to unzip Sumner's pants. *What the hell???*

"No, I don't think so," he protested as he pushed her back into her seat.

"Are you kidding? You really don't want me to give you head?"

How am I going to talk my way out of this? "No I don't. You were swapping spit with that guy and he didn't look too healthy. I think he might have syphilis." *That ought to do it.*

Tears began to stream down her face as she sobbed "I told you that guy is not my boyfriend, it…it makes me sick that he kissed me."

Sumner pulled up in front of her home. "Look, I'm just going to cut out. I'll talk to you tomorrow." He reached across and opened the passenger door.

"Unbelievable," she cried as she stepped out of the vehicle.

Sumner drove off as Ashley stood on the side of the street in front of her house crying. *She's just a little coke whore, why do I feel like hell?*

CHAPTER 18

S umner pulled into the parking lot at Del Mar High School. Several people watched as he drove to the east side of the lot and parked. He exited his vehicle and stood with his arms crossed leaning against the driver's door. A group of seven young men approached slowly.

"What are you doing here man," asked a medium height slender young man with long blond hair. Sumner ignored him. "Hey, I asked you a question."

Sumner stood up straight and moved quickly toward the questioner stopping inches from his face. "I'm here to meet someone." The others moved to encircle Sumner.

"Are you him?"

The guy looked around confused. The others looked at him and each other trying to make sense of the question. "You don't know who you're meeting?"

"I know his name...Bob Murphy. Are you Bob Murphy?" Sumner smirked as he thought to himself, *now that's funny...Robert Murphy is the Chief of the San Jose Police Department.*

"I'm not Bob Murphy," he replied somewhat bemused.

"You're not?" Sumner demanded moving closer, his nose less than an inch from the inquisitor. "Are you sure?"

"I know who I am," he pleaded dropping his gaze.

"What about you guys, any of you Bob Murphy?"

They all shook their heads in agreement that they were indeed not Bob Murphy. A tall, slender, long brown hair young man stepped through the group and up to Sumner. *This guy looks older…mid twenties I'd say. And he's tatted with prison ink.*

"You know, you look like a fucking nark," he said pounding the point of his right index finger into Sumner's chest. "And we got enough narks around here. So why don't you just get the fuck out of here." CRACK, came the painful sound of breaking bone as Sumner moved casually stroking his hair back with his right hand as his left hand shot up with lighting speed grabbing the man's pointing finger, snapping it back so it now pointed at him. The man screamed in agony.

"Hey that's not cool," screamed a younger, maybe 15 year old, female who had gathered at the edge of the small crowd.

"It's not cool to put your hands on someone you don't know," Sumner said calmly as he pulled a cigarette from his shirt pocket and placed it in his mouth. The crowd began to disperse as the bell rang, signaling the end of the lunch hour. The broken fingered man hobbled away assisted by two other young men. "Butch would have kicked his fucking ass," one murmured. "Shut the fuck up," replied the broken fingered one.

"You got a light?"

Sumner whirled around at the question to face a short, medium built young man with short brownish, blond hair. Sumner pulled a book of matches from his pocket and lit the requester's cigarette and then his own.

"Shouldn't you be getting to class?" Sumner asked.

"I should," he replied. "But I got expelled last year. Haven't been to class since."

Sumner let a crooked smile creep across his face. "You aren't Bob Murphy by any chance?"

"Huh, no. I'm Max Gardner." He extended his hand and Sumner shook it.

"So who is the welcome wagon chairman?"

"His name is name is Mark Hilton. He used to go to school here, but he got busted for drugs a few years back and went to prison. He hangs around here all the time selling dope."

"Where the fuck is he going now?"

"Sometimes he hangs out in the restrooms during class, gets high and does his deals."

"Who the hell is this Butch guy who would have kicked my ass?"

"Some big time gangster he's always talking about. He's got some kind of hero worship about the guy. Drops his name like an anvil. I think he gets his dope from him. I've never met him."

"Why did he get so touchy about me being here?"

"He probably thinks you're going to cut in on some of his action."

"That's funny."

"What's funny?"

"I could have been a customer for him. I'm here to buy, not sell."

"Yeah sure."

"Yeah sure what?" Sumner demanded.

"You may be here to buy today, but you're definitely scouting this place for market potential."

"Now why do you say that?"

"Because you don't look like the kind of guy who would hang around a high school just to buy dope from a bunch of punk kids. You look like the kind of guy who wants to cash in on their dumb asses."

"You may be right, but today I'm kind of dry and I need to score."

"Stick around. This place becomes a smorgasbord after school."

"Why after school?" Sumner asked somewhat confused.

"Because that's party time and that's when people need chemicals," Max replied shaking his head in disbelief.

I looked pretty dumb there. Need to recover. "Well then Hilton is smart to get here at lunch time and offer the early bird specials."

Max shrugged. "You may be right."

"Come on, I'll buy you a burger," Sumner announced.

"Cool, thanks."

During the next hour and a half Max enthusiastically filled Sumner in on who's who in drug ware marketplace that is Del Mar High School. *Unbelievable…ex-convicts, prostitutes, gangsters, motorcycle gangs. Nefarious characters of every conceivable sort. What the hell has happened to our high schools?*

As 3:00 PM approached Sumner and Max returned to the Del Mar High School parking lot. Sure enough, at least a half a dozen pushers were positioned about the premises. LSD on the south side, cocaine and weed on the eastside, speed at the center. *I need to find out more about the sources of LSD.* "Hey, I need some acid. Can you duke me in?" Sumner inquired of Max.

"Follow me," Max stepped off waving for Sumner to follow.

As they approached a purple Ford Fairlane parked near the gym on the south side of the parking lot, two slender young men in their early 20's began to shuffle uncomfortably. Max gestured a greeting and attempted to put them at ease. "Hey guys, how's it going?" "Joe, I need to introduce you to someone."

"Who the fuck is this guy, I've never seen him around here before," asked Joe, a medium height, white male with medium length straight light brown hair and long filthy fingernails.

"This is Les. He's my sister's boyfriend."

"What the fuck does he want?"

"He wants to steal all your dope, your money and fuck your girlfriend. What makes you so damned suspicious?" Max shot back sarcastically.

Joe flushed with embarrassment. Max pushed the issue. "He wants to purchase your wares if it's all the same to you. What the fuck are you here for anyway?"

"What do you want?"

"Acid, a quantity," Sumner answered.

"That's a lot of dope. You planning on going into business?"

"I've got a lot of friends."

Joe eyed Sumner suspiciously. He turned to Max. "You're sister's boyfriend huh? I didn't know you had a sister."

"You didn't know I have a dog either. He's a cool guy; I've known him for years."

Max certainly has the repartee down. And he's sticking it all out on the line for me.

Joe gave Sumner another look over. "You look familiar. Don't I know you?"

"Yeah, you look familiar too. You in the GED program at the Adult Ed Center?"

"Huh, no. No. You ever been locked up?"

"Juvie five years ago. For joyriding in the school principal's car. I did three days."

Joe shook his head laughing. "The principal's car?"

"The dumb ass used to leave his keys in the ignition."

"Two hundred." Joe handed Sumner a clear plastic bag containing clear crystalline tablets.

"Windowpane!" Sumner exclaimed as he handed Joe two $100 bills.

"Eight way windowpane. The best high there is," Joe replied proudly. "No nigger shit. My connection gets this directly from the Professor."

"The Professor," Sumner asked coyly.

"The dude used to be a chemistry professor at some university. He knows his shit. He manufactures the best acid."

"Now that's a guy I'd like to meet," Sumner probed.

"Not a chance. I don't even get to meet him. Only Andreas gets face time with him."

"Andreas?" Sumner asked.

Joe shot him a wary look. "Hey I don't even know you man."

"I'm just impressed. You're very well connected." Sumner could see Joe puff with a bit of prideful self-esteem.

"Yeah, and I protect those relationships," Joe announced with great aplomb.

The parking lot had grown crowded and Joe turned his attention to providing service to others who had gathered. Sumner gestured to Max that it was time to go. As he turned Sumner looked directly into the enraged face of Mark Hilton. Sumner instantly detected violent movement by Hilton and dropped both hands in a cross block toward his groin area.

CRACK...impact. Hilton had struck low with a knife attempting to plunge it into Sumner's stomach. Sumner stepped back with his right leg transitioning his block into a grab of the offending hand of Hilton which still held the knife. Bringing Hilton's hand high in a clockwise arcing motion Sumner snapped on a wrist lock that brought Hilton over head first and sent the knife flying from his grip. Sumner struck with a right kick landing it directly to the face of his assailant snapping his head back and his nose erupted in a geyser of blood. Sumner then brought his right leg around in a high guillotine like motion over Hilton and brought his heel crashing down on the back of Hilton's head, hammering him unconscious to the ground. Sumner grabbed the knife and, placing it under his foot, broke off the blade. As the adrenalin rush subsided and his blood pressure began to return to normal Sumner began to hear the commotion of the crowd that had gathered.

"Butt fucker!!! You butt fucker," screamed the young girl who had earlier chastised Sumner for breaking Hilton's finger, as she jumped up and down on the hood of a parked car in a lunatic rage, "you butt fucker, leave him alone." *I wonder what her parents would say if they saw their daughter now.*

Sumner nodded to Max. "Time to leave."

Sumner turned and surveyed the crowd assessing their reaction. They all stared in rapt astonishment. *They've obviously never seen two grown men engaged in a life and death struggle* he surmised. He took a last look at Hilton who lay unconscious in a rapidly growing pool of blood. He turned to walk away, then turned back suddenly. "I'm at least going to get something for my trouble," he announced. Sumner reached into the right front pocket of the unconscious Mark Hilton and removed a bag containing a half dozen bindles of cocaine. He patted, and then retrieved the contents of the left front pocket. More bindles. And from Hilton's waistband Sumner removed a one ounce bag of marijuana and a small automatic pistol. *A 32 caliber. Is that the only gun these crooks carry? And why the hell didn't he just shoot me?* Sumner stood and looked around at the speechless onlookers. "Mine by right of conquest!" he announced in a stentorian proclamation pregnant with drama. As he walked toward his car Sumner noticed several teachers near the buildings watching the commotion. *Guns, knives and exconvicts...no wonder they don't dare get involved.*

§

"Room 13, Sundowner Inn on The Alameda in thirty minutes. The Boss wants a face to face," Dreyer instructed.

"Why?"

"Because he's the Boss and he wants a face to face." Dreyer was in no mood to play twenty questions. *Something must be up.*

Sumner drove cautiously, checking for any tail or inadvertent encounter with a crook. As he arrived at the motel he pulled into the rear parking lot checking for a tail one last time. Upon reaching Room 13 he knocked on the door and was admitted by Sgt Dreyer and there Lt. Bertotti waiting impatiently. "Sit down," ordered Dreyer.

"The Chief got a call from the Principal of Del Mar High. The Principal wanted to know if we had any plainclothes officers working the campus," Bertotti explained.

"Why would he think that," Sumner asked suspiciously. "Do you think we've been compromised?"

"Oh, I don't know," Bertotti pondered in mock bemusement. "Maybe it's because of the way you handled Mark Hilton. Here's an ex convict who all the students, and the teachers for that matter, are scared to death of, and some guy hands him his ass like he's a cheap punk leaving him lying unconscious in a pool of his own blood. He just kinda figured it must be a cop."

"Boss, he coped a Sunday on me. Tried a prison yard shank to my gut. He got up close and brought the knife in low and fast. He almost got me. I blocked it with the point of the knife touching my stomach."

"But did you then have to take him apart like a surgeon at an autopsy? Those kids reported that it looked like Bruce Lee went to work on his ass."

"Boss I tried to end it as quick and clean as possible."

"Yeah, you did, by turning him into hamburger then taking all his dope and gun. And then you announced it was yours by right of conquest. What kind of theatrical bullshit was that?"

"I fucked up. I was scared and the adrenalin was still running. And somebody was going to lift his dope while he was out anyway...I figured I would go ahead and make the possession for sale case."

"He didn't come to for two hours," Dreyer replied.

Sumner looked back and forth at his supervisors. "Is the department in trouble here?"

"No," Bertotti answered. "The Chief fielded this personally. But he was not amused when the Principal informed him that the individual in question had been in the parking lot looking to buy drugs from a person named Bob Murphy."

"Sorry about that. The pressure of the job has caused my sense of humor to become somewhat perverse," Sumner replied apologetically. "But you've got appreciate the comic irony."

"No, I don't," the Boss said curtly.

"What's the down side?" Sumner asked.

"The Chief feels that the high school's staff is on alert that there might be a police investigation underway. These principals all talk and they will be covering their asses by reporting all suspicious activity from now on. It could get dicey for you out there."

"Nothing about this assignment has been as represented. I suppose I'll just have to go with the flow like I have all along."

"Well, it's only for a couple more weeks," Bertotti shrugged. He turned to Dreyer. "Brief him."

"Your sparring partner, Mark Hilton, is on parole for possession for sales of cocaine. Did three years at Folsom. His cell mate was a guy named Arthur Swearengen aka Butch Swearengen. Swearengen is bad news. Homicide is working him on two incidents. He did five years of a five to fifteen sentence for sales. Watch your ass if he shows up on the scene."

"I know Butch Swearengen. What else?"

"Your other crook is Joe Hamilton. He's done county time for drug offenses. But

we are very interested in this professor he mentioned."

"What about Andreas?"

"We can't find anything on him."

"Looks like I've got my work cut out for me for the next few weeks."

"Don't worry about those people. Just keep making buys from as many suspects as you can. We'll tend to them later," the Boss instructed.

"I'm going back to Patrol in less than a month," Sumner was confused.

"Maybe," said the Boss as he got up and left.

"What's going on?" Sumner asked.

"Nothing," replied Dreyer. "Get your ass to work. The City's not paying you to sit around bullshitting."

CHAPTER 19

"6:00 AM? Don't you ever sleep?" Dreyer asked through his car window as he yawned.

"This is the only time I know there are no dopers around. It's getting to where I can't go anywhere without running into someone I've bought dope from," Sumner carped. "Last Sunday when the wife and I were in church one of the little assholes was working as an alter boy."

"You've got over 450 buys from 209 suspects, some of them real heavy weights. Beckworth has about the same. The Boss is stoked at the production you guys are managing. You're each now getting up to three or four buys a day," Dreyer informed. "We're going to wrap this up in just a few days."

"Yeah, but this was supposed to be a high school operation and only a few of these buys were actually from high school students," Sumner pondered.

"That tells us exactly what we needed to know. Most the pushers providing drugs to the high schools are not students," Dreyer explained. "In fact, they all, for the most part, lead back to the same sources as for the rest of the dopers…HA's, Mexican Bob and Old Man Richard for speed, Rondal McGuire for Cocaine and the Sotello Organization for Heroin. It filters down through different channels, but essentially the same sources of supply."

"What about LSD?"

"All indications from your investigations, and that is the best source of information we have at this time, is that the main source is this guy The Professor."

"I don't think I will have time to get to him in the next week. I'm not even close."

"At least we have some good intel. The Boss wants you to start getting your complaints filed and your indictments and arrest warrants ready for MERGE."

"Does that mean I can get a hair cut and a shave?" Sumner's coarse dishpan blond hair had grown down to his shoulders. And his beard had grown in red and scruffy.

"Not yet," Dreyer instructed.

"Why the fuck not?"

"We may have a few more things for you to do."

§

One week later, the investigations completed and the complaints filed, the Street Enforcement Team, assisted by the MERGE/SWAT Unit fanned out through the city arresting the hundreds of suspects as well as individuals for any on site offenses. The total of suspects taken into custody came to 521, including Mark Hilton for Attempted Murder as well as possession of cocaine and carrying a loaded concealed firearm.

Sumner spent the next four months testifying in court. There were motions to suppress evidence, motions to dismiss the charges, motions to disclose informants and then the trials. When each and every matter had been adjudicated 100% of the suspects had either been found guilty or had negotiated a plea.

As had been planned, the simultaneous round up of this large number of suspects was extensively covered by the news media. And the psychological impact upon the community and the high school population in particular, was astounding, as had been anticipated by the architects of the operation. Everyone was sure that there were undercover narcs everywhere. The Mayor went on television and proclaimed that a major, perhaps fatal blow had been administered to the illicit drug trade in Northern California. But Sumner had learned during his daily performance of stagecraft through the malodorous purgatory of the shadow world of narcotics that he had not even touched the tip of the iceberg. He had come to realize that this matter of illegal drugs was far more pervasive and monstrous than anyone, the police, the traffickers or even the Federal Government, could even conceive much less comprehend. The war against drugs was far from over.

Chapter 20

"Headed to court?" the Boss asked.

"Yeah. I feel kind of silly in suit and tie with all this hair and beard," Sumner responded. "When can I get cleaned up?"

"Soon. I need to meet with you before you leave tonight. Be sure to come back here before you head home."

"I should be back in an hour or so. This is just a motion to discover."

Sumner left PAB and walked across the Police parking lot toward the Santa Clara County Municipal courthouse. He got off the elevator on the third floor where he found Deputy District Attorney Adam Babich waiting outside of Department 10, the courtroom of presiding Judge Wayne Kano.

"They're going to want to know if there was an informant in this matter," Babich advised.

"There wasn't one," Sumner replied.

"How did you meet the defendant?"

"I was at a party with a girl from Lynnbrook High. He was trying to hit on her all night. That's how we met."

"Was she an informant?"

"No, she was entirely unwitting."

"So she didn't know you were a police officer and she was not in the employ of the San Jose Police Department?"

"No. I met her while making a buy at another suspect's home. She introduced me to several dealers that she knew. I was her date at the party. As far as she knew I was a kid who used to live in the neighborhood and was staying with friends for a few months until I was to go into the Army."

"OK. Let's get it done," Babich replied opening the door to the courtroom.

After court Sumner headed back to the Narcotic Unit. As he cut through the parking lot behind the Police locker room he noticed several dozen marked Police cars parked by the back door. *Swing shift is getting ready to hit the street.* As he passed by a K-9 unit a 125 pound German shepherd leapt at the rear window snarling and snapping. Sumner jumped back with a start. "Damn that mutt!"

"Don't blame him, he's just doing his job," replied Ron Barron, the dog's handler. "After all, you do look like puke."

"I understand. He just startled the shit out of me."

"When are you coming back to Patrol?"

"Anytime now. I'm just finishing up all the court cases," Sumner explained. "If they would just put me back in Patrol working swing shift then all this court would be overtime instead of straight time."

"That's probably why they're keeping you up there. You're on the clock all day while you're going to court and they don't have to pay you overtime."

"Yep. But I should be getting cleaned up and back in uniform pretty soon."

"I'm working District 3. You're old hunting grounds," Babich informed. "We've got an empty car on beat 31."

"Who's the Sergeant?"

"Bill Bailey."

A good supervisor. "I'll see if I can slide in there," Sumner mused.

"We've got a good team. It would be fun to work together again."

"Yeah, I'm looking forward to it."

When Sumner arrived back at the Narcotic Unit Lt. Bertotti called him into his office. Sumner took a seat across the desk from the Boss.

"I had a meeting with the Chief and Deputy Chief yesterday," Bertotti advised. "They want to continue the program."

"The high school program? I think that pond is dry."

"Not the high school program exactly," the Boss explained. "They are very impressed with the quality and volume of cases you were able to make working deep undercover. They want you to continue in that capacity while expanding the scope of your investigations."

"You mean get to the sources?"

"As far as you can go. And also to provide intel to the Major Violators team."

"Dreyer verified that the supply sources of the high school drugs are all the same violators that the Buy Team and Majors Violators Team are already working. What do you need me for?"

"We feel that you might have a little more success in a deep cover capacity. At any rate they want to attack the problem from all directions."

"The Buy Team is already working the problem. Why don't you just cut them loose and let them infiltrate like I did. Why the hell do you need me?"

"You've already had success with this mode of operation. The Buy Team works with cover and body transmitters. They can only get so far into the culture."

"Well let them start working uncovered like I did. Believe me they'll learn fast."

"Our intention is to bring up more deep undercover operatives and have you train them."

"Train them?" Sumner was astonished. "Give them the same five days of training you gave me and throw them into the deep end of the pool. They'll learn to swim or they'll get the hell out of the water."

"What's the problem?"

"Boss, no two contacts were the same. It's a constantly moving target, I can't teach anyone to do this; they either can or they can't."

"Well you've proven that you can and we want you to continue in the deep cover capacity."

Shit! My home life is in shambles. My wife is emotionally distant, we have not been intimate in months and she is mortified to be seen with me in public because of my appearance. How could it get any worse?

"How much time are they talking about?"

"You will be permanently assigned to Narcotics."

Sumner's heart sank, "So basically until I burn out, fizzle out or cash in?"

"A few years up here, then you make sergeant and you go back to Patrol as a supervisor."

"Boss, deep undercover requires a great deal of time and I don't dare loose concentration. I have to socialize with these assholes, all the while being vigilant not to let myself get into a position where they will expect me to use the damn drugs or grow suspicious enough to terminate me. It's a full time job. I won't have any time to study for the sergeant's test."

"We'll get you a private tutor."

"Yeah, wonderful. So I'm permanently assigned to Narcotics and I am no longer the kiddy cop?"

The Boss raised his open hands as if handing something to Sumner. "It's all yours."

"If I agree, where do you want me to start?"

"That is entirely up to you. You're the only one who has ever done this type of operation so you've got a better idea of where to begin than anyone else. Who's the real power on the street? Of all the bad ass supplier's on the street, who has the biggest reputation?"

"Old man Richard? You expect me to get to him?" *You're out-a-your mind!*

Lt. Bertotti, scowled, "Well, no. We've been after him for years and no one's even gotten close; but there are others down the food chain who are reachable. We want you to dig in as deep as you can go."

"I'm sure my wife is going to be thrilled about this," Sumner contemplated the ramifications of accepting the assignment. He was deeply torn—far more conflicted than he was willing to reveal to his boss.

"Can I have some time to think this over?"

Lt. Bertotti leaned forward and looked Sumner square in the eyes. "I thought I made myself clear. Both the Chief and the Deputy Chief are *pleased* with what you've accomplished; and they want more—a *lot* more. Now, go home and tell your wife what a great job you've done and how the top brass has decided that you are indispensable. You need to change your appearance a bit anyway. So why don't you clean up a little, your wife will appreciate that."

"Yeah, that might soften the impact." "All right Boss. I...I guess, I'm in."

"Great." The Boss stood and reached across his desk and shook Sumner's hand.

"Yeah, great," Sumner shook his head slowly as he walked out of the Lt's office. "Yeah, that's just great."

As he made his way to his car Sumner thought of the crime maze he'd already uncovered. The assumptions that the department had made when he first went undercover were worse than naive. The drug distribution to high school kids had proven to be a small part of a much greater and far more dangerous criminal enterprise than anyone had anticipated. And real monsters lurked in the shadows. Old man Richard, the Professor...

Sumner was self confident, almost to the point of being cocky; but deep in his gut there was a cold hard knot of fear. *This isn't what I signed up for,* he thought, *I've got a wife and kids. Sumner,!* His conscience screamed at him, *how the hell did you get yourself into this?*

BOOK II

THE EARLY
YEARS

CHAPTER 21

Ted Sumner didn't grow up wanting to be a policeman. As a child he didn't play cops and robbers with his friends and didn't watch police shows on television. In fact, the police programs that he did occasionally tune in to, "The Untouchables" and "M Squad," he found somewhat disturbing due to the overtly violent content. As a little boy, he was much more interested in cowboys and Indians. He would sit for hours on rainy Saturday mornings watching "The Lone Ranger," "Lash Leroux," and "Hopalong Cassidy." Then at the age of seven, when he became eligible for Little League Baseball, he developed a passion for athletics, particularly football and baseball. His great childhood desire was to play football for the San Francisco 49ers.

Though a generally happy child, he learned at a rather young age that the world can be an unfriendly place. To compensate for his average size, he took up boxing in the YMCA program under the tutelage of Coach Denny Johnson. Denny, the son of a close family friend and business associate of his parents, discerned great talent in young Sumner and directed him to the boxing summer camp held each year at San Jose State University by the great Coach Julius "Julie" Menendez. Sumner greatly admired Denny and was shattered when he learned that he suffered a broken neck during a water skiing accident at the age of 22. Much to his despair, Sumner's first mentor and role model was to spend the rest of his life in a wheelchair paralyzed from the neck down.

Julie Menendez was the coach of the perennial NCAA Championship San Jose State University Boxing Team and had been Coach of the U.S. Olympic Boxing Team in 1960 where his most notable charge was a nineteen-year-old gold medalist named Cassius Clay, who would later become the great World Heavyweight Champion Muhammad Ali. Sumner blossomed as a boxer under the guidance of Coach Menendez and for a time considered entering Golden Gloves competition to test his abilities in consideration for a possible run at prizefighting. But fate would lead him in another direction.

On a late summer afternoon in 1963, he stopped by his alma mater, Shepherd Junior High School, to visit his eighth grade teacher, Dave Cardenas. Mr. Cardenas was a Korean War veteran and an avid boxer. He had taken Sumner under his wing and helped him to further refine his boxing skills. But on that particular day Mr. Cardenas was more interested in telling Sumner about his newest passion…Kenpo Karate. After an intense hour of discussion and demonstration by Mr. Cardenas, Sumner was convinced that he must learn Kenpo.

Sumner enlisted his good friend, the artistic prodigy Rick Harper, who was later to gain fame as a key member of the Disney brain trust, as his training partner, and both lads undertook the tedious process of convincing their parents of the great necessity of their learning this, then, obscure oriental form of self-defense. Finally winning their parents' approval, they enrolled in the newly opened "Tracy's Kenpo Karate School" where Mr. Cardenas was also a student. His training thus begun, Sumner continued his pursuit of excellence in the art with unremitting diligence.

When it came time to enter college, Sumner passed on a scholarship to the Ivy League Brown University (after all, he reasoned, who on the West Coast had ever heard of Brown University?), as well as an appointment to the United States Military Academy at West Point and settled on studying at San Jose State University in order to be close to home where he could continue his study of Kenpo Karate. Sumner was awarded his Black Belt in October of 1968, one week before his eighteenth birthday, thus shattering the long standing rule that nobody under the age of eighteen could attain the rank of Black Belt. This promotion was the single event that was to have the most impact on Sumner's life. Looking down for the first time at the Black Belt strapped around his waist, Sumner came to the realization that nearly anything to which he truly aspired was within his capacity. His confidence soaring, he knew that he had just been initiated, through the crucible of training and testing, into the very thin ranks of the most elite fraternity of martial artists on Earth, the Black Belts. He soon began work as an instructor for the Tracy Brothers, learning their cutting edge teaching processes that preceded by several decades the modern adult learning models to emerge in late 20th Century.

Though best known for its Schools of Engineering and Education, San Jose State University is also world renowned for its Administration of Justice Department where Law Enforcement Agencies from around the world sent their most promising people to study the most modern and cutting edge crime fighting sciences. And, while attending the University on a history scholarship, Sumner enrolled in several Administration of Justice classes as electives. Intrigued by the methodical scientific processes presented in the program, he became increasingly attracted to the possibilities of a career in police work.

But all that would have to wait. The United States Army beckoned and would not take no for an answer. Sumner had to put college and Kenpo on hold.

CHAPTER 22

As soon as he completed his active military service, he returned to civilian life and a job working for his family's business that supplied engineering equipment and supplies to the high tech industry in the Silicon Valley. He had intended to resume his studies at San Jose State University, but the school had changed the requirements in his major, dropping several classes from the curriculum. An additional year of study would be required just to catch up to where he had been. Instead, Sumner applied for admittance and was accepted to the academically conservative but scholastically incomparable University of San Francisco. A small Jesuit University located across from Golden Gate Park in the City by the Bay, USF offered an outstanding Law School, Medical School and, as luck would have it for Sumner, Liberal Arts School where he could complete his undergraduate studies in history, taking economic advantage of his still uncompleted scholarship.

Sumner soon found that his father, who was also his employer at this time, was in a state of complete disapproval of his choice of major and insisted that Sumner not waste his time on such trifles, but instead switch to a business major. Sumner's father, Frank L. Sumner, Jr., had grown up during the Great Depression, the youngest of five sons, on the family farm along the Snake River in Idaho, where his father Frank Sr. also owned a successful ready mix concrete company. Frank Jr. chaffed under the heavy handed supervision of his older brothers and finally escaped by following his dream, and the poems of Robert Service, taking a job with a construction company in the land of the midnight sun. But his adventure in Alaska was short lived when the Japanese invaded and Frank Jr. was one of the last Americans evacuated from Kiska Island. He returned home and enlisted in the United States Army Air Corps to do his part for his country in World War II. Frank Jr. became a gifted P-40 fighter pilot with natural instincts that made him a formidable aerial combatant. He was slated to deploy to the south coast of England where he was assigned to lead a squadron of fighters in low level support of the Normandy Invasion. However, at the last minute, the Army Air Corps realized that their losses would be high and new pilots would be desperately needed, so First Lieutenant Frank L. Sumner Jr. was reassigned to Luke Air Base as an instructor of fighter pilots. Lt. Sumner's squadron, without him, went on to England, where they were wiped out to the last man as they took on the Nazi flack towers of Hitler's Fortress Europe, clearing the way for the Airborne assault the night before D-Day. As the War raged on, with improvements in aircraft, fighter losses fell and there developed a surplus of pilots. Growing bored with inactivity; Lt. Frank Sumner asked for and received a transfer to a bomber flight crew whereupon he was assigned as a copilot on a B-29 Super Fortress Bomber. This transfer took him to Kirtland Field Air Force Base just outside Albuquerque, New Mexico. It was while stationed at Kirtland Field that Frank Jr. was introduced to the charming young Helen Paulantis, an Albuquerque native and recent graduate of University of New Mexico. They began dating and were wed shortly after the end of the War.

Returning to Idaho, the hotshot fighter pilot quickly remembered the reasons for which he had originally departed. After the heady experience of serving as an officer and a gentleman at the throttle of a high powered war plane, the prospect of working the farm for his older brothers was like a sentence to purgatory. Frank and Helen started making plans to move to a more cosmopolitan setting. They considered Salt Lake City and Denver, but finally decided on San Francisco, ultimately settling down in San Jose, fifty miles south.

Frank landed a job working for Kennedy Business Machines owned by the well connected and very astute business operative Roy Kennedy, who took a keen interest in the handsome, polished, young veteran with the country boy charm. Frank and Helen prospered in the postwar boom as the former farm boy learned the full particulars and intricacies of driving a business from the sagacious Mr. Kennedy. Inevitably the day finally came when Frank had to strike out on his own. During a disagreement over a calculation change in the commission schedule that gave more money to the company and less to the salesman, a technique which Frank later mastered and inflicted repeatedly upon the sales representatives of his own company, Frank looked his boss in the eye and stated flatly "What you are telling me is that I'm fired," whereupon he walked out the door never to return.

He was ready to go, but he needed funding. To his chagrin, Frank Sumner Jr. was compelled to borrow, in exchange for a share of the business, the required money he needed from Frank Sumner Sr. His family was once again in his business and his domineering and opinionated father Frank Sr. exerted his influence over Frank Jr. and the business until the day he died.

Ted Sumner stood firm against the wishes of his father, Frank Jr. as well as the pressures being exerted in the background by his grandfather Frank Sr. It was Ted's cherished belief that undergraduate studies would be the one and only time in his life when he would have the opportunity to study history, English, political science, and philosophy in a structured academic environment. He fervently felt that the acquisition of a classical education was essential to complete his initiation into manhood. He insisted that he could later pursue business studies in graduate school as well as during an "on the job training" modality, learning business practice and procedures directly from, and in total compliance with, the ethical schema of his father and grandfather. During one of their many discussions of disagreement over this matter, Sumner's father elected for the "nuclear option" by threatening to fire Ted if he did not comply with his wishes. Sumner replied, "All right, if that's how you feel, I'll go to work for the Police Department." His father made the monumental mistake of laughing.

Throughout his life, Sumner's accomplishments, particularly his athletic feats, had been belittled by his father. No matter how spectacular his performance, Frank Jr. would continually recall Sumner's one mistake in a football game, one error in a baseball game, and would talk on and on, laughing robustly about his son's failure to perform flawlessly. Though it was probably simply a perverse sense of humor that his father possessed, it was for this reason, Sumner began to discourage his parents' attendance at his athletic events. But something began to happen as Sumner plunged headlong into his study of Kenpo Karate. He began to gain confidence in his abilities, physical and intellectual. He began to mature into a person grounded in the realities of his own talents, as well as intimately aware of his short comings. He learned to maximize his strong points and minimize the effects of his weaknesses, real or perceived. He had learned to release and control the inner fury that martial artists refer to as the "warrior spirit" that drives a person after the body and mind have decided they can go no further. And through all this he had come to recognize that most anything that he was completely committed to accomplish was probably never entirely out of his reach. His father's mocking comments were stricken from Sumner's memory and his vocabulary. *Laugh it up; you're looking at a police officer.*

After submitting an application with the San Jose Police Department, Sumner decided to also apply with the Santa Clara County Sheriff's Department. The high profile trial of Angela Davis for conspiracy in the Marin County courthouse mass murders was soon to be held in the Santa Clara County Superior Court, and the Sheriff's Department was hiring deputies over their allotted strength in, what were referred to, as "unclassified positions" in order expand their ranks to meet the upcoming manpower needs. Ted Sumner finished second out of 1100 applicants on the written examination for the San Jose Police Department. He then passed the physical and background tests with flying colors. He had the same results at the Sheriff's Department. But to his utter consternation, he soon learned that the written exam for the San Jose Police Department had been challenged in court as being unfair to non-English speaking applicants and the hiring process had been put on hold until such time as the legal matter had been resolved.

At that time, the Sheriff's Department notified Sumner that they had an unclassified slot for him. They advised him that as positions on the department strength allotment became open, the unclassified deputies would he reclassified as "probationary" and would commence their one year probation as regular officers. Sumner took the job and was sworn in as Deputy Sheriff for the County of Santa Clara.

Sumner was soon transferred to the midnight shift working in the main jail. He worked there for the next year, getting to know many of the criminal elements of San Jose, as well as forming lifelong bonds of friendship with the deputies with whom he worked. He rated them as some of the finest officers he would ever meet. But the claustrophobic confinement and constant exposure to the culture of incarceration in the main jail was toxic to Sumner's spirit. As a result, his enthusiasm for law enforcement began to fade.

CHAPTER 23

The buzzer sounded at the swing shift Control Officer's station at the Santa Clara County main jail. That signal in the Control Cage inside the booking area alerted the Control Officer that officers were requesting admittance. Deputy Higginbotham looked up and verified that Deputies Sumner, Brown, and Lange of the graveyard shift had arrived at the window of the main gate. "Hig" pressed the button on the control panel within the "cage" and the heavy steel door slowly slid open. The deputies entered the entrance cell and the door slowly closed behind them, sealing them into the jail until dawn.

Prisoners being brought in for booking would be brought into the entrance cell, and then be placed into the "holding cell" and the gate would be automatically closed by the Control Officer. Police officers booking prisoners would then pass through a gate on the opposite side of the entrance cell. There, wall lockers were located where all weapons would be deposited and locked before the control officer would open the gate giving officers access to the main booking area. Sumner locked up his off duty Smith and Wesson 2 inch .38 caliber Chief Special revolver and his custom Gil Hibbin folding utility knife. The Hibbin blade was one of Sumner's prized possessions. Gil Hibbin was more than a master knife smith. He was also a student of Kenpo. Hibbin was first trained in Salt Lake City by Mills Crenshaw, one of Ed Parker's first Black Belts. Parker was the father of American Kenpo. Parker had also trained the Tracy brothers who had trained Ted Sumner. Hibbin had become famous throughout the Kenpo world for his superior craftsmanship in steel. He was also Sumner's friend. The knife had a long and illustrious history that Sumner treasured, but seldom shared. Once their weapons were secured, the graveyard shift officers then entered the booking area.

Sumner reported to the officer dining area of the main jail kitchen where the officers coming on duty were briefed by the shift sergeant. The midnight shift consisted of 14 deputies and one sergeant to administer a four story jail housing approximately a thousand prisoners. The midnight jail officers took their seats at the table as Sergeant Dick Min gave the assignments. Sumner was assigned, as usual when Sergeant Min was in charge, to second deck. The second deck comprised the showers and holding cell where prisoners were relieved of their clothing, given a shower, deloused, "dressed out" in the distinctive orange jump suit, issued bedding and assigned to a cell. Also located on second deck were the infirmary, medium security cells, and protective custody cells. Beyond the heavy bared gate next to the elevator was the second floor "east" wing of the jail manned by two additional deputies.

Sergeant Min had been stationed in Japan during his stint with the United States Air Force. While there, he had taken the opportunity to study Shito Ryu Karate. Min knew that Sumner was a newly promoted Nidan, second degree black belt, in Kenpo Karate and Min would spend several hours on second deck each evening passionately discussing theory and working technique with Sumner. Sergeant Min loved the Kenpo katas, which are exercise forms comprised of the myriad self defense movements in the art, as well as the self defense techniques, and often asked Sumner to demonstrate them. Those demonstrations were within clear view of the second deck prisoners housed in the west section, an area known as the "Snake Pits" and within the view of those prisoners contained in the south section that was known as "Siberia."

Sergeant Min was the consummate professional law enforcement officer. He had been assigned to the Sheriff's Departments elite "H" Car Unit prior to his recent promotion to the rank of Sergeant. The "H" Cars were unmarked; they were manned by plainclothes officers who worked what officers refer to as, "predatory law enforcement." These officers had no beat responsibilities, and as a result they were able to provide quick reaction to crimes in progress, follow up on open cases, and target career criminals. Sergeant Min and his partner Tom Sing virtually wrote the book on this type of law enforcement. Their tactical direction had made the Santa Clara County Sheriff's "H" Cars nationally famous.

Ted Sumner had great respect for Sergeant Min, and the opportunity to work on perfecting his Kenpo while on duty made the jail assignment almost pleasant.

Sergeant Min gathered the new shift around a table and briefed them. "Swing Shift conducted a shake down of the whole jail tonight," Sergeant Min advised. "They came up with all kinds of crap; Two laundry carts full of knives and other assorted weapons, drugs, hypodermics, even a zip gun" (a home-made device capable of discharging a 22 caliber bullet). Sumner looked around the table as the other deputies took it all in. "Deck Patrol, move and take the census," Min ordered.

The two Deck Patrol Officers were charged with taking a head count at the beginning of the shift to assure that all the prisoners were present and where they should be. This process was repeated at the beginning of each shift to assure that the oncoming shift was taking custody of the full compliment of inmates and that nobody had escaped during the previous shift.

"Sumner... St. Denis, since swing shift has sanitized the decks, tonight is a good time for you guys to replace the nightlights in the Snake Pits," ordered Min. The nightlights provided low voltage illumination inside the cells after "lights out." Enough for the deputies to see into the cells, but not bright enough to disturb the inmates sleep.

The inmates quartered in the aptly named "Snake Pits" were medium security prisoners, burglars, car thieves, petty drug dealers, and the like. These people lived in a twilight world where they perpetually strove to remain invisible to the police, whether on the street or in the jail.

Min explained, for the benefit of the new officers, that one of their favorite games was breaking out the nightlights. "They aren't satisfied just to extinguish the light," Min continued, "but they also use the light bulbs to clandestinely make coffee and hot chocolate." Min described how the prisoners would break lose the screw end of the bulb, and empty out the filament. They would then tear strips off their bed sheet and create a "sling" to hold the bulb. The empty bulb would then be filled with water and coffee or chocolate, stolen from the kitchen. Next they would roll up toilet paper and light it on fire while dangling the sling above the flames. *Clever,* Sumner thought as he listened to the sergeant's explanation. *They've got plenty of time on their hands to come up with this stuff.*

§

As Sumner stepped off the elevator onto the second deck, he noticed something different about the atmosphere. *The prisoners are louder and more agitated than usual,* he thought…*Must be upset about the shakedown.* Even in his short time on the job, Sumner had learned that, contrary to the conventional wisdom of command staff, the prisoners did not sleep at night. They slept all day and were awake all night, very much in keeping with the schedule they kept on the street for optimum criminal activity. *That way they do not disrupt their circadian cycle, and they can go right back to stealing when they get out,* Sumner thought.

Ted Sumner was not, by nature, an overly cautious man. But, for the moment he was on his best behavior. Two weeks earlier an incident had occurred that had earned Sumner a harsh verbal reprimand by the Jail Commander, Captain Ramos. A mentally disturbed prisoner had been placed in "the hole," one of four, eight-by-eight foot padded safety cells located on second deck. He spent the entire night standing at the door of the safety cell looking through the two inch by six inch window on the door. As he stood there, he would repeatedly chortle, "Haa haa haa haa haa" in a deep eerie baritone reminiscent of Renfeld in the 1930s film "Dracula." This prisoner's weird behavior thoroughly unnerved the prisoners of the "Snake Pits" located next to the safety cells.

At 4:00 AM the jail nurse, an unpleasant, disheveled little woman whom one prisoner described as looking like she had "just taken a direct hit by an ugly bomb" stopped at the deputies' station on second deck to pick up an escort before conducting "pill call." During these rounds she would administer any prescription drugs required by inmates as well as provide aspirin for the myriad headaches claimed by prisoners. Sumner drew the short straw and fell in with the nurse to act as bodyguard. Part of his assignment was to identify the prisoners who were actually to receive prescription drugs and to assure that all medications were consumed and not stashed away.

When Sumner and the nurse arrived at the safety cell that contained the mental patient, the nurse began preparing a hypodermic. "This patient is diabetic," she proclaimed. "You will have to restrain him while I administer the insulin." Once the nurse had the hypodermic prepared, Sumner cautiously unlocked and opened the safety cell door. The stench that assaulted their nostrils was overpowering. Sumner noticed that the prisoner had shed his orange coveralls and was standing naked in the corner hunched over as if ready to grapple. The prisoner, walls and floor were all smeared with the prisoner's feces. Sumner closed and locked the door.

"What are you doing?" demanded the nurse.

"In case you didn't notice," Sumner offered far more politely than he felt, "he is covered with his own excrement."

"I have to give him a shot," countered the nurse.

Sumner then opened the door wide and gestured to the deranged man, standing in the corner drooling, covered with his own waste and laughing like an idiot, "Go ahead." The prisoner was still in a combative posture awaiting a "wrestling match."

"You have to hold him for me," she demanded.

"He is covered with filth, madam," Sumner protested laconically.

"If he doesn't get this shot, he will in all probability die and you will have murdered him," came the nurses dire warning.

Resolved to the inevitably of the situation, Sumner took a deep breath and searched desperately for a solution. Then...spotting the fire hose on the wall, he formulated a plan to make this task a little less repugnant. He took the fire hose from its rack and turned on the valve, not realizing that this action automatically would trigger an alarm that dispatched to a minimum of three SJFD Fire Stations to respond to the jail.

He flung open the door and opened the nozzle to its maximum, letting the high pressure flow of water hit the prisoner. The blast of cold water pinned the deranged man in the corner of the safety cell. After washing the prisoner reasonably clean, Sumner shut off the nozzle, dropped the hose and engaged the prisoner. He spun the man with an open hand blow to the shoulder then applied a carotid restraint across the neck. The prisoner struggled for a second, then collapsed unconscious. The nurse quickly administered the shot and swiftly withdrew from the cell, followed closely by Sumner.

As Sumner began restoring the fire hose to the rack from which it had been taken, a very excited and agitated Sgt. McPeek arrived on the scene demanding, "What the hell are you doing?"

"Putting the hose back, we had a prisoner…"

"Don't you know that you set off the fire alarm when you turned on that water valve?" scolded McPeek. "San Jose Fire is responding from three stations with nine trucks."

Sumner stammered, "He was covered with his own excrement and he had to have…"

"The Sheriff and the Under Sheriff are en route as well as Captain Ramos" (the Jail Commander).

"But he was covered with shit," Sumner protested.

"Well, you are going to be in it up to your neck," warned McPeek. "Get some Trustees to clean this mess up," McPeek ordered as he strode past the gates of the "Snake Pit." The prisoners confined therein, were yelling, cheering, chiding, and protesting the evening's action.

After a thorough investigation and debriefing by the Under Sheriff, Sumner was issued a scathing verbal reprimand by the Jail Commander Captain Ramos. Fortunately for Sumner the verbal reprimand was "unofficial," although it was documented in the commander's report and could be used as corroborating evidence of "unfit for service as a deputy" if such conduct or use of poor judgment persisted.

The next time they met, Sumner asked Sgt. Min if he noticed Sumner to be walking funny or if his butt was somewhat misshapen?

"What are you talking about?" Min demanded.

"Well," Sumner replied sheepishly, "The Jail Commander pretty well chewed it off and I just wondered if it showed."

Min let out a raucous laugh that startled the snake pit inmates.

CHAPTER 24

Sumner had taken some good natured ribbing from the other Midnight Deputies. The next night they all reported for duty wearing raincoats. And at the beginning of that evening's shift, in a mock ceremony, they presented Sumner with a toy plastic fireman's hat. But despite the verbal rough housing, and even though they would never admit it, the other Deputies allowed a grudging respect for the "balls" that the young, "as yet unclassified" Deputy had shown in the face of such a violent and revolting situation.

§

Sergeant Min arrived on second deck around 2:00 AM, later that morning, carrying a mop handle. "I'd like to see that staff set you told me about," said Sergeant Min, handing the mop handle to Sumner.

In the open area in front of the elevator, using a mop handle as a staff, Sumner performed a Kenpo kata know only as "The Staff Set". When he had finished Sergeant Min asked several questions regarding the purpose and effectiveness of several of the movements in the set. As Ted explained the purpose and intent of the movements to his Sergeant, he noticed that the prisoners in the "Snake Pits," had their heads stacked up like cordwood at the gates of their cells. They were straining to see what Sumner was doing.

"That's the dude that took out that loony with a fire hose," one prisoner muttered to the others. Information moved through the population of the jail faster than a teletype. The prisoners often knew of events that had transpired in the jail before the other officers on duty.

"Beautiful. That was beautiful," praised Sergeant Min as he headed for the elevator. "Now, you guys get those nightlights changed," ordered Min as he climbed onto the elevator.

3:00 AM. Sumner and St. Denis arrived at the gate of Cell #1 at the entrance to the "Snake Pits" with a box of low wattage light bulbs and a ladder. In keeping with departmental procedures Sumner handed St. Denis his large "cell key" which opened every door and gate in the jail and which every Deputy carried. St. Denis then opened the cell door. Sumner entered with light bulbs and ladder as St. Denis locked the barred door behind him, all in compliance with procedural protocol.

"Sorry to interrupt your sleep gentlemen," Sumner said as he set up the ladder. "I will be done here in a minute and out of your hair," Sumner promised as he started up the ladder. As he neared the top, the ladder was suddenly and violently knocked from under him. *This is not going to end well,* thought Sumner as he plummeted toward the cement floor of cell #1.

Sumner landed as he had been trained by his Kenpo instructors and as he had drilled and practiced countless hours…*palms flat, meaty part of the forearms first, on the toes, don't let the knee caps strike the ground, and kiai* (a yell that constricts the muscles and controls the breath) *hard…*"Hiyaaa!" …Sumner kiaied on impact with the concrete. Before he could draw a breath three prisoners leaped on his back, then three more piled on as the remaining two stood kicking and punching at what they considered to be their target of opportunity, a downed Deputy. Though Sumner was unable to escape, his years of martial arts training took over. He drew himself into a "tucked" position using his well developed abdominal muscles to draw his knees to his stomach. As the prisoners continued kicking, punching and biting Sumner remained largely untouched, shielded from the onslaught by the bodies of the prisoners on his back. Those directly in contact with Sumner could not move because of the weight of those prisoners on top of them. Those on top, in effect, acted as shields that blocked the blows intended for Sumner. The inmates continued to kick, punch and bite each other until those absorbing the most punishment could endure no more and turned on their fellows.

One by one the assailants detached themselves from Sumner's back and turned their fury on their own tormentors until only two men remained on the fallen Deputy. At this point Sumner became operational. He tightened his "tuck" pulling his legs further under him. As the blows of the two remaining assailants began to rain down on his back Sumner used the large muscles of his legs to leverage himself to his feet. Once standing he utilized his considerable upper body strength in a series of pivoting movements. He swung his elbows above his shoulders, head high, striking both attackers and sending them reeling. The others inmates realized what had happened and turned to attack him as they had originally planned.

It was too late. Sumner had begun a series of movements known to Kenpo practitioners as "Chinese Swings". This was a weapon of last resort to be used when facing multiple opponents in a life threatening situation. "Once you unleash these," Jim Tracy, Sumner's Kenpo instructor had cautioned, "There is no controlling them. It is a doomsday weapon that will demolish your opponents…and your friends if they are stupid enough to get close," Tracy warned, "The situation better be dire".

This situation is dire, reasoned Sumner as he "uncorked the bottle and released the genie".

The battle was over in a matter of seconds. One by one, with brutal efficiency, the attackers were knocked to their bunks, the floor, or against the bars of the cell door. Several were unconscious, more were terrified at this display of empty handed destruction, but a couple stupidly thought they would try again and the first of them lurched toward the enraged deputy.

"Crack," the sound of the impact rang through the "Snake Pits" as Sumner's now unobstructed aim zeroed in on the attacker's skull. Down he went. The last prisoner standing raised his hands in surrender, quickly backed peddled to his bunk and lay down in a submissive prone position.

Sumner stood with his back to the gate in an offensive posture that warned with the clarity of a coiled rattlesnake, "You move, I strike." Just then the elevator door opened and St. Denis, called out, "Sumner's down,

Cell #1". From the elevator sprang Sergeant Min and the four most senior midnight watch Deputies who comprised the shifts "Tactical Unit". Deputies Brown, Shipley, Meeker and Day formed a phalanx around Sergeant Min as Min shouted orders, "Shipley, Day secure the gate, Meeker, Brown prepare for entry and extraction on me." Sergeant Min's commands were crisp, clear, confident and welcome.

The population of the "Snake Pits" had become riotous. It was always like this when there was a disturbance. The inmates reacted like ancient Romans at the Coliseum, clamoring for blood. The Tactical Team reached the gate and deployed for action. As Deputy St. Denis placed the key into the lock of the cell door, Sergeant Min noticed Sumner, standing on his feet with his back to the gate.

"We heard you had a little problem," said a relieved Min. "Looks like it's them that have the problem."

"Just let me out of here," pleaded Sumner as the adrenaline rush faded and he began to weaken.

As the gate opened Sumner backed out keeping a wary eye on his former sparring partners. Then, suddenly, the last reserve of adrenaline surged into his exhausted body. Sumner paused, took a breath and re-entered the cell. Swiftly, he set up the fallen ladder, picked up the light bulbs and climbed the ladder, hissing, "There will be fucking nightlights in this cell, assholes." Once installation of the bulbs was complete, Sumner climbed down, folded up the ladder and walked casually to the gate and his incredulous fellow deputies.

"Thank you gentlemen," offered Sumner casually, he then headed for cell #2 with his ladder and light bulbs. "Larry, we have work to finish," Sumner chided St. Denis.

As he walked away the heavy hand of Sergeant Min landed on his shoulder advising, "That's enough for tonight."

"We have to get this finished," Sumner protested.

"You're punch drunk," Sergeant Min whispered quietly into Sumner's ear. "Enough for tonight. That's an order!"

Enough for tonight; yeah, enough for tonight.

CHAPTER 25

"Sumner, Keyser…third deck," called Sgt. Bill Franks, the midnight watch supervisor in the Santa Clara County Main Jail. "It's Joint Night and the Transportation Unit will be taking one from Murder Max, so your other 'guests' may get a bit rowdy."

"Check," called Keyser.

Every Wednesday night was "Joint Night" in the Main Jail. That meant that those prisoners who had been sentenced to terms in the state penitentiary were to be removed to the California State Correctional/Medical Facility at Vacaville. There they would undergo a ninety day medical observation after which they would be moved for permanent housing to one of the state's prisons where they would serve out their term. The prisoners in the Main Jail who would be making the Joint Run were routinely removed from their cells by the Transportation Unit between 3:00 and 4:00 AM and relocated in the 2nd Deck dining area. There they received a sandwich and soup before being loaded onto the Sheriff's Department bus at exactly 5:00 AM and taken to Vacaville.

On this particular night a killer was to be taken from his cell in Murder Max on Third Deck. Though he had been sentenced to die in the gas chamber for the execution style murder of a key witness scheduled to testify in the trial of Angel Davis, he would instead be serving a life sentence due to the recent repeal of California's Capital Punishment statute. Murderers of this celebrity enjoyed rock star status among the other prisoners and when one was about to be removed to prison, it was a cause for raucous behavior.

"Deck Patrol, move out and take the census," ordered Sgt. Franks. "Sumner, Keyser, if it starts getting out of hand up, there don't hesitate to call for help."

"Affirmative," replied Keyser.

"Let's go to work."

Sumner and Keyser exited the elevator on Second Deck then climbed the stairs to Third Deck. Third Deck consisted of Murder Max, Max Row, Siberia, the two Trustee Dorms and a dining hall. At the morning feeding, Sumner and Keyser would supervise two feedings of 250 prisoners each. This was generally the most dangerous time of the shift. If prisoners were going to attempt any takeover, it would be then.

It was midnight, but one would think they were at the County Fair with the noise and activity in all the cells. Nobody was sleeping, and the inmates were sensing that something eventful was about to occur of which no one wanted to miss . Sumner took a quick walk through the deck to assess the mood of the population. *The natives are restless.*

At about 1:30 AM the phone rang at the Officer's station on Third Deck. "Third Deck, Deputy Sumner."

"Sumner, this is Cortez." Deputy Rich Cortez, who had attended high school with Sumner, was three years his senior and worked Patrol in the unincorporated section of East San Jose on swing shift.

"Rich, what's up?"

"My nineteen-year-old brother just got arrested for possession of marijuana. He's down in the Fish Bowl right now." The Fish Bowl was a large windowed holding area on the Booking Floor where all new prisoners were placed prior to either making bail or being housed. "He's waiting to be OR'ed, but I would like you give him a tour of the jail before he gets out." OR is when a prisoner charged with a minor crime is released on his "own recognizance."

"I understand," Sumner replied. "It's a good night to teach him a lesson, Joint Night."

Sumner phoned the Sergeant's office and advised Franks of the situation.

"I'll send Deck Patrol up to relieve you," Franks offered. "You got twenty minutes."

Sumner exited the elevator on the Main Floor Booking area. "Which one is Robert Cortez," Sumner asked Deputy Barton who was handling the booking area.

"I'll get him."

Barton called Robert Cortez to the Fish Bowl gate and escorted him over to the booking counter where Sumner waited.

"Hi, Robert," Sumner offered.

"Ted, this is no big deal," he replied. "Did my brother send you to get me out?"

"No, Robert, your brother asked me to give you a little tour of our facility here."

"This is no big deal. I ain't afraid of this place."

"Good, then you'll have a nice tour before we lock you up," Sumner smiled an evil grin.

As they exited the elevator on Second Deck, the prisoners were in high spirits. Sumner guided Robert down the hall into the Snake Pits. Prisoners on both sides of the hallway began reaching through the bars grabbing at young Robert yelling "Put the punk in here. 'Fresh meat,' 'My new sissy.' One rather large African American prisoner stood calmly at the gate of cell 8 and quietly asked "Is that white boy here for me to fuck in the ass?"

Robert was appalled. His faced turned ashen as he clung closer to Sumner. As they reached the Isolation Holding Cells at the end of the corridor, Sumner turned and asked Robert "Which cell would you like as your new home?"

"This isn't funny Ted. Get me out of here," Robert replied in trembling voice.

"It's not supposed to be funny."

"Is it always like this?"

"Yes, Robert, this is jail."

"Ted, I just want to get out of here. Please get me out of here."

"But you haven't seen the rest of the jail," Sumner replied. "Don't you want to see Murder Max and Queen's Row?"

"I just want to go home. You can get me out of here…my brother can get me out of here, just don't put me in with any of those guys," pleaded Robert as he stared in horror at the leering prisoners reaching through the bars salivating in anticipation of the arrival of 'fresh meat."

"All right, Robert, I'll give it to you straight," Sumner's gaze bore into young Cortez. "If I get you out of here, I never want to see you back again."

"No problem, I promise."

"If you do wind up in here again, and I don't care if it's for jaywalking, I will put you right into one of these cells…hell, I may even pass you around to the sex starved animals in each of the cells," Sumner laughed a demented chortle.

"You will never see me again," Robert panted in shear terror. "I promise."

Sumner returned Cortez to the Fish Bowl, then found the OR Officer. "Is he clear for OR?"

"Yeah, we were looking for him just a few minutes ago; his parents are here to pick him up."

"Make him sweat a little," Sumner explained. "His brother is a deputy and he wants to make sure he gets the message."

"Will do."

Sumner returned to Third Deck where Deck Patrol Officers Peters and Grant were anxiously awaiting his return.

"Finally," groused Peters. "We thought you stepped out for a beer."

"Thanks, guys," Sumner said. "I had to give a tour to someone's errant younger brother."

"Ah, good night for it," replied Grant.

"Yes, it is. The inmates performed magnificently. I don't think we'll see him this side of the bars again."

§

3:40 AM and the intensity of activity in the jail had not subsided as Transportation Unit Deputies St. Clair and Hooper arrived on Third

Deck. First order of business was to remove the convicted killer, Jesus Vallanon, to a secure holding cell near the dining hall on 2nd Deck East. Deputy Hooper produced the required paper work which was signed by both Deputies Keyser and Sumner. Deputy Keyser then keyed the intercom system to broadcast into Murder Max.

"Inmate Vallanon, standby the gate for transportation."

Sumner and Keyser then led St. Clair and Hooper to the gate that stood at the entrance to the row of cells known as Murder Max. The steel barred gate to Murder Max was operated electronically and required two deputies to open. The twelve cells of Murder Max all faced to the north and each was occupied this evening. Vallanon's cell was at the end of the row.

Keyser keyed the intercom at the entrance to the row.

"Vallanon, standby the gate for transportation."

"Fuck you. I'm not coming out!" shouted the voice from the end of row.

"Vallanon, standby the gate," Keyser called again.

"I'm not coming out until you send that punk deputy with the curly hair and cute rosy cheeks down here," he called out. "I'm going to fuck him in the ass and make him my bitch before I leave here."

The inmates in Murder Max roared their collective approval as they began to chant in unison "send in the bitch, send in the bitch." They then began to rake anything metal they could find across the bars of the cells making an incredible racket as they continued to shout "send in the bitch, send in the bitch."

St. Clair, Hooper, and Keyser all stared at Sumner in anticipation. The Santa Clara County Sheriff's Department did not have a formal extraction policy in place at that time. And though a challenge of this nature was rare, it could only be met head on and extinguished by the recipient of such a declaration of war in order to discourage such confrontationist behavior in the future.

"I think he's talking about you," said Keyser to Sumner.

The tension was thick as the deputies nervously watched to see what Sumner would do in the face of this defiance. Though three deputies could, and quite appropriately should, go in and take the prisoner out, all of them knew that unless Sumner answered the challenge and vanquished the provocateur that a great deal of the respect for authority within the walls of that jailhouse would vanish and more challenges would be forthcoming. People who have not worked or lived in an environment of incarceration do not realize that while it may appear that society has imposed it's collective will on those outside the law, on a personal basis it was very much the law of the jungle. Not to mention that Sumner's career in law enforcement would be at an end if the challenge was not answered as he would be regarded by fellow officers as too insipid for the job.

"I think you're right," said Sumner as he removed his key from his belt and handed it to Keyser. "Open the gate."

The gate creaked as it slowly opened and the inmates housed on Murder Max went silent. Curly blond hair, blue eyed, rosy cheeked, twenty-one year old Deputy Sumner stepped through the gate onto Murder Max looking every bit the stereotype of the sissy white boy that Vallanon was expecting to humiliate.

As Sumner took his first step forward, the entire row erupted in an ear splitting detonation of derision, disparagement and mockery as the inmates of Murder Max began to throw everything they could lay their hands on at the young officer. Spit, feces, cups of urine, left over food, stuffing from the mattresses...anything to show their utter contempt for Sumner as he slowly walked past each cell, ignoring the warm, if somewhat repugnant reception. *I'm not feeling the love here,* he thought.

As Sumner reached Cell # 12, he slowly turned and faced the gate, urine dripping from his uniform shirt which was also splattered with old food and human feces. Deputy Keyser, seeing that he had arrived, waited for a signal to open the cell door. Sumner nodded once, keeping his eyes on the inside of the cell. As the gate slowly opened, Sumner observed the object of his contempt at the back of the cell. The row had once again gone silent, waiting in rapt anticipation for his destruction, as Sumner stepped through the cell door. Sumner observed the prisoner crouched, ready to pounce, completely naked with a sock wrapped around each hand in which he had placed a bar of soap in order to act as a sort of brass knuckles.

The killer lunged, clearly attempting to slam Sumner back up against the bars of the cell door and off balance, a position from which he could then pummel the young deputy at will. But years of training in the martial arts ignited the engine of response, sending Sumner into action. As Vallanon lunged low attempting to strike Sumner just above the hips and drive him up and back, Sumner's left hand instantly swung around in a circular motion, the radius reducing, accelerating the movement as the heel of his left hand struck down on the occipital nerve at the base of Vallanon's skull stunning him. Sumner pushed firmly down on the head of the dazed killer as his right hand simultaneously swung around in a large 360 degree circle bringing his right elbow crashing down into the attacker's spine between the T5 and T6 vertebrae. Vallanon slunk to the floor followed instantly by Sumner right knee, which landed on the back of his head pinning him to the ground. Sumner quickly handcuffed the prisoner's hands and then rolled him over onto his back. His eyes were open and he appeared conscious.

"Get up," Sumner ordered. But the prisoner did not respond. "Get up, asshole!" Sumner yelled as Murder Max once again erupted in chaos. It was clear that, though conscious, the prisoner could not move. And though the row was going wild and St. Clair, Hooper, and Keyser could not see what was going on inside the cell, they made no move to assist Sumner. The stature and dignity of every deputy on the Santa Clara County Sheriff's Department was at stake and all they could do was wait.

Sumner looked around the cell and saw a towel hanging from the sink. He grabbed the towel and wrapped it around the ankles of the fallen murderer. He then exited the cell, dragging his vanquished foe behind him like a big game hunter returning from the jungle with his trophy. The row fell silent as Sumner, realizing the astonishment and awe with which this event was being viewed, slowed his pace to tantalize the agony of each and every prisoner as he passed slowly by their cells, dragging the fallen killer through the same urine and filth that had been heaped upon him. As he reached the entrance to Murder Max, he dragged Vallanon out the door and dropped the towel at the feet of the enraptured Transportation Deputies.

"He's all yours," Sumner said casually as he retrieved his key from Keyser.

Keyser smiled broadly as he fought back his urge to shout in triumph and celebration, but celebrating would be unprofessional and would earn them the undying contempt of every inmate in the jail as well as despoil the unspoken and begrudging respect that they all have for the men with the badge who are compelled to resort to the use of violence. "Let's get you cleaned up," said Keyser as he placed his hand gently on Sumner's back.

§

Sergeant Franks telephoned the Supervisor on duty at the Vacaville Correctional Medical Facility to advise that one of the lifers scheduled to be transported this morning had been injured in an attack upon an Officer. Accountability for the whereabouts of life sentenced prisoners must be diligently adhered to and any deviation from the scheduled delivery, such as a trip to the hospital, must be approved by the Department of Corrections once the transportation has begun.

"He was injured attacking an officer?" asked the Corrections Lieutenant.

"Yeah," replied Franks.

"Throw him on the bus; we'll have someone take a look at him when he gets up here."

Vallanon was duly deposited, in his current condition, naked and smeared with urine and feces, onto the floor of one of the security cells in the Sheriff's bus. He was then transported, in that state of utter humiliation in which he had planned to leave Deputy Sumner, to the state penitentiary at Vacaville. Vallanon was eventually examined by a prison physician and found to be suffering from a severe trauma to the spinal cord that had rendered him partially paralyzed. The paralysis turned out to be a temporary condition, and after several weeks he recovered. Six years after this humiliating night Vallanon (one of several aliases used by this criminal) managed to escape from the Deuel Vocational Institute, where he was serving his life sentence, by cutting through the prison bars with several hacksaw blades that he had stolen from the machine shop. He has not been seen nor heard from since.

§

As Sumner arrived home one February morning, frustrated after a long night working at the jail and suffering from an upper respiratory infection, one of the many illnesses passed among the inmates to the deputies in the confined spaces of jail, Sumner decided to check on the status of matters at the San Jose Police Department. He dialed the number for the Police Department and requested to be put through to personnel. After inquiring as to his hiring status, he was informed that he should have been notified by mail that the department was offering to hire him and he was to begin the Academy the following Monday. As he and his wife had moved from their apartment to their new home just weeks after he had applied to the SJPD, the letter had never arrived at his place of residence. Sumner was jubilant…and crestfallen. While his passion had always been to work the street for the San Jose Police, he felt a gut punch of guilt about leaving his fellow deputies in such an abrupt manner. But this was the opportunity for which he had been preparing himself, emotionally and psychologically. And while he felt remorse at leaving so hastily he was, after-all, still an "unclassified" deputy, and the Sheriff's Department had expended no resources in training him, so the quicker he made his departure, he reasoned, the better for all concerned. He tendered his resignation to the Sheriff's Department that afternoon.

§

Sumner reported to the San Jose Police Academy, along with thirty one other officers on the morning of February 13, 1972. He and his fellow officers were sworn in at 10:00 AM that morning. After several days of processing, paperwork, and orientation, the business of learning how to be a cop began in earnest.

Sumner took to this new environment as though he had been born to it. He was enjoying his job with the satisfaction and enthusiasm of a man perusing his favorite hobby. For the first time in his life, he enjoyed getting up in the morning and going to work. He excelled in academics, physical fitness, and (most important to his standing among rank and file officers) marksmanship. He had finely honed his abilities with firearms while on active duty in the Army and was the best shot in the Academy. Though most police officer never have to fire their weapon in anger, skill in marksmanship is highly valued and respected by their peers.

After graduating from the six month Academy, he and his fellow officers were assigned to the Field Training Unit for a three month period. During this time they were each assigned a Training Officer who wrote daily evaluations on the performance of their "Trainee." Sumner was once again assigned to the midnight shift and was scheduled to work with three of the top Training Officer's over the next ninety days.

§

Ted Sumner began his career with the San Jose Police Department eager as hell. His martial arts training had won him a few friends in the Academy and even more enemies. In the highly competitive atmosphere of the Academy, anything that resulted in an edge cut two ways.

Once he graduated, he had the good fortune to draw Ben Kephart as his training officer. Kephart was a no-nonsense, by the book, professional who added common sense to his understanding of departmental rules. As a result, Sumner started out with a clear eyed understanding of where the boundaries lay. The excitement of his recent graduation was beginning to fade, and the lessons of his first training week were beginning to sink in. It was the last day of his first week in the Field Training Program. They were working the graveyard shift on the west side of town. It was just after midnight when the call came in.

"8216," their call sign came over the radio.

Kephart nodded for Sumner to answer the call. Sumner grabbed the pen from his clipboard, keyed the mike and responded, "8216."

"8216, investigate report of a 415, 1072," (10 code for disturbance and stabbing) "at The Phase Three Bar, corner of Moorpark and Saratoga…handle code two ."

"8216, 10-4."

As Sumner re-hung the mike, Kephart had already flipped the light bar switch and was already making a U-turn. He resettled himself in the seat and hunched forward over the steering wheel. His tone of voice was the one he used whenever there was a point he wanted to make sure his young trainee understood.

"Ted, what do you know about The Phase Three Bar?"

"Uh, nothing— never heard of it."

"Umm, — OK, listen-up. Phase Three is a biker bar, bad rep...worse people. Keep your head up and your mouth closed. Don't act tough but don't get pushed around either. There's nothing you can say that will impress any of these animals. They're always on the prod. We watch each other's back, AT ALL TIMES. Clear?"

"Clear."

The warm glow of apprehension started in Sumner's gut and worked outward. It wasn't fear, but rather the anticipation of combat...that hyper awareness that put all his faculties on high alert. His Kenpo instructors had taught him before a match to control that apprehension and channel his energy by controlling his breathing. He took several deep breaths, then held his breath and counted. *20 seconds, still in a shallow breathing pattern.* He took several more deep breaths and then held his breath, repeating the process until he could hold his breath for sixty seconds. This put him into a deep breathing pattern that energized his body and focused his mind. He was now ready for action.

The almost deserted streets raced by, the patrol car's flashing lights reflecting off store windows. Kephart turned onto Saratoga Ave. and immediately pulled into the Phase Three parking lot. Sumner spotted two men standing just outside the entrance and pointed toward them. Kephart nodded. He grabbed the mike and reported in.

"Control...8216, 1097."

"8216, 10-4."

Both officers exited the patrol unit and approached the two men standing at the bar's entrance. "You make the call," Kephart asked.

The taller of the two stepped forward, "Damn straight...that som'bitch had no call to knife the guy. He weren't caus'n no trouble...just up 'n knifed him like he was a hog or sumthun."

"Where is the victim?" Sumner asked.

The smaller of the two men jutted his chin in the direction of the street and offered, "He crawled off down that way."

Sumner looked at his training officer with a questioning look.

Officer Kephart nodded and turned to his clipboard, "We appreciate your cooperation, sir. Let me get some personal information."

Kephart took down witness's personal information as Sumner switched on his flashlight and began to sweep the parking lot, starting at the entrance. He quickly located a trail of blood. At a brisk walk he followed the trail of blood across the parking lot, down the street, and into a family pizza parlor.

Cautiously, he entered the warmth of the restaurant and was confronted by the unconscious, bleeding body of the victim lying face down on the floor of the foyer. The appalled patrons had reeled back in horror from this ghastly intrusion on their evening, but no one had thought to render aid to the wounded stranger in their midst, or call the cops.

Sumner grabbed a man wearing an apron by the arm, shook him once to focus his attention and took a field card from his blouse pocket and handed the card to the employee.

"Here," Sumner said firmly, "call this number...it's police dispatch. There's an ambulance on its way to the bar down the street. Tell them the Officer Sumner wants it rerouted here. Tell them that the officer and victim are here, then give them your address. Got that?"

The man nodded enthusiastically and turned to the phone by the cash register. Sumner turned back to the man on the floor and attempted to stop the profuse bleeding. He ripped the man's shirt into bandages and packed the wounds as best he could. One forearm wound required pressure, so Sumner removed the man's belt and tightened it just enough that the bleeding slowed to a slight oozing.

When the ambulance arrived, he left the work to the EMTs and returned to the bar.

As he approached, Kephart asked, "What have we got?"

"Multiple stab wounds to the abdomen. He's in pretty bad shape," Ted reported, "but the EMTs think he'll pull through."

"Hum-m," Kephart responded. "We'll put it down as an attempted murder. I've got the personal data on the witnesses, you take down their statements. They can identify the assailant." "As soon as our fill gets here, we'll go into the bar and take him into custody."

Sumner tucked his five cell Kel light under his left arm took a Form 2 Crime Report from the bottom of his clipboard, clipped it in place, and began writing down the witness's statement. As he was writing, he noticed a large white male in his mid-twenties had moved into position on his right. Instinctively, Sumner shifted his position slightly so as to have an unobstructed view of this new individual out of the corner of his eye. The guy was ripped, obviously a weightlifter. The tight "T" shirt he wore said he tried to impress people with how powerful he was. Suddenly the subject took a step forward and slammed a punch into the witness's mouth, shattering his teeth.

In an instant, Sumner had dropped the clipboard, snatched his Kel light into his right hand and pivoted to face the attacker, who had now raised both clenched fists into a classic boxer's stance. The sneer on his face clearly stated his intent.

The assailant dropped his shoulder as he began a roundhouse punch at the officer. With lightning speed, Sumner brought his light slashing down on the attacker's right fist, shattering his knuckles. He then whipped the light around in a tight circular motion, striking the man's left wrist. Continuing the motion, he this time struck the left elbow, and continued the motion, finishing with a blow to the attacker's left knee knocking him to the ground.

By now bikers began pouring out of the bar, some wearing Hells Angels "colors." Without preamble, they began punching and kicking at both Sumner and Kephart in a mindless attempt to liberate Sumner's prisoner.

Sumner yanked his handcuffed prisoner to his feet and used him as a shield as he and his training officer fought a retreating action in the direction of their car. At that moment came the unmistakable roar of the 440 cubic inch engines of police cars. No music had ever sounded as sweet as the snarl of those high powered engines.

From the shadows directly across the street three unmarked police vehicles roared across street into the parking lot screeching to a halt at the edge of the melee. The doors flew open and from each of the unmarked cars emerged four battle hardened members of the elite San Jose Police SWAT Team known as MERGE. Each SWAT officer was equipped with a 42 inch boken stick with which they proceeded to systematically and

methodically pummel the perpetrators of what had become a rapidly es-
calating riot. The business like precision with which the SWAT officers
demolished the riot was a marvel to behold. Sumner would carry that
picture in his mind for the balance of his career.

Sumner's appreciation was cut short when his training officer yelled,
"Let's get him out of here!" They threw their prisoner in the backseat
of the patrol car and headed for the hospital to get his injuries treated
and to check on the disposition of the victims. As they pulled out of the
driveway, Sumner glanced back and caught a glimpse of the SWAT Team
dispatching the remaining fragments of the crowd with the precision of
a Spartan phalanx.

As they drove toward the hospital, Sumner glanced toward his training officer for any sign of reproof or encouragement. Kephart might as
well have been a model for the Sphinx.

They arrived at Valley Medical Center Hospital at the same time as
their "fill unit" that had taken the stabbing suspect into custody at the bar.
They escorted the prisoners, under guard, to the treatment room where
they were shackled to the bed while undergoing emergency treatment.
Sumner's prisoner was treated for five broken bones in his right hand, a
broken left wrist and a sever contusion on his left elbow. Sumner used the
desk in the hospital waiting room to work on his report. While writing his
report, he heard his training officer telling another veteran officer, "...the
kid took on his first rat."

"Yeah, the kid tangled with the Prez," replied Officer Lipski.

"No shit, the Prez?!" asked a surprised Kephart.

"Filthy Phil himself."

Later, on their way to the station, Sumner asked, "What did he mean
about my taking on the Prez?"

Ben Kephart turned to his trainee in mock surprise, "You don't know?
Why kid, you arrested the head rat. Phil Cross, aka Filthy Phil. He's the
president of the local chapter of the Hell's Angels." Then Ben Kephart
threw back his head and laughed out loud, which was the first time Sumner had ever heard his training officer laugh.

In Retrospect

The stabbing suspect, who had been arrested by the back up unit at the conclusion of the SWAT Team's annihilation of the crowd, was convicted of attempted murder and sentenced to five years to life in the state penitentiary. Phil "the Prez" Cross was charged with assault and battery, as well as interfering with a police investigation. He was bailed out of jail by the club's attorney and never seen again. Two years later he made the FBI's Ten Most Wanted List.

§

Day 88 of the Field Training Program—as the briefing began, the sergeant looked long and hard at his room full of rookie officers. "Sumner," he called.

"Here."

"8102."

Sumner was being honored as the first recruit of his Academy class to be "cut loose." And he was assigned the great honor of working alone, not with another rookie. None of the rest of his class had been released from their Training Officers at that time. Even though it would be another three months before he would complete his probationary period, Sumner felt that evening that he had finally achieved the prominent stature of San Jose Police Officer.

CHAPTER 26

San Jose is a nice town, a family town; but it does have more than its share of low life bars and hangouts. That's probably a good thing, because they tend to be gathering places for ex-cons, crooks and thugs. That at least keeps them out of family neighborhoods…most of the time.

Ted Sumner spent a major portion of his law enforcement career in those sections of town. Not that he enjoyed it; but because he was very good at his job. He was needed there. He was working patrol on the "swing" shift in the downtown area of San Jose, (Once the sun goes down, in the downtown area of San Jose, it becomes a jungle.) when he got a call.

"8501," the dispatcher broke into Sumner's reverie. "415 Fight at the Cozy Bourbon, 142 East Devine."

"7115, 10-4." Sumner made a left on St James and headed toward First-Street which crossed East Devine. The *"Cozy Bourbon"* was one of the lowest of the low. It was a known hangout for crooks and drug dealers. When he arrived, Sumner found the place in shambles and an angry bartender picking up overturned tables and chairs. He approached the bartender who cursed under his breath that everything happened on his shift.

"Excuse me sir," Sumner asked politely, "What seems to be the trouble"

"The *trouble*," the barkeep replied with an angry jerk of his thumb, "booked it out the back door into the alley just before you got here."

Sumner looked cautiously out the open door that led to the alley and saw no one. As he stepped out into the alley and the foggy, dank, February night he detected movement to his left. A dark shape sprang from behind a dumpster and rushed in his direction. He caught a glint of steel as the large figure emerged from the darkness and struck at him with an overhead blow. Instinctively Sumner drove his left arm upward at a 45 degree angle in a movement he practiced virtually every day. In Kenpo Karate the move is known as an upward strike. As the blow landed he felt a sharp pain across the fingers of his left hand; the hand in which he was holding a five celled, steel, Kel flashlight.

Damn, Sumner thought, *he's got a wrench or piece of pipe or something!* Believing that he'd had been struck by a blunt instrument, and that the suspect was without a firearm, he transferred the flashlight to his right hand and years of training took over. Using a technique, known in the art of Kenpo as "Five Swords," he slashed the suspect on the right wrist with an inward strike just as the attacker attempted a second blow. Without pause he then struck the suspect across his right temple and continued the motion to his hip, gathering inertia at which point he drove the end of the light into the man's solar plexus. The suspect dropped to one knee in excruciating pain, just as Sumner swung the light around striking his left shoulder, then his left elbow and finally onto the occipital nerve at the base of the skull. The attacked collapsed in a shapeless heap.

As Sumner fought to regain his breath, he became aware of blood covering the suspect as well as his own hands. He was confused...he'd been careful to strike at targets and in a manner that should not have caused any bleeding. He was perplexed by the presence of the blood. Never the less, the suspect was now his prisoner and he was responsible for the in custody's well being.

Sumner dragged the unconscious body to his patrol car and over the radio advised his district sergeant that he had a badly bleeding suspect in custody and inquired as to whether he should stand by for an ambulance or transport the suspect to the hospital himself. The sergeant directed him transport "code 3", with red lights and siren. The sergeant did not sound pleased.

As Sumner arrived at the Valley Medical Center Hospital, he found a medical team was waiting outside the Emergency Room door with a gurney. As he skidded to a stop the medical team removed the suspect from the back seat of Ted's patrol car and began treatment on the spot At that moment Sumner's sergeant, Jerry Albertson, who had been one of Sumner's instructors in the Academy, pulled alongside. The sergeant was clearly agitated.

"Sumner," he demanded, "how did you let this thing get so far out of hand? You're supposed to be some big shot karate guy, right?"

As he stammered, searching for a reasonable explanation the Emergency Room physician stepped up and stated, "this guy's OK. A little bruised up, but what the hell happened to you?" Pointing at Sumner's gloved left hand.

Sumner held up his left hand and noticed, for the first time, that the three end fingers had been slashed by a blade and cut half way through the bones. Suddenly his left hand radiated pain at the realization that the blood was his own and his fingers had been very nearly severed from his hand.

The medical team instantly went to work on Sumner's hand. As the medical team worked to save his fingers Sumner turned to Sergeant Albertson and requested that the sergeant handcuff the suspect to the gurney so that he not walk off.

Ultimately the suspect, a resident of the nearby City of Oakland, was convicted of assault with a deadly weapon and sentenced to five years to life in the state penitentiary. Sergeant Albertson wrote a "Letter of Commendation" praising Officer Sumner's professional and efficient handling of the dangerous, potentially lethal, situation.

CHAPTER 27

"Sumner?" called the briefing sergeant.

"Here."

A wry smile crept across Sgt. Alberto's lips. "6103," he smirked as he looked toward Watch Commander Captain Morgan.

"Having him downtown should keep the snakes and swimming pools safe," Morgan quipped for the benefit of the sixty men attending the swing shift briefing.

The room erupted in laughter. Then, Officer Gary Scardino stood and walked to the podium at the front of the briefing room. He stood between Sergeant Alberto and Captain Morgan.

Scardino cleared his throat and proclaimed to the swing shift: "In honor of his fearless encounter with a large rattlesnake, the officers of the swing shift present to Officer Sumner the Great White Hunter Award." Scardino held up a Field Interrogation card with a "snake load" bullet taped to it. He presented the prize to Sumner, who graciously stood, turned and bowed to the guffawing collective. A "snake load" is a .38 caliber cartridge, but instead of a lead bullet it is armed with "bird shot" pellets making it all but impossible to miss and assuring a kill when shooting at a snake.

§

The role call (levity) drama was the result of a call for assistance to which Sumner had responded the night before. He had been working beat 14 on San Jose's affluent West Side. When he arrived at the residence of the complaining party, a short balding gentleman in his forties, Sumner was informed that there was a large rattlesnake in the family's empty swimming pool. Sumner followed the man to the backyard to the pool.

"We're having some work done on the pool and had it drained," explained the man. "The snake must have been trying to get at the water left on the bottom of the deep end." The weather had been hot and dry and it wasn't unusual for a variety of wildlife to come down from the surrounding hills in search of water. There was about six inches of water left in the deep end and the snake had apparently entered the pool to get a drink, but now could not get out.

"Why didn't you call animal control?"

"I did, but nobody was in. The operator forwarded the call to the Police Department," explained the man apologetically.

With the exception of the Police and Fire, all other departments of the City of San Jose worked weekdays from eight to five. After business hours, all complaints and calls for service are forwarded to the police.

"What do you want me to do?" asked Sumner.

"My wife and kids won't sleep with that thing in there," explained the man "Can't you just shoot it?"

Sumner looked at the man with a measure of incredulity.

"You want me to shoot the snake?" he verified.

"Yeah," confirmed the homeowner. Sumner shrugged his shoulders and drew his Colt Python 357 Magnum revolver.

"Cover your ears," said Sumner as he took aim.

BOOM! The explosion was followed by lead, smoke, and flame. A large chunk of the middle of snake's body was blown away as well as a square foot of plaster from the bottom of the pool.

Sumner looked down at the snake, which, though wounded, continued to slither about the bottom of the pool. "Looks like the pool's going to need some repair on the plaster," shrugged Sumner. "What do you want me to do?"

"Well, the damage is done, go ahead and finish that damn thing off."

Sumner took aim and fired again. BOOM! The resounding explosion was made all the more ear splitting by the reverberating echo off the cavernous walls of the empty pool. The snake was blown into two pieces but continued to slither about. Sumner took careful aim at the head of the snake and with his next shot put the animal out of its misery…together with blasting away another square foot of plaster from bottom of the pool.

Sumner looked at the resident contemplatively. "Don't touch any part of that snake," Sumner instructed. "It's just as dangerous dead as alive. Animal control will be out Monday to remove the carcass." The gentleman looked on speechless as Sumner completed his "Form 2" Incident Report and left.

It was a warm summer evening and the city was hopping. Sumner raced from call to call until about 11:00 PM when he heard over his radio "6214, 1087 Watch Commander, Blue Hills Center."

"10-4". *What the hell does he want?*

Four minutes later Sumner arrived at Blue Hills Center on the border of San Jose and the posh community of Saratoga. He pulled his patrol car next to Captain Morgan's, the front of his car facing the rear of the Captain's so that the officers could face each other while remaining seated behind the wheel. While this particular encounter was discouraged by the training division as not conducive to "officer safety," it was a common practice when officers needed to talk.

"What the hell happened out there?" demanded the Captain.

"Where?" inquired Sumner.

"That snake call," Morgan said. "You discharged your weapon."

Sumner handed the Watch Commander his report on the incident. "The guy and his family were afraid to be in the house with a poisonous snake in the pool, he asked me to dispatch the thing."

"Wasn't there anything else you could have done?"

Sumner sighed. "Alligator wrestling and snake handling are beyond the scope of my MOS," Sumner explained. MOS refers to Military Occupational Skill, which is the method by which jobs in the Army are referenced and is used by many veterans of the military to describe any job.

Morgan shot Sumner an accusing look. "Three shots?!" asked Morgan. "And you're on the pistol team."

"I hit it with all three shots," pleaded Sumner, "but I'm not a hunter. I didn't know you could blow it in two and it would still be alive."

"Well, under the circumstances, if they were that frightened and he insisted you shoot it, he will just have to live with the consequences. I don't imagine it did his pool a whole lot of good."

"Blew the hell out of the plaster," Sumner replied. Morgan just shook his head and drove off.

§

Roll call ended with Alberto's customary command, "Let's hit the streets!"

Sumner removed one of the bullets from the bandoleer on his gun belt and replaced it with the snake load he had been "awarded." *Handy thing to have* he thought.

CHAPTER 28

"6103, respond to a disturbance at the Winchell's Donut shop, Seventh and Clara." The directive that came over the police radio was crisp and demanding.

"In route," Sumner replied into the microphone. He was on his "overlap night" and working "in the hole." San Jose Police Patrol Division works four ten-hour workdays. One day of the week two teams would "overlap," meaning that there were two officers to fill each beat. Every other week one team would work "in the hole," meaning they would be spread across the city to fill beat requirements left vacant due to illness, vacation, and military leave. On this evening, Sumner was in the hole working the swing shift on beat 3 just east of downtown.

It was just after 11:00 PM. The midnight shift should be hitting the street soon. *I'll finish this call and go Code 10-7 (dinner break)* Sumner thought in response to his growling stomach.

§

Winchell's Donut shop was a twenty-four hour a day business located at the northwest corner of the parking lot of the Safeway Store at the corner of Seventh St. and Santa Clara Ave. As Sumner pulled into the parking lot, he observed a chaotic melee underway in the donut shop. A large black man, 6'8" and no less than 275 pounds was "cleaning house." There were two men down in the parking lot lying amid the broken glass that had moments before been the donut shop window. Just outside the front door of the shop, two more hapless men were locked firmly in the grip of the behemoth.

Damn! This must be Bo Mosley. During roll call, there had been an announcement that the notorious Mr. Mosley had recently been released from the state penitentiary after serving a seven year sentence for assault with a deadly weapon. Bo had spent his days and years of incarceration lifting weights and working out. He had succeeded in loading layer upon layer of muscle to his enormous frame. It was reported that Bo's thighs were 34 inches around and his biceps 20 inches. Sumner was about to find out.

He exited the patrol vehicle and grabbed his nightstick. The nightsticks issued by the department were solid oak, painted black. Sumner preferred polished cherry wood. Cherry wood was much more durable and could withstand far more impact and not splinter or split. It was also slightly heavier. Based on his martial arts experience, he had his cherry wood nightstick custom lathed to one quarter inch less diameter than the standard issue. This allowed him more maneuverability and the ability to generate greater baton "head speed."

After a year working with inmates as a deputy in the Santa Clara County jail, he felt he was somewhat familiar with mind set of "institutionalized" individuals. Mosley had only been out of prison for a couple of weeks, so Sumner reasoned that he may still be locked into that institutionalized mind set. He approached the shattered front windows of the donut shop.

"Hold it!"

"They started it," Mosley shook his head slightly to clear the sweat from his eyes. "I didn't do anything until they started it."

"Let go of them, lock you fingers behind your head, and walk this way backwards," Sumner commanded.

Mosley released his adversaries, but didn't comply with the other orders. "They started it man," repeated Bo as he walked straight toward Sumner.

"Hold it right there," growled Sumner holding up his left hand like a traffic cop.

Mosley raised his hands behind his head and Sumner stepped forward grabbing Bo's left shoulder with his left hand in order to turn him around so he could apply the handcuffs. Suddenly Mosley moved with unexpected speed. He grabbed Sumner's left arm with his right hand. Sumner struck with his right arm aiming for the radial nerve on Bo's right arm, but Mosley moved like a cat. He scooped up Sumner's right leg just above the knee and effortlessly lifted Sumner up over his head.

Sumner looked down from nine feet above the ground at the concrete surface of the parking lot where he was about to be slammed. Years of martial arts had helped Sumner develop excellent falling skills, but the combination of gravity and Mosley's almost superhuman strength were going to make this a potentially disastrous landing.

Sumner felt Mosley's grip tighten. He tried to prepare himself for the pain to follow, when a police siren suddenly rent the air. Mosley turned, brandishing Sumner above his head just as Officer Mark Louis and his rookie trainee skidded to a stop three feet from Bo. Sumner couldn't suppress the image of himself as a victim in a "B" movie, in the clutches of a great ape. Bo gave an anger filled growl and with a grunt hurled Sumner directly at the windshield of Louis's patrol car. The effort was like a child throwing a broken toy with which he had become angry.

The reduced distance to impact allowed Sumner's falling skills to save him from serious harm. His chin was tucked tightly against his chest, and he "kiaied" (yelled) loudly as his forearms slammed down on the hood and windshield of the police car and his back slammed into the glass, shattering the windshield. He shook his head and heaved a heavy huff to restart normal breathing.

In a controlled rage, Sumner leapt from the hood of the patrol car, drew his nightstick and engaged the now rampaging Mosley. Officer Louis approached to assist, but Sumner waved him off. He did not want anyone getting in the way or risk being inadvertently injured. He was about to do what he was one of the best in world at doing. With the grace of a bull fighter, he sidestepped Mosley's lunge and struck a blow across Bo's right knee. Mosley screamed in agony and reached out with his massive hands for the object of his fury. But in matters of physical combat, Sumner never made the same mistake twice. He had let Bo get a hold of him once, but would not repeat that error.

With surgical precision Sumner smashed his nightstick down on Mosley's left hand. With the emotional detachment of a butcher carving a roast, he proceed to strike Mosley's left wrist and continued the circular movement of the stick and slammed the rapidly accelerating head of the weapon into Bo's left elbow. Mosley limped toward Sumner, his rage slackening as pain began to overcome adrenalin.

"Kneel down, place your hands behind your head, and interlock your fingers." The order was clear, but Bo still had fight in him. He lunged again at Sumner, this time with his right hand. Sumner stepped clear of the big man's grasp and repeated the treatment he had just meted out to Bo's other side. The big man was starting to teeter as Sumner repeated the order. "Kneel down, cross your legs, and place your hands behind your head and interlock your fingers." Bo's anger flared, and he made one last desperate lunge just as Sumner's nightstick slammed against the inside of his left knee. Bo dropped to his knees.

"Please don't hit me anymore," Bo pleaded.

"Cross your legs, place your hands behind your head, and interlock your fingers," Sumner ordered in a thoroughly detached monotone. When Bo didn't comply, Sumner struck again against his left elbow and repeated the order.

Bo began to weep as he begged "Please don't hit me anymore." Sumner's order was again ignored and the cherry wood nightstick careened off Bo's left shoulder.

Officer Louis looked on unemotionally as his trainee remained seated in the driver's seat of the patrol car behind the shattered windshield, recoiling in revulsion at what was unfolding before him. This was Sumner's show and he was calling the shots. Sumner had been used as a bouncing ball already and he was not going to again risk himself or any other officer. Sumner's nightstick would continue to encourage Mosley to comply with his lawful commands.

"Please, Mr. Policeman, don't hit me anymore," Bo pleaded through clenched teeth and tears of pain streaming down his face.

"I'm not going to hit you anymore, Bo," Sumner said drawing his revolver "if you won't do as I say I'm just going to have to shoot you." Bo's eyes widened to the size of saucers as his expression went from weepy to one of stark terror. He quickly crossed his legs and interlocked his fingers behind his head.

That worked rather well. Sumner removed his handcuffs from the case on his gun belt and handed them to Officer Louis. "Cuff him for me, Mark," Sumner asked.

Sumner kept his pistol trained on Mosley as Officer Louis moved behind and attempted to apply Sumner's handcuffs.

"They won't fit," said Louis. "His wrists are too big." Louis sprinted to his patrol vehicle and retrieved an 18 inch plastic tie down that the police use as auxiliary handcuffs. "This will do it." He applied the restraint and stood Mosley on his feet.

Sumner holstered his weapon and took custody of the prisoner, walking him to his patrol car and placing him in the backseat behind the prisoner cage.

"That was a little rough," said Louis, inspecting the damaged windshield of his vehicle. "Are you OK?"

"Well, I wouldn't want a steady diet of that kind of treatment, but I think I'm OK," Sumner replied. "But your partner doesn't look so good, you better tend to him."

"Yeah, you need a Form 3 from me?" Louis asked.

"If you don't mind," said Sumner "a lot of people saw what went down and to the uninitiated it might have looked a bit excessive."

"No problem. I got it covered."

FOLLOW-UP

Mosley's parole was violated, and he was returned to prison for an additional two years of weightlifting and bodybuilding. Officer Louis's young trainee was so shaken by what he had witnessed that apparently he had second thoughts about his career choice. At any rate, he failed to return to work the following day...or ever.

CHAPTER 29

There were times, when dealing with the public, that police officers became disgusted with the citizens with whom they interact. One of the private jokes between officers working some of the sleazier parts of the city was that they were going on 10-91 (animal) patrol. The sad truth was that animals usually treated each other with more dignity than many, so called humans did.

Ted Sumner was working swing shift patrol on the poorer east side of town one fall evening when he received an urgent call.

"6323, 6321," the dispatcher was summoning Sumner's unit. He responded and was told to assist unit 6321 on the scene of a 10-91V (vicious) dog bite incident. He responded to the call, but shook his head as he changed course heading toward the given location. Vicious animal calls tended to be a no win state of affairs. If the situation was bad enough that County Animal Control couldn't handle it, it typically became a public relations nightmare. Sumner had had more than his share of those of late. He wasn't an animal hater. In fact, at home there was a little long haired tabby female named Mia who felt she owned Sumner, but on the job, animal calls tended to morph into nightmares.

§

When he arrived on the scene, he observed another San Jose Police officer, Don Archibald, an excellent police officer, striking the head of a pit bull that had its jaw locked on the arm of a twelve-year-old girl. A crowd had formed, and a County Animal Control Unit was on the scene, but could do nothing until the police got the dog off of the girl's arm. The blows from the officer's heavy steel flashlight were having no effect, and the girl was slipping into shock. Sumner's first response was to demand why the Archibald had not shot the dog with his firearm.

"Look at this crowd," Don responded. "A ricochet might strike the girl or one of the bystanders." *At least he was thinking*, Sumner thought.

"OK," Sumner directed. "We're going to put an end to this. Move the crowd back and get ready to shoot the dog the instant I got the animal off the girl's arm."

"How are you going to get the dog to release her?"

"I'll handle that. You just get ready to shoot…and please don't miss."

Sumner then quickly removed a road flare from the trunk of his patrol car. He lit the flare which he then concealed at his side; then he gave Archibald a nod, signaling that he was ready. Sumner whirled in a lighting like movement plunging the burning flare into the eye of the dog. The reaction was instantaneous. The animal squealed in agony as it released the young girl and began snapping blindly and wildly with its vise jaws at anything that moved. Officer Archibald, taking careful aim, fired two quick shots into the skull of the tormented animal as Sumner carried the girl to the nearby awaiting ambulance. The animal collapsed dead.

The girl was in a serious state of shock as the ambulance attendants began treatment to stabilize her condition and clean and dress her wounded arm, which looked broken. Now the difficult work began. Sumner knew that a full accounting of events would be required to justify the discharge of firearms in a residential neighborhood, particularly in the presence of hundreds of onlookers. And there would be animal lovers who would be more concerned for the fate of the dog than the damage to the girl.

He quickly grabbed the department issued camera from his "beat pack" and photographed the victim's wounds as well as the dead animal.

He then briskly moved through the crowd, obtaining the names and addresses of witnesses before they departed the scene. His plan was to contact them individually and obtain statements, but first he had to deal with the owner of the dog and handle the disposition of the crime scene. He then got a statement from the Animal Control Officer.

Sumner was firm but polite with the animal's owner. Animal control had issued a citation, and Sumner made it clear to the owner that he was responsible for the injuries his animal had caused.

"I'll handle the Form 2," (SJPD Incident Report). "You cover your part in a 3," (SJPD Supplemental Report) directed Sumner.

Though Archibald had been the case officer originally dispatched to the incident, Sumner felt that his own decision to invoke the use deadly force placed responsibility for the conduct of the case fully in his hands. Archibald, emotions still elevated from the shooting, had no arguments with that reasoning.

"I'm heading to the hospital to get a statement and check on the condition of the victim," Sumner said. "See you later for coffee."

"You buy" shot back Archibald, who was engaged in briefing District Sergeant Rich Cadnaso, who had just arrived.

§

Upon arrival at Valley Medical Center Hospital, Sumner was confronted by the victim's extremely agitated parents who demanded to know why such a vicious animal was running loose on the street. In order to avoid a possible public relations nightmare, Sumner took twenty minutes to explain to the parents that the Animal Control Officer had issued a citation for violation of city ordinances requiring dog owners to control the animal at all times and not to allow dogs off the leash in public. He also advised that a follow-up investigation would be conducted by both the police and Animal Control to determine if any other laws had been violated by the dog's owner. While not happy, the parents were placated enough to cease their tirade long enough for Sumner to get an injury report from the attending physician.

The emergency room physician was a Stanford University Medical School student completing his residency at Valley Med. He was young man in his twenties who made no secret of the fact that he would much rather be a police officer.

"How is she, Doc?" Sumner inquired.

"The arm is broken, there is severe trauma, but the most dangerous part of this is that she is in severe shock. If they had gotten her here any later, we might have lost her. And, she has a burn on her shoulder," he explained, somewhat confused.

"That was from the road flare," Sumner stated in a matter of fact tone.

"Road flare?" The doctor responded in undisguised bewilderment.

"The only way we could get the pit bull off of her was to stick a burning road flare into its eye."

The young police officer "wanna-be" contorted his face in revulsion. "You really did that?" he asked again.

"It was that or we could have brought the dog in here with her," Sumner replied sarcastically.

"Is the dog OK?"

Amazing, or maybe not, the man is after all a healer. "The animal had to be destroyed. We did it quickly, the dog only suffered for a second or two." Sumner was both touched by the compassion of animal lovers, and astonished at how little concern those same individuals seem to have for their fellow man.

§

Back at the scene, officers had dispersed the crowd. Animal Control had removed the dead animal, and a fire unit had thankfully washed the blood down the sewer, a compassionate gesture to remove any reminders of the day's unpleasantness.

Archibald cleared the scene and keyed his mike "6323, 6321, 1087," (meet me at) "Sambo's Coffee Shop."

"10-4," Sumner answered.

§

Sumner and Archibald enjoyed a cup of coffee and decompressed while writing the initial Form 2 and Archibald's Form 3. Over the next few days, Sumner obtained statements from the many witnesses which were filed in subsequent Form 3s. The San Jose Police Shooting Board cleared Officer Archie and Officer Sumner of any wrong doing or violation of Department or Administrative orders as well violations of the California Penal Code. Officer Archibald, upon Sumner's recommendation, received a commendation for the precautions he had taken to preserve the lives and safety of the public.

Ted Sumner's concerns had been reinforced. Animal calls were a bitch.

Exhausted by the high emotion of the evening's happenings, Sumner was relieved when the end of the shift finally came. 2:30 a.m., time to head for the barn. He stifled a yawn and reached for the quart of milk he'd picked up at the 7-11. Coffee cried out to him, but he wanted to sleep when he got home. His routine was important; home by 3:00a.m., up by 10:30 and ready to head to the gym by 11:30 a.m. Keeping physically fit was as much a part of the job for a police officer as were staying proficient at the many other tasks for which officers are unceasingly summoned. He didn't want to think about the pressures that would build on his home life when he soon transferred to his new assignment in the Narcotics Unit and began his work as a deep undercover operative.

He took a circuitous route back to the station, avoiding the freeways and staying on the surface streets in order to continue the high profile that marked police vehicles provided. He swung past River Glen Park, slowed at the intersection of Bird Ave., and turned left. If his patrol unit had been a horse, it would have known the way. Follow Bird to Willow, turn east to South First Street, then head for the barn. He would vary his pattern for security, from time to time and might possibly stumble across a crook, busy at his nefarious work. Suddenly something in the east grabbed Sumner's attention. He scowled out the driver's side window and grabbed the mike.

"Control, 6321."

There was a short pause, then dispatch responded.

"Go ahead 6321."

"Does fire have a 904 (fire) working in the area of Willow and Palm?"

"Negative 6321."

Sumner thought for a moment. Central Fire, the County of Santa Clara's Fire Department, was the agency that handled all fires in the unincorporated areas of the County of Santa Clara, where the City of San Jose was located, as well as fires in their own "contract" cities. The smaller incorporated cities didn't have the tax base for their own fire department, so they contracted for fire protection from the county. *This fire may be located in the unincorporated sector of San Jose* , he thought to himself.

"Control, 6321, please check if Central is working anything in that area." There was a pause.

"Central Fire reports no activity in that area."

"6321,10-4. I will be investigating a suspicious glow emanating from that area." The dispatcher hesitated as Sumner was two districts over from District 3, in which his beat, 21, was located.

"10-4, 6321."

Sumner checked for traffic, and then floored the accelerator. There was no traffic at that hour, so he covered the ground in less than seven minutes. As he turned on to Palm, the source of the skyline glow became obvious. Sumner screeched to a halt in front of an older, two story Victorian home that was fully engulfed in flames. It was a classic scene from a disaster film. People were moving about inside the house as fire raged and hungrily reached out through the windows.

Sumner keyed the mike as he kicked open his door.

"Control, 6321, I have a fully involved 904 structure at 643 Palm Avenue. Dispatch Fire Code 3."

"6321, 10-4."

"Control, be advised this is a fully involved," (burning to the ground) "904 residence with an unknown number of occupants. Dispatch ambulance units. I will be affecting rescue." Not waiting for a reply, he sprinted for the front door.

This was unknown territory for Sumner. He had never arrived on the scene of a major fire where the firefighters were not already in charge and seeing to the rescue of any occupants. He was staggered by the scorching heat as he entered the house. The blast of hot air instantly dried his eyes and he was forced to turn away and rehydrate them by blinking rapidly.

Concern overcame caution and he bolted through the front door. He headed upstairs where he had observed people moving about. He vaulted the stairs two at a time until he reached the landing and confronted the man of the house huddled there with his wife and three children.

"Is there anyone else in the house?!" he yelled.

"No!" the husband shouted over the roar of the flames.

Sumner scooped up one of the children into his arms and took one final look around to ensure that no one had been left behind. The heat was unbearable, so he hunched over to shield the child turned and followed the parents and the other two children down the stairs at a dead run. At the bottom of the stairs, he ran toward the front door and ran head first into a support beam in the middle of the room. All he could see was a blinding white flash as he fought to remain conscious. His legs lost their strength, and he felt a knife like pain shoot down his spine. He gritted his teeth and made a determined plunge for the front door as the floor of the second story came crashing down into the room he had barely vacated.

Once they reached the safety of Palm Street, he handed the child to its distraught mother and opened the doors to the patrol unit so the family would have some place to sit. He turned just in time to see the homeowner heading back into the burning building. Painfully, Sumner chased the man down and grabbed him roughly just as he was about to enter the front door.

"Where the hell are you going?" Ted demanded.

The disoriented man stammered, "I have to get my stuff." Sumner dragged the man back to the patrol unit and through clenched teeth he assured him there was nothing in the house worth dying for. As the family huddled together in unit 6321, Central Fire units rolled up and began the process of extinguishing the fire.

At the point at which the firemen were spraying down the few remaining hot spots, the Battalion Commander approached Sumner.

"Nice work, officer," he offered quietly. "If you ever want a career in fire fighting…"

Sumner looked at commander through pain filled eyes, "Thanks, but what you guys do is too dangerous for my taste." The older man chuckled, extended his hand and then turned back to the smoldering ruin.

For several months after this incident, Sumner was plagued with neck and upper back pain. The city doctor diagnosed his condition as a cervical sprain and recommended rest and aspirin.

Aftermath

Twenty-five years later during a comprehensive physical exam, Sumner's physician entered the examining room carrying X-ray film of his upper spine and asked, in a matter of fact manner, "When did you break your neck?"

Sumner was stunned, "I have a broken neck?" The doctor shrugged and explained that it was an old injury… that it was completely healed, and then he held up the X-ray and pointed to the place where the fracture had occurred many years ago when Sumner had dared to play fireman.

CHAPTER 30

Ted Sumner and his partner Steve Schmidt took their seats for the graveyard shift's Saturday night briefing. It was the summer doldrums and as was to be expected, the San Jose Police Force was shorthanded. The shortage of personnel was caused by more than earned vacations and military leaves. That weakened the shift, but the other major cause of the extremely "thin blue line" was the flood of transparent "sick outs," who, when they were unable to secure a night off because the department was short handed, defiantly called in sick.

Sumner and Schmidt were assigned to work 8331 (8 indicates midnight shift, 3 indicates district 3 and 31 is the beat number). District 3 was San Jose's near east side. Beat 31 was one of the toughest beats in town. They would be working "the district from hell," four men short on a hot July night.

The briefing sergeant was about halfway through his list when the night lieutenant interrupted. "Let's hit the street, gentlemen. The city is falling apart and the swing shift is really catching hell out there."

"I had a feeling about this one partner," grumbled Schmidt. "It's going to be a long night." Sumner shook his head in disgust and the two men headed to the garage to "saddle up" their patrol unit.

Sumner climbed into the driver's side and Schmidt went through the brief check list. Then he keyed the mike,. "8331, 10-8," Schmidt said into the microphone.

"8331, 10-8" cooed the velvet voiced female dispatcher. "Respond to a 415 fight outside Cliff's Bar, 983 Alum Rock Avenue," ordered the dispatcher.

"10-4," replied a smiling Schmidt. He replaced the mike, slapped his knee and howled, "Let's get this night started!"

Cliff's Bar had a well earned reputation. It was not the kind of establishment that any officer entered alone or approached without making sure his "six" was covered.

It was frequented by the meanest black gangsters and ex-cons in the area.

Sumner turned the key, and the 440 Hemi powering the patrol car sprung to life. He hit the gas and the tires let out a sharp chirp as they left the police parking lot and hit the street.

Three minutes later they skidded into the parking lot next to Cliff's. As they exited the vehicle approximately, thirty men, who had been watching a scuffle, scattered. No time for the spectators; there were two men engaged in what appeared to be mortal combat, one wielding a knife, the other a straight razor. With a subtle gesture, they divided the combatants and moved quickly up, each approaching one of the combatants from behind. Simultaneously they slapped on a carotid restraint across the neck and took control of the weapon wielding hand. Timing was of the absolute essence. If one officer was late in subduing his suspect, the other officer might get slashed or stabbed.

It was only a matter of seconds before both suspects were unconscious and on the ground handcuffed. A voice from the darkened doorway of Cliff's Bar cried out, "Damn, did you see those cops?" Another deeper voice said, "Stay in here! Don't go out there!"

A quick interrogation revealed little. Both men, now conscious, regarded the incident as mutual combat and neither wanted to make any complaint. Sumner said, "I'll check with the bartender," and entered the bar. The stale smell of beer and cigarettes permeated the air. The individual behind the bar was a giant of a man. He stood 6'5 and Sumner estimated that he weighed at least three hundred pounds. There was no question in Sumner's mind that the bartender was none other than Cliff himself. Sumner nodded at the owner and asked, "Any damage here? Do you want to make a complaint?"

"No, no complaint," drawled Cliff, "but I don't want dem niggas back in my place tonight."

"No problem. We'll handle it," Sumner assured him.

When Sumner returned to the parking lot, both subjects were in the backseat of the caged patrol car and his partner was reporting in. "10-4, we will be 10-49 to county with subjects in custody." Schmidt, standing at the passenger door snapped loose the key of the mike. He looked at Sumner with raised eyebrows as if to say, "What gives?"

Sumner shrugged and responded, "He doesn't want to make a complaint, but he doesn't want these two assholes back in his fine establishment tonight."

"Well, problem solved," replied Steve. "Both our scrappers have misdemeanor warrants." Sumner smiled broadly and slid into the driver's seat.

As they sped toward the county jail, Schmidt expedited the process by calling ahead, "Control, please have warrants forward hard copies to booking." The warrants were ready and waiting and the booking process took no more than twenty minutes. The troublemakers would not be able to make bail until they came before the judge on Monday morning. *Soul on ice*, Sumner thought, *likelihood of recidivism this weekend...zero.*

They arrived back on the beat just after 12:30 AM. Traffic was heavy and the bars busy. This night was not going to end early. "Look out," shouted Schmidt as he lifted his arms in anticipation of collision with white Ford Granada pulling an illegal U-turn across all four lanes of Alum Rock Ave. Sumner sharply swerved the patrol car right, narrowly missing a collision with the Granada and the parked vehicles on the side of the road in front of the "Tampico" Mexican restaurant and bar. As the Granada sped off eastbound on Alum Rock, Schmidt turned on the red lights mumbling, "Let's see what this moron has to say for himself."

The 440 Hemi roared in answer to Sumner's demand. When they caught up to the vehicle, it was traveling 65 mph in a 35 zone. At first the driver refused to yield and continued eastbound. Sumner pulled to within 10 feet of the runner's back bumper and asked, as much to himself as to his partner, "Should we put out a pursuit?"

"Naw, he's pulling over," Steve said.

As the vehicle rolled to a stop, Schmidt finished his call to dispatch. "Control 8331, 1195, Sharf and Alum Rock, California X-ray, victor, zebra, 7, 2, 5." He then lit up the vehicle with one of the two spotlights mounted between the window and windshield of the patrol car.

Driver officer Sumner dismounted and moved forward to make contact with the driver, as Schmidt took up a covering position behind the opened passenger door of the patrol car. Sumner unsnapped his holster and drew his 357 Magnum Colt Python revolver. As Sumner approached the vehicle he observed, *One occupant, check the backseat, hang back…make him turn in the seat to face you.*

The driver was a young man in his early 20s with red hair and freckles. He turned his head toward Sumner, squinting into the light from Sumner's flashlight. The hair on Sumner's neck stood up as the driver faced him with a peculiar, almost saturnine smile on his face. *What the hell?* Ted thought, then at that instant, he saw it! Flame and smoke thundered from the barrel of the pistol the man was holding in his right hand. He had cradled it in the crook of his left elbow which was resting on the window of the car. That posture had partially hidden the weapon from view.

The bullet ripped past Sumner's right ear, the powder searing into the pores of his right eye. His perception of sound dropped off even before the crash of the first shot echoed past. Everything went into slow motion as Sumner reeled back raising his own weapon. He was certain that he was moving too slowly to return fire before he would be hit by the inevitable second shot. His sight picture had just lined up when he saw a massive flash from the rear of the vehicle. The flash clearly illuminated the profile of Officer Schmidt poised in the crouched combat position, weapon aimed. There was a series of flashes as Schmidt fired again and again. Schmidt finished his fourth shot as Sumner returned fire, blindly into the driver seat. Five shots fired by each officer with no return fire. Sumner had been deafened by the assailant's first round. The only sensation of sound he could register was the rapid beat of his own heart, racing from a sudden surge of adrenaline. As his heart rate slowed, he could make out the faint sound of someone screaming. Little by little the volume of those screams rose as his head cleared.

Through his left eye Sumner could see the redheaded suspect on the passenger side floor board of the vehicle screaming for the officers to stop shooting. Unbalanced by the blinding of his right eye, Sumner stumbled to the driver door in time to see Schmidt dragging the suspect from the vehicle through the open passenger window. The suspect was quickly handcuffed, searched, and deposited into the backseat of the patrol car.

Sumner felt his partner's strong hands grab him by the shoulders, guiding him to the sidewalk. "Are you all right, do you need and ambulance?"

"No, no. My right eye got burned a little," Sumner responded shakily, "but I'm OK. What do you think that was all about?"

"I think we got a crook. A 211," (armed robbery) "just went down at the liquor store by the drive-in. It looks like this is our "percolator." (Police humor for perpetrator) "8332 is bringing the victim here for positive ID. You sure you don't want an ambulance?" Schmidt asked, observing his partner's oozing right eye.

"No. But why isn't that asshole dead? How the hell did we both miss him?"

"I think I can tell you," it was the sagaciously steady voice of Sergeant Bill Shurm. Sergeant Shurm had arrived on the scene and conducted a cursory investigation of the vehicle. Shurm, a former Crime Scene Detective, was an expert on reconstructing shooting scenes.

"After the suspect fired on you, Schmidt opened up. His first shot shattering the rear window which compromised the trajectory of his round. At that instant, the lucky crook dove to the floor of the passenger side. Schmidt's next four shots would have gone through the back of his head had he not bailed so quickly. All five of your shots went right into the driver seat where he was sitting, but it's small wonder you couldn't see he wasn't there…that eye looks bad. Do you want an ambulance?"

"No!" Sumner replied .

"Well, that was some damn good shooting. If he hadn't moved, he'd be fully dispatched," replied Shurm.

§

The gunman was positively identified by the store clerk as the perpetrator of the liquor store armed robbery. The suspect was then transported to the hospital by unit 8107 for examination. Once he was cleared by the emergency room physicians at Valley Medical Center, the suspect was transported to PAB (Police Administration Building) where he was interrogated and booked by the Night Robbery Detectives.

Schmidt drove his partner to Valley Medical, over Sumner's ongoing objections. There, Sumner was attended by ER physicians. His right eye was irrigated with a solution of saline and boric acid, and his right cheek was scrubbed to remove the embedded gun powder. They then proceeded to PAB to write the crime report and brief the detectives.

The San Jose Police Shooting Board cleared both officers of any misconduct. The Board found that both Officer Sumner and Officer Schmidt had conducted themselves within the parameters of the regulations and administrative orders of the SJPD as well as the laws of the California Penal Code. They were returned to duty.

The armed robbery suspect subsequently pled guilty to violation of section 211A of the California Penal Code, Armed Robbery and Section 245A Assault with a Deadly Weapon on a police officer. The suspect was sentenced to fifteen years to life under the California indeterminate sentence law.

CHAPTER 31

Sumner sucked in the warm spring evening air as he piloted his police cruiser among the posh retail businesses along Saratoga Avenue on San Jose's affluent west side. He was relaxed and feeling contented. He had had an excellent workout with Doc Meyer that afternoon during which he had set a new personal record on their five mile run. And the warm spring night air and the smell of the cherry blossoms this time of year always filled Sumner with a renewed peace of mind. He was working the midnight shift on a training team. Though he was not a field training officer, he had been selected to work alongside the training units by his former training Sergeant, Rich Gerrod, who was now a Lieutenant and commander of the midnight shift Field Training Unit. Slater preferred to have officers that he knew and trusted working the non-training cars in his area, as they would often be working with and around the impressionable rookies who were fresh out of the Academy. He held Sumner in high regard.

"8216, fill with 8210, Stevens Creek Blvd and Monroe."

8210, normally a car manned by a Field Training Officer and his trainee, was, on this evening, a unit consisting of two rookies in their tenth week of field training. As the top performers on their team, these two officers had been honored by becoming the first of their class to be "cut loose" from their training officer and allowed to work on their own.

"8216— from Stevens Creek and Saratoga." Sumner gave his cruiser a bit of gas as he pushed to shorten his ETA. He barreled along Stevens Creek, the wide boulevard that cut through the heart of West San Jose from Highway 17 to the foothills of the Coast Range that runs from San Francisco to San Luis Obispo. He steered his vehicle across the three wide oncoming lanes and into the parking lot of the fashionable Valley Fair Shopping Center. Spotting the police car, Sumner then noticed the two rookies grappling with a large muscular individual who was easily over-powering their every attempt to subdue him. Grabbing his baton, Sumner exited his vehicle and approached the melee. As he approached, the sus-pect flung the two rookies to the ground and postured himself to engage the new threat.

"Place your hands on the top of your head, interlock your fingers, and turn around," Sumner ordered.

"Fuck you! I didn't do anything," growled the suspect.

"Then you've got nothing to worry about," Sumner replied. "You'll be released after the officers positively identify you."

"Fuck you...you got no right touching me."

As Sumner got closer, he took stock of his adversary. *6'3", 235 pounds easy, muscle bound and extremely hostile. Steroids and probably some cocaine.* For some reason athletes who use steroids to build muscle also develop a fond-ness for coke. And if the steroids don't make them antisocial enough, mixed with the cocaine, they become downright misanthropic.

As the two rookie officers regained their feet, Sumner signal*f*ed for them to hold back and let him handle the situation. Most of the injuries that Sumner had ever sustained as a police officer had been inflicted by other officers trying to help. When engaged in altercations that could eas-ily escalate into a life and death struggle, Sumner preferred to rely on his own skills as a martial artist, developed over decades of training, rather than the untested abilities of a new officer.

Sumner repeated his command as he moved closer. "Place your hands on your head, interlock your fingers, and turn around."

"Fuck you...fuck all of you," the suspect lowered himself into a wres-tler's stance and prepared to charge into Sumner. *Well, this guy has absolutely no intentions of cooperating. Show time!*

Sumner positioned himself in a partially closed stance with his right foot forward and in his right hand raised his nightstick, pointing it inches from the approaching behemoth's nose in what can only be described as an unfriendly and intimidating gesture. The suspect slapped the baton away with his right hand as Sumner spun backwards in a pivoting movement, accelerating the nightstick along its 360 degree trajectory to a blinding velocity. The dense cherry wood baton crashed into the suspect's right shoulder with a sickening crack that sounded like a homerun ball leaving the bat of Willie Mays. The suspect screamed like a wounded animal as Sumner then unwound his pivot accelerating the stick along the same trajectory in an opposite direction bringing it rocketing around, slamming into the suspect's left elbow.

The suspect's knees buckled from the acute pain as Sumner stepped back and casually took aim, again sending the cold wood, like an aimed missile streaking to its target on the side of the man's neck, hammering into the vagus nerve and rendering the suspect instantly unconscious as he tumbled to the ground.

"Cuff him," Sumner directed the rookies as he wiped his nightstick with his gloved hand. "What an asshole. What did you stop this guy for?"

"Deuce," said, Ray Gray the blond haired officer. Deuce is police slang for driving under the influence of alcohol or drugs.

"My cuffs won't fit around his wrists," said Joe Esparsa, the Hispanic officer.

"Then use the plastic restraints, that's what they're for, but do it quick. He's going to be in a real bad mood when he wakes up," Sumner instructed.

Esparsa strapped on the restraints and then patted the suspect down for weapons and some form of identification. As he removed the suspect's driver's license from his wallet, his jaw dropped. "Hey, this is Brian Ogelthorp!"

"No shit?" replied Gray as he grabbed the driver's license. "I'll be dammed, it's Brian Ogelthorp."

"Who the hell is Brian Ogelthorp?" asked Sumner.

"He's an Olympic shot putter," explained Gray. "He's favored to take the Gold Medal next year."

"This dumb ass will never get past the Olympic Committee's required drug test," Sumner said disgustedly. Ogelthorp groaned as he started to regain consciousness. Sumner rolled him over and pulled open his right eyelid exposing the eye. He then ignited his flashlight and introduced the beam into the eye. The pupil remained fully dilated, indicating the presence of a strong stimulant such as amphetamines or cocaine. "I'm guessing coke. These steroid heads just love coke." Several of the bodybuilders who trained at the same gym as Sumner used steroids to accelerate their physical development and they often discussed their fondness for cocaine. *I don't know, maybe steroids enhance the appetite for that stuff.*

Ogelthorp was now fully conscious, but very groggy. Gray and Esparsa guided him into the backseat of their vehicle for transportation to preprocessing where he would be tested for the presence of alcohol and drugs in his system prior to his booking into the county jail.

"I'll cut a Form 3," (supplemental report) Sumner advised. "Get a hold of me when you guys finish booking his ass."

"See you later. Thanks for the help," replied Esparsa.

§

"8216, 10-8," Sumner spoke into his microphone as he pulled from the parking lot heading westbound on Stevens Creek Blvd. back toward his beat.

"8216, 10-4." "82-16 respond to an 1179 Stevens Creek and Lawrence Expressway, ambulance in route." *Traffic accident, unknown circumstances.*

"8216, 10-4, request clearance for Code 3 response."

"8216, standby," replied the dispatcher who was obviously checking with the watch commander before authorizing use of red lights and siren. "8216, respond Code 2, Santa Clara PD is on the scene."

"10-4." Sumner was still pushing his speed as far as he dare.

As Sumner approached Saratoga Ave., the radio crackled, "8216, 1022, the incident occurred in Santa Clara jurisdiction."

"8216, 10-4." *Good, I hate messy traffic accidents.*

As he reached Saratoga Ave., he turned southbound approaching the Garden City Card room. He suddenly noticed a white Chevrolet El Camino leave the parking lot at a high rate of speed, the rear tires breaking traction and squealing as the vehicle speed off southbound on Saratoga Ave.

Sumner accelerated to close the distance. Checking his watch he noticed the time. *2:25 AM…could be a deuce.* As he continued accelerating, he noticed that he wasn't closing the distance. As he crossed Moorpark Ave., he saw that he was passing fifty miles per hour and still accelerating. He was reluctant to turn on his red lights at this distance. He had been taught and learned through experience that a suspect with any thoughts of attempting to evade a police stop is greatly encouraged to do just that if the officer initiates the stop from too great a distance. He hit the gas and kicked it up to 65 mph. The suspect vehicle actually began to pull further away.

"Control, 8216, 1195, possible failure to stop," he called into the mic. Sumner turned on his red lights and spinner.

"8216, 1020?" the dispatcher replied.

As Sumner reached to turn on his siren to initiate the pursuit, the white El Camino suddenly hit the brakes and pulled abruptly to the right hand curb skidding to a stop.

"8216, the subject is stopped. Saratoga south of Doyle."

"8216, 10-4."

As Sumner pulled to a stop behind the vehicle, he observed the driver door to open and a white male adult in his 40s exit quickly and approach Sumner. *Shit,* thought Sumner as he quickly put the police cruiser in park and alighted swiftly from the car. The last thing a patrol officer wants on a stop is to be attempting to exit his vehicle with a hostile suspect standing at the door. The officer is at an extreme disadvantage. Sumner quickened his exit.

"Thank god, thank god, it's you," effused the middle aged man as he approached Sumner with his arms extended as if he were going to embrace him with a big hug. "Thank god it's you."

Sumner extended his left hand in a gesture communicating to the approaching subject that he should stop. "Please step up on the sidewalk, sir," Sumner advised.

"No problem. Thank god it's you," huffed the man, his level of excitement obviously very high. "I thought someone was after me."

"May I see your driver's license and registration please?"

"Sure, yeah, no problem. I'm just so happy it's you," the man went on as he dug his license out of his wallet. "I was sure it was them after me when I saw your headlights coming up on me."

"Who was after you?" asked Sumner as he examined the driver's license. *William Maxwell, 42 years old, lives on Livorna Ave, about a half mile from here.* "Who did you think was after you, and why would they be chasing you?"

"I've been at the Garden City playing cards all night," Mr. Maxwell explained. "I've won over $25,000 tonight."

"That's a lot of money," Sumner whistled.

"I was playing a bunch of out of town card sharks, a rough looking bunch," Maxwell explained. "I thought they might be trying to get their money back."

"What the hell did you think you were doing?" Sumner demanded. "Where were you going."

"Home," he replied.

"So if a bunch of toughs were following you, you were going to lead them to your home, so they would know right where you live…and what about your family, do you have a family?"

"Yes," answered Maxwell contritely. "I guess that wasn't too smart."

"Mr. Maxwell, I understand your concerns, but your best course of action would have been to remain at the card room where there's other people and lots of witnesses and called the police for assistance," Sumner explained. "You might have had to wait for an available unit, but you would be safe and the police would be happy to see you safely home."

"Will you follow me home now?"

"Yes, Mr. Maxwell, I will, but first I am going to issue you a citation for excessive speed and for running the red light at Moorpark, that was just plain reckless."

"No problem, no problem, at all officer. I'm not even going to contest the ticket. I know I deserve it, just get me home safe," Maxwell begged.

Sumner followed Mr. Maxwell's El Camino through the affluent west side neighborhoods, carefully watching his mirrors for any signs of vehicles following. As they turned onto Livorna Ave., Maxwell pulled into the driveway of his two story home. *Nice house.* Maxwell opened his garage door remotely and pulled his vehicle in, then trotted back down the driveway to where Sumner was stopped.

"Thank you, officer. Thank you so much."

"No problem. Just be careful when operating a motor vehicle," Sumner cautioned. "I did not detect anyone following us, but I'm going to remain in the neighborhood for a while and make sure we did not pick up a loose tail."

"Thank you, thank you so much, officer."

CHAPTER 32

Sumner maintained a comprehensive patrol of the surrounding neighborhood for the next thirty minutes. The place was as quiet as a cemetery .

"All units, Santa Clara PD advises 10851," (stolen vehicle) "hit and run suspect fled from scene at Lawrence Expressway and Steven Creek approximately 0230. Be on the lookout for a WMA 5-10 to 6-2 medium build, with long brown hair, possibly injured. Last seen running southbound toward Steven Creek."

"8216, 10-8."

"8216, 10-4."

At 3:12 AM Sumner pulled onto Williams Road just west of Saratoga. A vehicle with all lights extinguished pulled from behind the closed service station across the street and proceeded eastbound on Williams. *Let's see what this is all about.*

Sumner pulled onto Williams, maintaining a discrete distance as he followed the vehicle that was still running without headlights. As the vehicle slowed to a stop at the red light at Saratoga Ave., the headlights suddenly came on. Sumner accelerated up directly behind the suspect vehicle.

"8216, 1195 Saratoga and Williams, Cal license plate XYZ123."

"8216, 1195," control confirmed.

As the light changed to green, the suspect vehicle slowly proceeded across the intersection and into the area of apartment complexes east of Saratoga Ave. Sumner ignited his front red lights as he lit up the interior of the vehicle with his spot light. *Two WMAs, one clean cut, the other with long brown hair.* The suspect continued slowly on Williams before turning right on Colonial Ave. and coming to a stop at the right hand curb. Sumner fixed his spotlight on the interior of the suspect vehicle, fully illuminating the inside compartment.

He approached the suspect vehicle warily. The driver side window lowered slowly. "Good evening, sir. Would please step out of the vehicle?" Sumner shined his flashlight on the face of the passenger. "Please remain seated right where you are, sir." The passenger stared blankly forward in an almost catatonic state.

Sumner directed the driver to the sidewalk at the rear of the suspect vehicle where he could keep an eye on the passenger. The driver produced his driver's license and registration. *Gary Robey, lives in Santa Clara.* "Is this your current address?"

"Yes, sir."

"Where do you work?"

"Apple Computer."

"Who's your passenger?"

"I met him at a party and he looked like he had had a little too much to drink, so I offered him a ride home."

"Are you in the habit of offering rides to intoxicated strangers?"

"Well, he's a friend of the person who was throwing the party," he squirmed.

"Where was the party?"

"Over in Santa Clara."

"What's the address?"

"I don't remember."

"You don't remember the address that you drove to earlier this evening and from which you just left, huh?"

"Well uh," he stammered.

"What is the name of the individual who was hosting the party?"

"Uh…"

"What is the address where you are taking your passenger?"

"He said he lives on Apple Blossom, just around the corner."

"Mr. Robey, you don't seem to know very much about what you have been doing this evening. What were you doing behind that gas station?"

"He was using the phone booth."

"Why were you driving with no headlights?"

"Well, uh, I…"

"Mr. Robey, place your hands on head and interlace your fingers," Sumner ordered as he patted him down. Finding no weapons, Sumner handcuffed Robey and placed him in the backseat of his police car.

Sumner opened the passenger door of the suspect vehicle. "Please step out of the vehicle, sir," Sumner ordered. Sumner directed the passenger to the sidewalk. *WMA, 6 foot, 185 pounds, long stringy light brown hair.* "May I see some identification, please?"

"Uh, I lost my wallet."

"What's your name?"

"Bob, uh, Bob Roberts."

"Bob Roberts," Sumner smiled broadly. "Mine, too."

"Who is this guy you're with?"

"I don't know. He picked me up hitchhiking."

"Where did he pick you up?"

"Over on Stevens Creek."

"Where you coming from?"

"The Hofbrau. I was having something to eat."

Sumner noticed dried blood in the hair behind his left ear. "What happened here?" asked Sumner as he moved the hair away from the suspect's ear with the back his gloved right hand. The suspect swung wildly with his right hand attempting to strike Sumner in the head. Sumner brought his left hand straight up deflecting the blow, stepping quickly forward bumping the suspect with his body, knocking the suspect off balance, as he struck with the open palm of his right hand smashing into the suspect's nose.

The suspect reeled back, stunned by the blow, as Sumner moved forward to place him in custody. As the suspect continued to reel back, Sumner saw a uniform covered arm suddenly apply a sleeper restraint across the neck of the suspect. The suspect began to shake uncontrollably as he lost consciousness. *Schmidt, my old partner.*

Officer Schmidt applied plastic restraints supplied by Sumner. "Thanks, buddy. Where'd you come from?"

"I'm working district one on channel one," he explained. "They sent me on a call over on beat 12 so I switched to channel 2. I heard you going out on the stop as I was clearing the call and I knew I better fill with you before you got yourself into trouble."

"I'm glad as hell you did. How the hell were you able to walk up on me without me seeing you?"

"That's always been your blind spot pal," Schmidt said knowingly. "As you prepare to go into battle, you become hyper focused on your adversary and quit looking around."

"Yeah, I guess it goes back to my days as a competitive fighter."

"What's with this asshole?"

"I've got a hunch he's the 10851, 20002." (auto theft, hit and run) "suspect Santa Clara is looking for."

"Today's payday. You can buy me a beer at Bruni's Tap room in the morning."

"I'll be there right after I deposit my check."

Schmidt departed as Sumner placed the shackled suspect in the back-seat of his police car and moved Mr. Robey. "You had better be completely honest with me, Mr. Robey. Who is this guy and where did you pick him up?"

"Aren't you going to read me my rights?"

"As it stands right now, you're not a suspect in any crime other than being stupid. However, if you wish to invoke your right to remain silent, I will be more than happy to book you into the county jail as an accessory to auto theft and felony hit and run driving." Sumner smiled like a Cheshire Cat. "It's entirely up to you, sir."

"I picked him up running along the road on Stevens Creek just past Lawrence. He said he was a hitch hiker passenger in a car that had been involved in a collision. He told me he ran away because the thought the driver was drunk and he didn't want any trouble. He was afraid he might loose his job."

"And why did you lie to me?"

"I didn't want him to get into trouble."

"What business is it of yours? According to you you've never seen the guy before."

"I just didn't want the guy to get into trouble, you know?"

"No, I don't." replied Sumner. "He is a car thief who may have injured someone badly in a collision and you actively helped him to flee. In addition to that, you aided and abetted his escape by lying to the police during the conduct of an investigation."

"I'm sorry. I was just trying to be a nice guy. I really didn't know."

"Mr. Robey, I am going to release you with a citation for driving with no lights after dark, however I am certain the Auto Theft and Traffic Investigation Detectives will be in contact with you. You made some poor choices tonight, Mr. Robey."

"Oh, god," he wept as he covered his face with the palms of his hands.

CHAPTER 33

"Control, 8216."

"8216, go ahead."

"Is Santa Clara still at the scene on Lawrence and Stevens Creek?"

"8216 stand by. 8216, affirmative."

"Please advise them that I am 1049 with a possible suspect."

There were still fire trucks and two trucks on the scene when Sumner arrived. Santa Clara Police Department Officer Bob Sadler, with whom Sumner had attended San Jose State University, approached flashing his million dollar smile that had made him a favorite among all the sorority girls while in college.

"You got our perp, huh?" asked Sadler, good-naturedly mussing Sumner's hair with his right hand as he had always done whenever they met up in college. Sadler was two years older than Sumner and had always been a sort of big brother figure.

"Maybe."

"Let's see," said Sadler as he held up a California driver's license and looked at the photo, then the suspect and back at the photo. "Randy, how you doing?"

"You found my wallet?" asked the suspect contritely.

"Yes, we did. You dropped it about fifty yards from the accident scene."

"He's all yours," said Sumner, removing Randy from the backseat of his patrol car and exchanging handcuffs with Sadler.

"How'd he get the bloody nose?" asked Sadler.

Sumner shrugged, "He must have hit his head on the steering wheel, right, Randy?"

"Yeah, I hit my head on the steering wheel," he agreed. Sumner had counted on the tough guy not wanting to disclose that he had been bested by the police while attempting to resist arrest, and thus save Sumner four to five hours attending him while he was treated at VMC. Now it was Santa Clara's problem.

Sadler smiled. "You were always quick with your hands."

"If you don't want him, I'll handle the case and take the collar."

"No, no, we'll take care of it."

"Bye bye, Randy," Sumner waved.

Sumner obtained all the pertinent information he needed to complete his report from Sadler. "Here's my case number." Sumner wrote the number down on an FI (Field Identification Card used to record information on subjects encountered in the field). "I'll forward a copy of my report directly to you."

"Outstanding, buddy. Thanks for the help on this one."

§

The rest of the evening was relatively uneventful. Sumner finished his reports over a cup of coffee at the Maple Leaf Donut Shop on Saratoga Ave. Though the shop was closed, the owner started work making donuts at about 3:00 AM each day and liked to have the police stop by for coffee. They not only provided him some company but made him feel safer. Sumner drank his coffee with cream as the shop owner rattled on about everything from the poetry of Keats and Shelley to Keynesian economics. While an intelligent and well educated man, he would occasionally make an historical reference that Sumner, more often than not, would have to correct.

At 6:00 AM. the owner opened the shop. Sumner departed just as the first customers were arriving. Commute traffic was already clogging the roadways on this warm spring Friday morning. At 7:00 AM Sumner requested clearance to go 1019 (return to station). With clearance granted, Sumner began a circuitous route back to PAB avoiding the freeways and passing by the world famous Rosicrucian Museum of Egyptian Artifacts located on the edge of the historical Rose Garden area of San Jose. He loved the Museum and had visited regularly since he was a boy. Arriving back at the police garage, he advised communications he was 10-7 OD (off duty).

He turned in his reports and joked with the other Midnighters gathered in the Bureau of Field Operations Report Writing Room.

"Boy, you really earned your pay check this month," commented his District Sergeant, Bob Slater, as he perused Sumner's activity sheet.

The officers then proceeded to the briefing room where an Inbox was assigned to each officer for receipt of any mail, correspondence, messages, and of course, the officer's paycheck. It was payday, and none too soon for most of the married guys. But Marge, the Chief's secretary who was in charge of distributing the paychecks, took a sadistic delight in delaying the delivery of the checks as long as possible. She would shuffle through the pile of checks claiming that she needed to organize them before she could make distribution. So the officers sat and cooled their heels for several hours, joking, talking, and making fun of the single officers, most of whom didn't even know it was payday and had not even cashed their last two checks.

Mercifully, on this day the checks arrived at 9:05 AM, several hours earlier than usual. It turns out that Marge was out ill, and one of the other secretaries had seen to the delivery of the paychecks.

Sumner drove to the Bank of West around the corner from PAB on the corner of First Street and Hedding. He parked in the rear parking lot and entered the bank. After filling out a deposit slip and marking the "less cash" box allowing himself twenty-five dollars for the week he got into the teller's line to make his deposit.

The lines to the tellers lengthened as Sumner waited. When it was finally his turn, he stepped up to the teller's window and presented his check and deposit slip. The teller, an attractive young woman, did not respond, but rather stared at the customer at the next teller's window. He waited patiently, but the teller didn't move. He cleared his throat, but the teller was frozen. Sumner looked around, finally glancing at the customer next to him. *Damn, he's robbing the bank.* The skinny man with greasy curly black hair was holding a gun on the teller.

Sumner discreetly let his right hand drop to his side as he looked forward, then in a lighting fast movement brought his hand up, under his shirt, drawing his gun and bringing it to bear on the robber.

"Drop it," ordered Sumner. But the robber didn't move.

"I said drop it, or I'll shoot," Sumner repeated the order slowly and with more force. But the perpetrator stood frozen.

"Set the weapon down gently and step away or so help me I'll send you to your maker," Sumner offered one last warning.

"I don't know what to do man!" pleaded the nearly hysterical robber.

"You move and I'll burn you to the ground," Sumner heard the distinctive voice of Officer Karl Bothello from the other side of the robber. *Karl must be here making a deposit also.*

"Please don't shoot. I just don't know what the fuck to do," pleaded the frantic perpetrator.

"Karl, it's Sumner," he called to his fellow officer.

While Sumner had been ordering the suspect to set the weapon down, Bothello had warned him not to move. The man was in a desperate quandary not knowing what do to avoid getting shot.

"Sumner, I got him covered!"

Realizing that they were in crossfire, Sumner called to Bothello. "Karl, I'm going to disarm this guy, if he moves..."

"Yeah, yeah, get that weapon away from him. Don't you move asshole," he warned the robber.

Sumner stepped behind the suspect, leaving Bothello a clear shot if anything went wrong and reached around with his left hand, gently grabbing the barrel of the perpetrator's weapon. Before he made any further movement, he gestured to the nearly catatonic teller, a young man no more than twenty years old, to move out of the line of fire. Sumner then lifted the pistol out of the suspect's hand as the crook stood petrified with fear. Sumner placed the weapon, a Beretta 380 semi automatic, on safe, and tucked it into his waistband. He then removed his handcuffs and cuffed the prisoner. The entire bank heaved a giant collective sigh of relief.

"We're secure, Karl," Sumner called.

"Kool," said a slightly agitated Officer Bothello, as Sumner reached out and shook his fellow officer's hand.

"That was some nifty work, buddy," Sumner praised. "I was zoned out until I realized the clerk was in a state of abject terror. But you already had the drop on the crook."

"Yeah, well, nice recovery," said Bothello as he slapped Sumner on the back.

"The police are on the way," panted the hyperventilating bank manager. "Thank god you guys were here."

"Can we hold him in your office until the uniforms get here?" Bothello asked.

"Of course."

Sumner and Bothello walked the suspect into the bank manager's office and sat down. "The FBI are on the way," advised the assistant bank manager, a pleasant looking blond woman in her late 30s. *The FBI, great.*

Two FBI agents arrived five minutes later and took custody of the suspect under the jurisdictional authority of the United States Code which makes Bank Robbery a Federal Crime.

"Do you want our case number?" Sumner asked.

"That's not necessary, officer. Thank you for your assistance," the agent replied, somewhat condescendingly as they removed Sumner's handcuffs and applied their own. They then walked the suspect to a waiting vehicle parked in the red zone in front of the bank.

"Just like that?" Sumner asked the two San Jose Police Robbery Detectives who had just arrived.

"Just like that," replied Sergeant Denton of Robbery. "However, if there had been no suspect in custody, they would classify the crime as a local matter and probably would not even have showed up."

That evening the newspaper's and television news reported that the FBI had apprehended a bank robber that morning at the Bank of the West in San Jose. There was no mention of the San Jose Police or the actions of the two off duty officers who had foiled the robbery. Neither Sumner nor Bothello ever heard another thing about the case. *Such is the way of the much venerated FBI.*

§

Sumner and Bothello recited the events of their morning banking adventure to at least a dozen different groups of officers who came and went from Bruni's Tap Room that day. Laughing, embellishing, and mischaracterizing each other's participation as they grew progressively more intoxicated by the beer being purchased for them by fellow officers eager to hear the details of the incident, they told and retold the story.

At about 4:00 PM Officer Steve Schmidt, who had patiently listened to each and every recitation of the continually aggrandizing saga, packed Sumner and Bothello into his Chevy Stepside pickup and drove them to their respective homes.

"Thanks, pal, I can always count on you," said Sumner as he stumbled from the cab of Steve's pickup truck.

"No problem, buddy. I always have your back."

Sumner made his way upstairs and into bed completely clothed, determined to get a few hours of precious sleep before his family arrived home, fully satisfied that on this one night he had indeed earned his paycheck.

BOOK III

DEEP COVER
COP

CHAPTER 34

Damn, *there is no mistaking that profile. Norm Perkins,* Sumner thought to himself. While waiting for the San Jose Police Department to organize a new Academy, he had been contacted by the Santa Clara County Sheriff's Department and offered an "unclassified" position as a Deputy Sheriff. The Trial of Angela Davis was to be held in San Jose and the Sheriff had been authorized to hire forty-five "unclassified" Deputies to assist with the new manpower needs. These Deputies were to then be moved into classified positions and begin their one year probation as permanent employees of the Sheriff's Department. Upon being sworn in he was assigned to the Main Jail, graveyard shift. The midnight Sergeants usually assigned him to 2nd Deck. This was where the prisoners were sent after being booked. There they received a shower, delousing and were dressed out in the distinctive orange jump suit and assigned to a "house" (jail lingo for cell. Norm Perkins had been Sumner's Trustee on 2nd Deck).

Jail Trustees were prisoners who were considered reliable enough to be let out to do much of the "dirty work" in the jail. They undressed and showered incoming prisoners who had soiled themselves with vomit or feces, swept and mopped and did some of the light administrative work.

Norm had been in charge of "housing" the new inmates. Because he had spent so much of his life in and out of jail he knew who should be

183

housed where to prevent violence, conspiracy and general unpleasantness. None of the inmates argued with Norm, he was 6'3", 210 pounds
and had had a promising career as a professional boxer until the Light
Heavyweight Champion of the World, Archie Moore knocked more that
a few wires loose in his head.

Sumner, now with the San Jose PD and working as a deep undercover
narcotics operative, was at Bini's Bar, in the midst of a nest of thieves,
cutthroats and drug addicts with a man staring at him who could blow
his cover in an instant. When Norm made no move to uncover him or to
warn anyone Sumner decided to cast fate to wind and engage him. On
that evening he was working alone hanging out at the known haunts of
drug dealers and users attempting to make a contact. This was a very difficult way to penetrate a drug supplying organization but he had mastered
the technique. Many of the individuals who had sunk to this antisocial
level were insecure loners who did not make friends easily. Armed with
that knowledge Sumner went out of his way to befriend such individuals. It did not matter who...the bigger the loser the better. This invariably led to introductions to many others as these "new friends" wanted to
show everyone that they had a friend and were, therefore, not such losers
themselves.

Sumner climbed up on the stool at the end of the bar next to the man
with whom Norm was talking. A black man in his late 20's, very slender,
5'10, distinctive odor of
ammonia...had all the look of a methamphetamine user.

"Don't I know you?" Sumner asked Norm.

"I don't think so," replied Norm as he looked around the room suspiciously. *Now it is time to acid test my cover or at the least smoke Perkins out* he
reasoned.

"Yeah, you were the Trustee at County when I did those nine months
for possession of LSD".

Norm was very much into LSD, that and having his brains scrambled
by Archie Moore just might prevent him from recognizing the former
Deputy.

"Oh yeah, I think I remember you" said Norm.

"Les," Sumner extended his hand as Norm shook it.

"Norm, this is Leroy" he said gesturing toward his companion.

Sumner called to the bartender "Give me a Bud and set these guys up" gesturing to Norm and Leroy.

"Thanks man" said Norm.

After several hours of talking and Sumner buying drinks, the conversation came around to drugs. "I am out of the know," Sumner explained. "I've been in New Mexico for the last couple years" Sumner informed his new friends.

"I know a cat who I can duke you into" said Leroy "come by my pad tomorrow". Leroy then wrote down the address of his residence…an apartment building owned by his father. *What the hell else can go wrong with this caper* Sumner thought to himself?

§

When he arrived at Leroy's apartment, Leroy introduced Sumner to his wife, a very pleasant white woman, but ugly as hell.

"You smoked any dope today?" asked Leroy. *It's 10:00 o'clock in the morning for god sake…*

"No."

Leroy tossed Sumner a bag of marijuana.

"Roll us one." *Sumner could not believe it. Did he actually believe the old wive's tale that Narcs did not know how to roll a joint? That was the first thing Dreyer taught the rookies when they came up to Narco. That was the kind of thing Sumner expected when working the High School drug scene. Not from a heavyweight. Next thing he will do is try to get me high, he thought. The dopers believe that if you get a Narc high and ask him if he is a Narc he will tell the truth…like truth serum.*

"Will do" Sumner rolled him a nice fat two paper joint.

"Dam" said Leroy "that's a championship roll".

For the next several hours they talked, Leroy asked a lot of questions about who Sumner was, where he came from and what he was planning to do, relative to the connection he was going to make me. They stopped at a rib shack for lunch while running several errands for Leroy's wife.

At 5:00 PM it was time to leave for the Green Parrot.

§

Undercover operations were always hairy. The risks were outweighed only by the fact that there was no other way to gather information that would lead to the arrest and conviction of some of the worst criminals on the planet. The deep cover officers constantly walked the razor's edge between their deep cover assignments and criminal activity. Deep cover meant that the officer could not carry a wire, could not be under surveillance and could not call for backup if their lives were threatened. Success often required the Wisdom of Solomon and the patience of Job. Through careful, step by step progress, Sumner had successfully gained the confidence of a bad guy named Leroy Baglin. Over time Sumner had discovered that that Baglin *might* lead him to the elusive source, known on the street as, "Old man Richard." The old man's reputation was that of one of the most violent, ruthless and successful drug dealers in the country. The department had been trying to bring him down for years. No one even got close. Each time warrants had been issued they had been quashed by the court. Sumner wanted to be the first to bring the old man down; but deep down there was an element of dread when he thought about working his way deep enough into that enterprise to finally confront that shadowy figure in person.

Leroy had finally arranged to introduce Sumner to his supplier who he hoped would take him one step closer to Old Man Richard. Sumner had convinced Leroy that he had the capacity to move large quantities of product and that he needed to purchase a larger supply of the narcotic in order to finance his own addiction by selling to other addicts. Leroy was so greedy for the commission he would earn, that he set aside his usual hypersensitive advanced precautions.

Leroy set the meeting at a black bar on the east side of San Jose known as the "Green Parrot." The Parrot was frequented by drug addicts and cutthroats of all criminal persuasion. It was located in the sleazy area near the food processing factories on the north east side of town. When they entered the darkened bar, it took two minutes for their eyes to adjust to the dismal atmosphere. When Sumner could finally see, he assessed his surroundings. There were about thirty patrons in the bar, with him standing out as the only white person present. *Wonderful,* he thought. He cocked his head toward the end of the bar and quietly suggested that they grab a beer while they waited.

Years of defensive training dictated his next move. Sumner settled himself at the end of the bar where it turned the corner. He was facing the length of the bar with the paneled wall behind him. In this position no one could sneak up behind him, and he had a commanding view of the entire watering hole. He motioned for Leroy to take the seat to his right. Now the end of the bar was relatively secure.

While sipping a beer and talking with his unwitting informant, Sumner noticed three men standing at the other end of the bar. They were engaged in an animated conversation when one of the men casually walked around behind the bar as if he were going to serve the other two men. Suddenly the man behind the bar reached over and grabbed the wrists of the man who had been in the center. The move pinned the man's hands down on the bar. As he struggled like a fly in a spider's web to free himself from the pin, the man to his right produced a switchblade knife, flicked it open, and stepped behind him, raising the blade and in one fluid stroke cut the victim's throat from ear to ear. The victim's head rolled back, as dark blood poured from the wound. He staggered back from the bar as he turned and looked straight at Sumner with an expression that silently screamed the terror with which he was seized. He then collapsed to the floor in a pool of blood. The act had been extremely violent, and yet it had been accomplished in the silence of a prayer meeting.

The two perpetrators then slowly stared down the patrons of the establishment, one by one, finally settling their gaze on the one white guy in the place. Sumner carefully assessed his situation, first noticing that the assassin had simply dropped the knife and that both killers were casually holding semi automatic pistols at their side. Sumner could sense their hair-trigger tension, and their dead fish eyes warned of their psychotic disregard for human life. Sumner sat motionless, considering his options. He was unable to draw his meticulously concealed weapon without drawing their immediate response.

OK, Sumner, he thought, *it's your move, and if you make a bad choice it could be your last.* Decision time. He rolled the dice and simply looked away for several seconds, which seemed an eternity. When he looked back up, they were gone. The message he had sent by looking away told the killers that as far as he was concerned he had seen nothing.

The bar's patrons then began to quietly get up and head for the exit. Sumner was torn. He knew that he needed to get a license number or at least a description of the perpetrators' vehicle in order to assist the homicide detectives, but he also had to protect his cover. He turned to Leroy and whispered, "Your guy isn't going to come into this mess. Let's get the hell out of here."

As Sumner started out the door exited by the murderers, his informant grabbed his arm and urgently noted, "No, man, we needs to go out the back."

Sumner realized that there was nothing that he could do for the dead man and that his job was to maintain his cover until such time as he could safely and discretely make contact with the homicide detectives. At that point he could provide a detailed description and all the pertinent information he had. He nodded and followed Leroy out the back door

§

Later, when he was alone, Ted contacted the homicide detectives. He didn't know what to expect, but he was reasonably certain that they would be eager to learn that a member of the force had been an eyewitness to a cold blooded murder. The response he got was an eye opener. The detectives told him thanks, but the victim was an ex-convict and drug dealer and they felt that the murder was a turf war hit. The detectives made it clear that this case had very low priority. Life and death on the street— each person's life counts, but some count more than others.

The murder at the Green Parrot caused a change in Ted Sumner's life. In the martial art of Kenpo there is a self defense technique known as "Anvil." Anvil is a specific defense against an attack where the assailant grabs both of one's wrists. Sumner had never felt this technique to be of great value until the day of the incident at the Green Parrot. From that day forward, however, he not only practiced that defense diligently, he went out of his way to make sure his students understood the threat and could perform all of the essential components of the defense.

CHAPTER 35

Methamphetamines are a "family" affair. There are small bastard groups, of course, that struggle to survive, but their risks are great and their rewards are seldom commensurate with those risks. The cold, hard realities are if you are a meth user or distributer, your chances of survival are significantly greater if you keep things within the "family" …if you're Anglo, and you want to speed, you're going to have to ride with the Angels. That is, unless you happen to be African-American, in which case your life will belong to "Old Man Richard." But if perchance you are Hispanic, the fast track leads to the door of "Mexican Bob."

Unlike the Angels, who had their own "cooker" and produced the drugs locally, "Mexican Bob" was a "Mule" who brought the stimulants in from outside the area. His source and the specifics of from where the merchandise came and when it was delivered had been a matter of heated speculation by local law enforcement agencies for over three decades. Veteran Narcs were convinced that he had contacts along the Mexican border. These contacts, it was reasoned, brought the drugs into the U.S. and quickly offloaded the shipments to "mules" like Bob. Mexican Bob was an entrepreneur. He had visions of expanding to the point that he could retire. To that end he was grooming his two sons to take over the family business. Jose, or Hosa, as he was called, age twenty-one, and his brother Jesus, age nineteen, were learning the ropes from their father. But unlike their father, they both brought to the business a ruthlessness that seemed to be very much a part of the new generation of *"Californios."*

§

Ted Sumner, in his deep cover role of "Leslie Sheffield," sat on a bar-stool sipping a Dos Equis at "Arturo's," a dive bar located in the New-bury's Center at the intersection of King and Story Roads on San Jose's east side. That undercover identity was Sumner's favorite. Sheffield was a self styled, bad ass stock car driver. Sheffield had once led Sumner on a high speed pursuit after he had failed to yield to the red lights and siren during a car stop for speeding. When he had finally crashed his vehicle, Sheffield had attempted to attack Sumner with a piece of steel rebar. That proved to be a serious mistake that resulted in Sheffield sustaining a fractured skull. He wound up suing the city, claiming that Sumner was too violent when making the arrest. The city settled for $5,000 rather than undergo the expense of a trial. Sumner loved using Sheffield's name.

Arturo's was ground zero for illegal activity amongst the south bay's Hispanics. Sumner had completed "Operation Kiddy Cop" in early June, with a massive roundup of hundreds of pushers who had, until their cap-ture, been using the high schools of San Jose as their drug mall. They had been supplying all manner of illegal substances to high school students with seeming impunity. The high profile police roundup of drug dealers was reported on the front page of the local newspapers and on television news for seven days running. The crackdown was conducted the week before graduation. This operation had been intentionally timed by SJPD Chief of Detectives Ed McKay. His intent was to send a clear message to the drug dealers, users, and the community as a whole that the San Jose Police would not tolerate drug trafficking on or around their high school campuses.

The daily headlines describing the high school narcotic investigations of the San Jose Police Department had earned the department the en-mity of both "Rolling Stones" and "High Times" magazines. Both pub-lications had run derogatory articles berating the SJPD for using "Kiddy Cops" to nab drug dealers in the high schools. The veteran officers of the Narcotic Unit gleefully seized upon this characterization and hung the nickname "Kiddy Cop" on Sumner. At first he shrugged off the alias as good natured kidding, but over time he began to chafe at what he perceived as jealously based harassment.

Sumner's Kiddy Cop days were long gone. . Deep undercover meant that Sumner did not work the informants developed by the Narcotics Unit Street Enforcement Team, or "Bulls" as they were referred to by the drug world. Sumner was alone, exposed, and could not count on any assistance if anything went wrong. As a deep undercover operative, Sumner stayed away from Police Headquarters or PAB as it was known. At a designated time each day he would check in with his handler by phone and brief his "handler" on his operations, the progress of specific investigations, and submit any information that needed to be analyzed. This usually involved passing all available information to his handler to aid in the process of identifying street contacts and criminal subjects. The handler had access to the extensive SJPD Narcotic Unit database as well as CJIC (California Criminal Justice Information Center), NCIC (National Criminal Information Center), and many other resources. If Sumner needed to book evidence or submit reports, he would arrange a discreet meeting with the handler and there turn over those items, obtain "buy money" for the purchase of drugs and any other tools necessary for the successful completion of the job. Sumner's job now was to work the streets and develop entry contacts, or meet and befriend people who could give him entry into circles of criminal drug activity.

§

"What are you doing here asshole?" demanded a sharp faced Hispanic man in his mid twenties. He was less than Sumner's height, cokehead thin and wild-eyed as a skittish colt. He held something to the right side of Sumner's head, but Sumner made no move see what it might be.

"Minding my own business; You ought to try it," Sumner replied coldly. The man then shoved Sumner off the bar stool. Sumner gained his balance and stood to face his assailant. The man shoved Sumner's right shoulder with his left hand and brought the knife he'd been hiding up under Sumner's nose.

"I'll cut your fucking nose off," he threatened "What are you fucking doing here, Holmes?"

Sumner could feel the razor sharp blade under his nose cut slightly into his skin. He made a quick analysis of the situation. *Five inch fixed blade, razor sharp, MMA (Mexican Male Adult), 5-9, 165lbs, prison tattoos, turn left and your nose comes off. Right it is.* With the speed and precision of a well practiced Kenpo Karate instructor, Sumner turned his head sharply to the right, disengaging the blade. Simultaneously, his left hand slammed into the attacker's right wrist moving the knife past Sumner's face. In one continuing fluid motion Sumner pivoted, slamming his left forearm into the assailant's right forearm hyper-extending the man's elbow. Continuing the movement, he slipped his left elbow over the knife arm and up under the attacker's armpit, exacerbating the hyperextension of the offending limb up to the elbow. Sumner then used his hips to apply torque and slammed the attacker's head into the heavy wooden bar. *Four more sitting in the rear of the bar...probably his friends. Overwhelm this guy, terrify him, but do not injure him badly. Don't need a blood feud. Need to make friends, not mortal enemies.*

Sumner, with precision timing, reversed his movement locking the wrist that still held the blade, turned left slamming the attacker to the floor. *No knee to the chest could cause damage to the heart or lungs. Arm pit!*

The instant the assailant hit the floor, Sumner's right knee dropped his full weight into the attacker's right arm pit, neutralizing the knife wielding arm and pinning him to the ground. In the same movement, Sumner drove the attacker's knife hand to the floor just behind the attacker's head.

It had only been a second or two when the four other patrons of the bar reacted to their associate's distress. They rose quickly to their feet. Sumner was now aware of the new threat. He momentarily returned his attention to his attacker. *You're not hurt enough. You need something to remember me by.* In a quick, sharp movement, he pushed the attacker's right forearm forward and slammed his right palm down on the attacker right elbow. SNAP! The man's wrist broke, as he screeched an intense squeal of pain, and released the knife.

Sumner picked up the knife and brandished it in the tear stained face of his vanquished attacker. The man's eyes widened in terror. Sumner turned to face the approaching gang. They stopped cold as they surmised what Sumner was about to do to their buddy. Sumner then slowly looked down at the agonized aggressor and scolded, "Your mother should have taught you some manners." Sumner then reached across his body, placing the blade of the knife under his boot. In one sudden movement he pulled upward, snapping the blade off the handle. He then stood over the fallen man like a possessive lion standing over its kill and stared down the four patrons. He then dropped the handle of the broken knife on the prone attacker's chest. In a final act of defiance, he turned his back on the four murmuring, half to himself, "Adios" as he walked out the door into the late summer afternoon sunlight.

§

"Hey, where did you learn that, Holmes?" the inquisitive voice came from behind Sumner.

"Man, you really handed Flaco his ass. Who taught you that?" Sumner didn't turn, but out of his peripheral vision he could see on his right, a diminutive Hispanic man in his late teens or early twenties running alongside him. Sal Lopez was one of those "invisible" individuals, 5'2" maybe 110 pounds, dark skinned with a mop of straight black hair, and he was absolutely that last person you would notice when you walked into a room.

Sal had been at the end of the bar during the recent unpleasantness, where he had just finished sweeping out behind the bar. Sal worked part time for his wife's brother who was one of the bartenders at Arturo's. He was an easy person to underestimate, as Sumner was soon to learn. Sal was a highly intelligent and cunning individual.

"Really man, where did you learn that?" Sal persisted.

"My father was a Marine," Sumner growled as he kept walking. "He taught me some stuff."

"No shit, man, that was really cool. I love the way you tossed Flaco around like an old rug," Sal gushed. "Hey, my name is Sal," he offered as he bounded along trying to keep up with Sumner's pace. "Hey, what's your name man?" Sal inquired.

"Les," Sumner grunted, shaking off the last vestiges of his recent adrenalin rush.

Sumner reached his vehicle, a nondescript tan Volkswagen bug, and inserted the key to the driver side door.

Sal ran around to the passenger door asking, "Hey, give me a ride home, man."

"Fuck off," came Sumner's curt reply.

"Come on, man You never got to finish your beer," Sal implored. "Give me a ride to my crib and let me buy you a beer." *This couldn't be going better any better,* thought Sumner as he climbed into his vehicle and unlocked the passenger door.

"All right, where to?" Sumner asked as if thoroughly bored.

§

Five minutes later they were at Sal's apartment. It was located in a seedy corner of the ghetto in the projects off Poco Lane, which was one of the chronic trouble spots for the SJPD. Sumner had worked this beat for six months while assigned to the Patrol Division and had spent many an evening quelling violent disturbances here. His new appearance was so un-cop like, that Sumner felt invisible.

Uncharacteristically, for the area, Sal's apartment was clean and tidy, kept that way by his young, pregnant wife. She was a small statured woman given to openly demonstrating her adoration for her husband.

"Mia (my love), would you get us a beer" Sal said to his wife. "You should have seen this machista (tough guy) handle Flaco (a nickname which means skinny) when he pulled a knife."

"A knife!?" She reacted with concern. "Are you all right? Do you need a bandage?" She scrutinized Sumner with a corpsman's eye.

"I'm fine. It was no big deal," said Sumner.

"Yes, it was," protested Sal. "It was like bam, bang, boom," intoned Sal as he went through wild gyrations in his interpretive reenactment of the encounter.

"I'm Irma," offered Sal's wife as she handed Sumner his beer.

"Thank you. I'm Les," replied Sumner. Over the next two hours Sumner found Sal to be an open book. He was a surprisingly intelligent and complex young man, but he seemed to possess no guile. He held nothing back. Sal was, for the most part, dismissed by his peers. Because of his diminutive size, he was overlooked, treated as insignificant, and with disrespect. Given an opportunity to be treated as a peer, he demonstrated an active intellect that offered flashes of brilliance, although he governed those displays with a caution born of a keen awareness of his environment, the realities of his physical limitations, and a discernment of the daily dangers that life presented. It was clear that he considered Sumner as a potential strong ally.

Sumner laid out his cover, that he had been living in New Mexico for the last three years, working construction as a hod carrier (this tended to allay suspicions about such a muscular build on a doper), had saved up some cash, and was looking to get into dealing some crank to his old doper buddies if he could find a reliable source and a reasonable price.

"I might be able to help you," offered Sal enthusiastically. "I know a dude who is solid."

CHAPTER 36

Friday night, 10:00 PM, Sumner met Sal, as agreed, at the Quiet Village, a Latino bar on Capitol Ave near Alum Rock Ave. The bar could not have been less like its name. It was a raucous place filled with the dregs of San Jose society. The purpose of the meet was for Sal to introduce Sumner to a possible meth supplier… an acquaintance of Sal's. Sumner had survived on the street by being cautious. The bar was packed, and Sumner's long, coarse, blond hair and red beard make him stand out. True to his strategic custom, he took a seat at a booth against the far wall facing the door. Music blared from the jukebox loud enough to mask most conversations. Sal excused himself and walked across the bar. Sumner watched him shake hands with a young Latino man. Sumner mentally catalogued the man's distinguishing features, *Medium build, 5-8, 170, black wavy hair.* The man followed Sal back to the table. Sal then introduced Sumner as "Buffalo." *Buffalo? What's that all about?*

"This is Hosa." Sal's introduction was quiet and respectful, a detail Sumner noted and filed away. Sumner motioned for them to sit, and ordered three beers. The three men were making small talk, cautiously feeling things out, when Sumner suddenly spotted a woman with whom he was all too familiar. *Oh great,* Sumner groaned internally, *it's B-36.* B-36 was a woman in her mid-twenties named Eileen Chavez, and she was headed toward the table. She had been arrested for possession of a hypodermic syringe and being under the influence of heroin during the dragnet to

197

arrest the dealers Sumner had targeted during the high school operation. The charges against her had been dropped on the condition that she co-operated in acting as a reliable informant for the Narcotics Division. The "B" designated her as a female and "36," appropriately enough given her ample figure, was her identification number. She had been assigned to work with Officer Miguel Mendoza targeting heroin dealers on the East Side. Sumner looked quickly around the room, but he didn't see Mendoza anywhere. *Miguel must be keeping banker's hours* Sumner thought; *she could burn me to the ground right now.*

"Mi Corazon," sang B-36 to Sumner. "You are breaking my heart. You promise to have a drink with me but you always disappear." She climbed into the booth and put her arms around Sumner's neck snuggling up against his arm. Sumner noticed Hosa's look of respect and his nod of approval. "You have to promise to spend the rest of the evening with only me," chirped the perky B-36 as she tried to kiss Sumner on the mouth, but could only make contact with his cheek as he turned his head. Sumner ordered more drinks and the small talk continued until B-36 excused herself to go to the ladies room.

"You do all right, Buffalo," said Hosa. *There's that Buffalo again. What the hell is that all about.*

"Why do you call me Buffalo?" ventured Sumner.

"That's what Sal calls you," he answered. "Buffalo Blanco." *White Buffalo.*

"Why?" Sumner's curiosity overcame his caution.

"Because that's what you look like," the answer was confusing. Hosa took a sip of his beer, noting the quizzical look on Sumner's face. "Next time you're in front of a mirror, look at the back of your head," said Hosa. "All that hair looks like the back of a Buffalo."

At this point Hosa looked around and, satisfied they couldn't be over-heard, leaned forward and got right down to business. He made clear that he could handle any Meth orders up to multiple pounds. Good quality crank he promised and reasonable prices, if there was money.

"I got a good stash of cash," Sumner assured. "I been working con-struction for a couple years in New Mexico."

"You been carrying bricks," Hosa chided. "But I don't care how you got the money, just so it's green." "Normally…twelve hundred dollars a piece (ounce), but for Sal's amigo, El Buffalo, it's only a thousand dollars."

$1000 IS the going price you thief, thought Sumner. Hosa handed Sumner a folded bindle of paper under the table. "Try this. If you like it, we can do business," Hosa concluded. "Now I better go," said Hosa. "It looks like this is your lucky night," he added, gesturing to B-36 as she approached the table.

"How do I get a hold of you?" asked Sumner.

"I'll get a hold of you," was the answer. And Hosa was gone.

§

The next day Sumner met with his handler Sergeant Dreyer. Dreyer was the supervisor for the undercover team, but personally acted as Sumner's handler. They had attended high school together and were friends socially. Sumner turned over his reports and the bindle of meth that had been supplied by Hosa. "Check this for purity ASAP," said Sumner. "I need to know if he's paddy hustling me or if he's on the level." A paddy hustle is where minorities who feel ethnically superior in street smarts to white boys sell "bunk" or extremely diluted drugs, or even substances other than what they claim, such as Ajax for cocaine.

"That was Jose Castellano you connected with last night," said Dreyer with a hint of trepidation in his voice. "Mexican Bob's oldest kid," he went on. "You be very careful. These people are heavyweights."

Mexican Bob's kid! What a stroke of luck Sumner congratulated himself. "What's with B-36? At first I thought she was going to give me up, but she played along and provided me some great cover," Sumner informed Dreyer.

Dreyer snickered. "Miguel said she is really getting into this whole CI," (Confidential Informant) "thing," Dreyer advised. "She saw you and felt the need to fill with you," said Dreyer, as he broke into outright laughter. Fill is a term patrol officers use to denote a unit that acts as an assist to a unit that is engaged.

My fill unit, B-36, just dandy, Sumner thought.

CHAPTER 37

Sumner spent several hours each day with Sal, driving him to work, helping him out with whatever project he was occupied with, cementing the friendship, and solidifying his position in the social strata of this drug culture.

"Hosa wants to know how you liked the stuff," said Sal. *So this is how he is going to get ahold of me*, thought Sumner. *I've got to get Sal out of the middle*.

"Let him know it was great," said Sumner. "And tell him I want to cop a piece. Have him contact me directly," said Sumner, handing Sal a piece of paper with a phone number written on it. "I live with my cousin. If I'm not home, he'll answer," said Sumner. The number he had given was to the Batphone, which a phone at the Narcotic Unit located in a soundproof booth inside the unit commander's office. When that phone rang whoever was present to answer knew a crook was calling for one of the undercovers and to go into character.

"He wants to work through me," advised Sal.

"Not a chance pal," Sumner replied. "You'll get a cut, but you have a baby on the way and I don't want you getting into trouble if something goes wrong," Sumner stated flatly. "Hosa will have to deal directly with me."

§

Later that afternoon Sumner checked in with Sergeant Dreyer. "Message on the Batphone...Hosa wants you to call him at this number," advised Dreyer. "The Boss," (unit commander Lt. Bertotti) "is really stoked about this, but I want you to be very, very careful," warned Dreyer. "These guys are not poopbutts," he cautioned. "Poopbutt" is a term used by Narcotics Detectives to characterize small time players of relative insignificance.

Sumner hung up the pay phone, deposited another dime, and called the number provided by Dreyer.

"Hello."

"Hosa?" Sumner asked.

"Just a minute."

A moment later Hosa answered.

"That was primo shit. You got a piece I can score today?" Sumner asked.

"No problem," Hosa advised.

"Where do we meet?" Sumner asked.

"I want to go through Sal on this," Hosa said. "I don't know you."

"Well, you better get to know me," chastened Sumner. "We're going to be making a lot of money doing business together."

After a silent pause that seemed to last forever came, "River Glen Park, one hour."

Sumner knew the drill. River Glen Park was located in the middle of the pleasant residential area of San Jose known as Willow Glen. The park had quiet residential streets on all sides and was surrounded by a cyclone fence with entry openings every fifty yards or so. It was a favorite place for drug dealers to do business because of the lack of access by the police. If the police came in one way, the dopers would exit the other side of the park. Every now and then an ambitious patrol sergeant would attempt to organize his team to hit the park in a coordinated, well timed assault from all directions, but the park was so large that all the dopers had to do was move to the center and destroy any contraband before the police reached them. It was an interesting problem in tactics...something Sumner would attend to later, but at the moment, his mind was on Mexican Bob's son.

§

Sumner arrived at River Glen Park fifteen minutes early to survey the environment. *Three kids, ten years old or so, playing catch near the south west corner of the park. Some high school kids smoking pot near the picnic tables. Let's see how much cover he brings,* Sumner thought. He removed his pistol and locked it in the glove box. This could wind up being close and personal, no need to spook anyone, Sumner reasoned. He pulled his Gil Hibbin custom Profolder combat knife from inside his boot and slipped it into his pants pocket. He then proceeded to the center of the park where the meeting would no doubt take place.

§

Two vehicles leading a black Mustang pulled up on Pine Ave. A white Ford proceeded to the southwest corner followed by a blue Gremlin. *Blue Gremlin?!* Sumner thought, *these guys have no class whatsoever.* The Gremlin pulled up and stopped at the northwest corner of the park. *Well done,* Sumner silently processed his situation, *clear line of vision, unobstructed field of fire and if anything goes wrong I am in the open, in a crossfire.*

With the cover in place, the black Mustang proceeded slowly up Parkside Drive, parking behind Sumner's Volkswagen. Hosa exited and walked slowly toward the gate, entered the park and approached Sumner. As Hosa got to within five feet, Sumner sensed a growing tension and impending danger. He suppressed all his instincts, training and reflexes thinking, *you brought it this far, it is going to have to play out.* At three feet Hosa moved clumsily, drawing a nickel plated Colt Model 1911 .45 Caliber automatic pistol. *What a clod,* thought Sumner *This guy would be dead on the battlefield.* With his left hand, Hosa grabbed Sumner's right arm, and with his right brought the pistol to bear pushing the barrel up under Sumner's chin.

"Who the fuck do you think you are, man?" Hosa screamed. "I decide how the deals go down, not you, chump." Hosa then shoved Sumner to the ground. As Sumner landed on his back, Hosa stepped up, straddling Sumner's chest, pointing the pistol at his forehead.

"Screw that," hissed Sumner. "I worked too long and too damn hard earning this money. Two years carrying those damn bricks up and down the ladder in that heat, putting up with those asshole masons; nobody touches my money until I touch product," Sumner ranted. "That's the way it's going to fucking be, man, that's the way it's going to be."

Hosa lowered himself down on his right knee over Sumner's chest, pushing the barrel of the .45 onto Sumner's forehead. "You're pretty bold, Buffalo," Hosa allowed himself an evil serpentine smile. "I could kill you, you know," boasted Hosa.

"Yeah, well, you wouldn't have long to celebrate," answered Sumner as he let the blade of his knife, positioned in his right hand over the femoral artery of Hosa left leg, slide forward, slicing through Hosa's Levi's. The razor sharp blade lightly severed the tender skin of the inner leg and sent a stinging warning.

"Aye-yah, you fucker," yelled Hosa as he jumped to his feet. "That could have fucked me up really bad."

"Could have," said Sumner matter-of-factly getting to his feet as he calmly closed his knife, placed it in his pocket and casually brushed the grass from his clothing.

Hosa stepped back in a rage, but then that cool malevolence crept back over and self control returned, along with that evil smile. He stepped up grabbed Sumner around the neck, hugging him roughly. "I'm starting to really like you, Buffalo. You got some real huevos." Hosa then gestured toward the blue Gremlin waving the nickel plated pistol above his head. *What an idiot,* Sumner thought. A young Hispanic man in his late teens or early twenties exited the American motors classic vehicle and walked slowly toward the men.

"This is Jesus, my little brother," said Hosa, grabbing the man around the neck and roughly hugging him. "This is the Buffalo," Hosa informed his brother. "A real bad ass." "The money," demanded Hosa as his brother handed him two rolled plastic bags. Sumner handed him two thousand dollars in cash as Hosa handed him the bags. "This hombre is going to make us a lot of money, hermano."

Sumner departed, emotionally drained by the experience but gratified with the success of the operation. Looking down the barrel of a .45 caliber pistol has a way taking the fun out of the rest of the day. He wanted to go have a beer with his fellow officers and decompress, but that is not a luxury available to a deep undercover operative. He still had reports to write and needed to connect with Sgt. Dreyer to turn over the evidence and get briefed on any new information that might have surfaced. Sumner found a pay phone and called in to his handler. They arranged to meet in the parking lot of the Garden City Hofbrau in thirty minutes.

Later that evening Sumner lay on the sofa in the family room of his home reading Bram Stoker's *Dracula,* feeling very much like Jonathan Harker. *I must get to the mobster's lair…but how?* He pondered.

CHAPTER 38

It was Wednesday and Dreyer had attended a 7:00 AM staff meeting in the Chief's conference room with all the command staff. Following that meeting, Dreyer called an early meeting with Sumner in the parking lot of Valley Fair Shopping Center.

"The Boss is only going to let one more buy from Hosa walk." "If you can't get to Mexican Bob on the next buy, the Boss wants to bring in the State," Dreyer's directive was delivered without enthusiasm. "The State" meant agents from the California Bureau of Investigations and Narcotic Enforcement who were far better funded for such operations than the SJPD. They were nice enough guys and good officers, but they operated differently from Sumner, and he felt that they cramped his style. And it would become a State case—no longer under Sumner's direct control.

I don't like that Sumner thought.

"Take a look at this," said Dreyer, handing Sumner a small box. Sumner opened it to find a brand new Smith and Wesson model 59, nine millimeter fifteen shot semi-automatic pistol. There had been a great deal of talk about this high capacity firearm. It was being introduced to police departments across the state and everyone was dying to get their hands on one. "The Chief now considers this as our primary duty weapon and several of us have been given one to evaluate," Dreyer commented with more than a little pride.

205

Sumner dropped the magazine out and jacked back the slide assuring the weapon was unloaded. As he admired the pistol, his mind suddenly went into overdrive. "I need this for an hour," Sumner demanded.

"I can't," pleaded Dreyer. "That was issued directly to me by the Chief."

"I need this," Sumner reported. "Meet me back here in an hour and I'll get it back to you safe and sound."

"I can't, I really can't!" Dreyer implored.

"See you back here at noon," said Sumner as he drove off.

§

"Hosa, there's something big coming down," Sumner reported excitedly into the pay phone. "I need to show you something right now."

"Where?" asked Hosa in a sleep laden voice.

"Make it easy on yourself," said Sumner. "I'll come to your place."

After a pause came a deep exhale, "What the hell," said Hosa. "1638 White Oaks."

"I'll be there in fifteen," said Sumner.

That address was a two acre lot with a small adobe house built in the late eighteenth century. It was located in the unincorporated area of the City of Campbell just outside the San Jose City limits. Sumner arrived and drove slowly off the road onto the dirt driveway that led to the house about fifty yards from the street.

§

"Buffalo!" greeted Jesus.

The two men shook hands as Sumner asked, "Where's the boss?"

Jesus answered quizzically, "If you mean Hosa, he's coming, but there is only one boss...Patrón," asserted Jesus.

"What's up?" asked Hosa.

Sumner held up the box containing the Model 59 pistol. He opened the box, dropped the magazine, and locked back the slide. Handing it to Hosa, he said, "I can get twenty five hundred of them for thirty thousand."

Mexican Bob stepped from the kitchen, gently taking the pistol from the hands of his son, as if receiving a baby from its mother. "Nice…very nice," admired Mexican Bob.

"This is Buffalo, Patrón," said Hosa.

"Buffalo?" Mexican Bob's eyes widened. "The famous Buffalo," said Bob. "I hear you are muy valiente. Now how exactly are you going to get twenty five hundred of these?" Bob asked point blankly, staring Sumner directly in the eyes.

Sumner looked Mexican Bob squarely in the eyes and offered a story of reasonable plausibility about how the guns belonged to the Army and had been smuggled out of Cambodia by an old partner who was a pilot.

"They are in the long term storage area of a warehouse in LA and he has to off load them before someone discovers them," Sumner concluded.

Bob nodded his head thoughtfully, "And this one is mine?" Bob inquired ruminatively.

"I can have one for you in two days," Sumner advised. "But that one has been tricked out for someone who will find me and use it on me if it is not delivered back to him in one hour." *And there is no doubt Dreyer would do just that*, thought Sumner.

Mexican Bob took one last admiring look at the pistol as he handed it back to Sumner who placed it back in the box.

"I think we should do business," Bob said to his sons. Turning to Sumner he ordered, "You get me the exact details on how the merchandise is to be transported, when and where."

"Sir!" Sumner snapped. *Damn that military discipline, I'm burned.* Bob's eyes widened as he turned to his son's. *They smell a rat*, Sumner thought.

"Now that is respect," Bob said to his sons. "Something you two need to learn." Bob placed his right hand on the top of Sumner's head and mussed his hair as an affectionate parent would a child. Sumner smiled.

"Oh…speaking of business." Sumner then produced two thousand dollars in cash and presented it to Mexican Bob. "I need two more bags," said Sumner. "That primo shit is selling like hotcakes."

Mexican Bob stood with his hands and his side, looking down at the money Sumner offered. *If they figure out what you're doing you just may finally get your fool head blown off* Sumner thought. Slowly Bob's hands came up as he gingerly took the money.

"Respect! Do you see that?" Bob demanded of his sons. "This muchacho (boy) knows who the boss is," scolded Bob. "Get him his product."

CHAPTER 39

Sumner arrived back at the rendezvous point at 12:01 to a nervous and visibly agitated Sergeant Dreyer.

"Give me that damn gun," Dreyer ordered. Sumner placed the two bags of methamphetamines on top of the box and handed it through the window to his handler. Dreyer's jaw dropped.

"Don't tell me," he mumbled. "You just made a hand to hand buy from Mexican Bob."

"My report will be in the mailbox at your house by midnight," Sumner promised. Sumner would often complete his reports, and then place them in a manila envelope and pay a neighborhood kid to deposit the envelope in the mailbox at Dreyer's home two blocks from his own home.

"You know the Boss is beginning to think that there's nobody you can't get to," Dreyer praised. *If the Boss knew how close I've already come to getting killed on this operation, he'd shut it down and send me back to Patrol,* Sumner thought.

§

Sumner met later that day with Sal. Sumner handed Sal two hundred dollars in twenties. "You're cut amigo," Sumner said.

"Why are you cutting me in?" asked Sal.

"Because you're my partner and I never Welch on a partner," assured Sumner.

"All I did was introduce you," protested Sal.

"And if you hadn't, I'd be nowhere. Take your wife out to dinner and then give her the rest of the money to put away for the baby," suggested Sumner.

"I'll do that, Holmes," beamed Sal.

§

"Fourth Street Bowl, back of the dining room," called Dreyer.

"Ten minutes," replied Sumner then hung up the pay phone. The Fourth Street Bowl, curiously located on Fourth Street just north of Highway 17, had a large dining room that served lunch, but was only open for dinner on Saturday evenings. There was a small banquet room in back where the officers could meet in relative privacy and safety.

"The Boss wants to bring in Jonesy as the gun man," Dreyer advised. "He has his own plane and we can set the deal up to go down at the airport where no innocent bystanders will get hurt if the deal goes bad and the shooting starts." Jonesy was Officer Russell Jones, a veteran undercover narcotics operative and a former combat helicopter pilot who had flown over 600 missions in Viet Nam. Jonesy was unflappable. Nothing could appall him. Those who knew him often said if he were ever shot, he wouldn't bleed; he would merely leak ice water. In any situation, he could be absolutely counted on when things got dicey. "The Boss wants you to get one more hand to hand buy from Bob before we do this caper and wrap it up," ordered Dreyer.

"Tomorrow," answered Sumner as Dreyer handed him an envelope containing buy money.

§

It was 6:15 PM when Sumner arrived at the home of Mexican Bob and his sons. It was mid-October and the sun would be setting in fifteen minutes. Sumner knew he may earn the wrath of Mexican Bob for just dropping by, but it was the only way to make sure that Bob would be involved in the sale of the drugs. Hosa answered the door with an expression of surprise and irritation,

"Que pasa," asked Hosa.

"I got news," replied Sumner.

Hosa opened the door and Sumner entered.

"What's the news?" asked Hosa.

"No offense Hosa, but your father ordered me to report directly to him and he is not someone I want to piss off," replied Sumner. He heard footsteps behind him as a hand came to rest on his right shoulder.

"This hombre knows how to follow orders," said Bob to his sons. "Something you two need to learn."

"My partner is going to bring the merchandise by plane," informed Sumner.

"When?" asked Bob.

"He wants to meet you first," said Sumner. "He wants to fly up tomorrow and meet at the airport out in the hangars." Suddenly Sumner noticed movement outside the front window of the house. A tall, slender, long haired man moving stealthily toward the house from the road. Then two more men.

Oh shit! Sumner thought. *Undercover officers from the Santa Clara County Narcotics Task Force.* This was a countywide Narcotic Unit comprised of officers from all of the county's police forces, except San Jose. The unit was funded by the federal government but administered by the Santa Clara County Sheriff. And right now Deputies Will Browne, Charlie Belvedere, and City of Santa Clara police officer Ted Kane were moving into position to attempt a raid to catch Mexican Bob holding dope.

"It's a rip, boys!" bellowed the booming voice of Mexican Bob. *He doesn't know they are cops,* Sumner realized. *He thinks they are dopers here to rip him off and he is going to make a fight of it...shit!* "Help out," ordered Bob, handing Sumner a Smith and Wesson .38 caliber revolver. BOOM, BOOM, BOOM Hosa's opening shots made a deafening roar and shattered the front window. Sumner could hear Jesus in the bathroom running the shower, the bath tub, the sink, and flushing the toilet. *There goes a couple of hundred thousand dollars worth of dope,* mused Sumner as a bullet crashed into the wall behind his head, return fire from the officers outside.

This is crazy, fretted Sumner. *I can't shoot at the cops and I can't take Bob and*

his sons down by myself. I'm going to get my ass shot off by fellow officers. He ducked down behind the wall just below the window. "Shoot, Dammit," ordered Mexican Bob. A bullet crashed through the wall just below Sumner's nose. *This wall is not going to stop a 357 round,* Sumner came to understand. He then moved behind the couch as the gunfire continued unabated. *I've got to do something,* Sumner's mind raced. "They're cops!" Sumner yelled. "I think they're cops!"

Bob and Hosa stopped firing looking suspiciously at Sumner as a marked Sheriff Department's patrol car pulled into the driveway.

"I knew it!" yelled Sumner. We been shooting at cops and now they're going to kill us!"

"Police officers!" the demand came from outside. "Throw down your weapons and come out of the house with your hands up!"

"Nobody goes anywhere until Jesus is finished," ordered Bob.

CRASH the front door was literally knocked off its hinges and the officers stormed in, crouched with weapons at the ready. Suddenly the three lead officers spotted Sumner and stopped, stood straight up and almost smiled. Mexican Bob and Hosa exchanged knowing looks as the officers, realizing that they had just compromised an undercover operative decided to set right what they had wronged. Two officers grabbed Sumner, pulling him to his feet as a third punched him in the stomach. Another kneed Sumner in the groin then, grabbing the back of his head, slammed his nose onto his knee as the other two punched his kidneys. Sumner was then handcuffed and placed in the backseat of one of the three marked units now on the scene. Mexican Bob, Hosa, and Jesus were also cuffed and placed in other patrol cars. All the units then proceeded to the Sheriff's Department where the prisoners were taken to the Detective Bureau and placed in separate interrogation rooms.

Sergeant Dick Pereira entered the interrogation where Sumner sat with his nose bleeding and both eyes swelling and blackening. Pereira had been one of Sumner's first supervisors when he had worked in the jail as a deputy sheriff before going to work for SJPD.

"They did a good job roughing you up," Pereira smiled. "That should protect your cover."

"Not a chance," groaned Sumner. "I don't think they gave a damn about my cover. I think they just wanted to work over a San Jose Officer."

"You're probably right," laughed Pereira. "Dreyer is on his way and we'll figure out where he wants to take this," advised Periera as he left the room. Sergeant Dreyer arrived twelve minutes later.

"Damn!" exclaimed Dreyer as he looked at Sumner's face. "They really did a number on you."

"Yeah, and one of them really went to work on my kidneys," said Sumner. "I'm going to be pissing blood for a month."

"Well, why are we wasting this? You've taken the beating, let's move Bob in here and see how he reacts to you," ordered Dreyer. A moment later the door opened and Mexican Bob was escorted into the room and seated next to Sumner. The officer then left the room, locking the door.

Bob said nothing, not even giving Sumner eye contact. Several moments passed before Mexican Bob said "That cop knew you."

"What are you talking about? I don't know any cops," protested Sumner.

"When they came through the door, that first cop stopped and looked at you just like you were his old friend," accused Bob.

"I didn't see that," protested Sumner. "Maybe I was too busy getting the shit beat out of me."

"They just did that to make it look good," Bob stated flatly, "You're heat." Just then the door opened and a uniformed officer entered and escorted Bob out of the room.

A few minutes later Sergeant Dreyer entered the room, accompanied by Deputies Will Browne, Charlie Belvedere, and Officer Ted Kane.

"I thought for sure working him over would have protected his cover," mused Brown. "Maybe we should beat him up some more and bring Bob back in," suggested the comical Kane.

"I want to thank you assholes for at least leaving my nose on my face," came Sumner's sarcastic reply.

"Oh, come on," said Belvedere, "You know if you got a chance to give one of us the business in the line of duty, you wouldn't pass it up."

"Not me," joked Sumner. "I am the epitome of the professional law enforcement officer. Hell, no…I'd just shoot you in the ass."

"Well, let's get out of here and go get a beer," said Browne, affectionately known as "the carrot" for his red hair and ruddy complexion.

"What about my nose?" Sumner growled.
The four officers stood looking pensively at Sumner's face for a moment.

"I think it's an improvement," said Kane, as they all laughed, slapping each other on the back in approval of each of their high brow senses of humor.

§

The operation could not be revived at this point. Mexican Bob and his sons were kept incarcerated until their trial several months later. All three were convicted of possession of methamphetamines, sales of methamphetamines, possession of illegal firearms, and assault with a deadly weapon. Mexican Bob was also convicted of maintaining a place for the purpose of engaging in the sale and use of controlled substances. All were sentenced to the state penitentiary.

CHAPTER 40

Sergeant Lawrence "Nails" Farnsworth shuffled his chair closer to the red and white checkered table, brushed the pizza crumbs over the edge so he had a reasonably clean spot to rest his elbows, and leaned in for a more confidential conversation. He looked around before beginning his instructions. Satisfied that they were alone, he unloaded the unwelcome news, "Jeannie Tye is back in town," he said apologetically. "The Boss wants you to work her."

Great, thought Sumner. *Jeannie, her husband Taylor and his brother Donald "Cowboy" Tye were all certifiably nuts.* Every undercover who has worked those crazies had spent most of his time intervening to keep the members of that totally dysfunctional family from killing each other.

"Why me?" groaned Sumner.

"Taylor and Donald are back in prison, so it shouldn't be too bad," said Nails. "And you're the only white undercover available."

Sumner had had the misfortune to work with Jeannie and Taylor a couple of years back. While they made a number of high profile cases, there had been a boatload of stress. Working deep under cover with a confidential informant always involves risk. Not the least of which is the fact that the CI knows that the officer is "uncovered" and could at any time rat the officer out to cover their own "six." Or, if they were short of cash, they would blow the officer's cover for a sufficiently attractive enticement. Every encounter brought with it the risk that the officer was

215

walking into an ambush. It was dangerous work and not for the timid or faint of heart.

Nails handed Sumner an envelope containing buy money. This was no longer a discussion. He was now assigned to buy illicit drugs. "Meet Jeannie at Little Chef Café tomorrow at 11:00 AM," ordered Sergeant Farnsworth. "The Boss wants you to start by targeting the dealers at the Methadone Clinic."

The Santa Clara County Methadone Maintenance Clinic was located on the edge of the grounds of the county's Valley Medical Center. Methadone is a synthetic opiate used to maintain heroin addicts at their current level of addiction. By dispensing free methadone to heroin addicts, the theory goes, the addicts will remain heroin free and secured against the excruciating pain of withdrawal by the synthetic drug. Again, the theory held that this substitute would allow the addicts to lead productive lives and not be engaged in the illegal activities that addicts invariably resorted to in order to support their ever-growing heroin habit. Since the clinic was where the addicts were required to report in order to receive their dosage of methadone, the parking lot outside became a target rich environment for providers of heroin.

§

"Hey, dumb ass." There was no mistaking that Tennessee accent. Jeannie Tye was in the house. Steam and the smell of grease and burned coffee filled the air of the Little Chef as Sumner walked between the tables toward Jeannie, who had taken a seat in the back.

"When did they let you out?" Sumner chided.

"That's dead and stinkin," shot back Jeannie. "I ain't never been locked up."

"Just kidding," assured Sumner. "Why is this place so popular?"

"It's welfare day, everyone got their checks today," explained Jeannie. "They eat here and then go get their methadone. It's the perfect time to see who's dealing over there." She filled Sumner in on what she and her husband Taylor had been up to for the last year and a half. They had moved back to Tennessee, but that triggered a parole violation for Taylor, who was still under sentence in California for drug violations and possession of stolen property. When they returned last month, Taylor made contact with his parole agent, who immediately violated him and returned him to Folsom Prison to finish the last year of his sentence incarcerated. Donald "Cowboy" Tye had gotten himself arrested by the San Jose Police for possession of heroin and possession of a hypodermic needle after getting into a fist-fight at a local dive bar where he had just scored a spoon. Cowboy was apparently beginning to withdraw and was in an agitated state, when another addict in similar condition tried to relieve him of his recent heroin buy. The ruckus brought the local beat officer who, after administering a generous dose of attitude adjustment with his nightstick, booked both of the addicts, who were now in total withdrawal. Cowboy's parole agent had agreed to allow him to remain on parole, contingent upon his cooperation with the San Jose Police Narcotics Division. Cowboy had been assigned to work with Officer Rob Grant, who made no secret of his distaste for hypes, as those addicted to heroin are referred to by narcotics officers. The arrangement had gone sour and upon the recommendation of Officer Grant, Cowboy's parole had been violated by his parole agent and he was returned to San Quentin Prison to serve out the remainder of his sentence.

"Who are we likely to encounter over there?" inquired Sumner.

"Maybe Shirley Rodriguez, or Raul Guerra, and maybe Monte Mc-Cueston," mused Jeannie. "We'll see."

After choking down a stomach-churning cup of stale coffee that tasted like it had been reheated for the last three days running, Sumner paid the bill and he and Jeannie left.

§

The parking lot of the methadone clinic was an anthill of activity with patients of the clinic coming and going in endless streams.

"Park right up front," directed Jeannie.

Sumner pulled the VW Bug into a parking space east of the front door of the clinic. Jeannie exited the vehicle and was soon talking with three men near the front of the clinic. Moments later she returned with two men, one of whom she introduced as Monte.

"Just moved to town?" asked Monte.

"Been living in New Mexico, but the sunshine and clean air were getting to me," joked Sumner.

"What do you need?" asked Monte.

"Two," replied Sumner. Monte took two bags from his boot and placed them on the seat next to Sumner. A bag is doper term for a single dosage of heroin that is universally a measured one quarter of a tablespoon. It is almost always packaged in a toy balloon, which is then rolled into a ball. Bag, balloon, quarter, all were terms used to describe a single dose. Sumner laid thirty dollars on the seat and picked up the balloons, which he placed in his boot.

Monte picked up the money and stood, looking at Jeannie Tye. Suddenly his face went ashen. He laid the money back down on the car seat and in a near frantic voice demanded the return of the heroin.

"Not a chance," replied Sumner. "Gimme that stuff back, for all I know you might be a narc," ordered Monte.

"It's mine and I need it," Sumner truculently shot back. As Sumner turned to start the vehicle, Monte produced a revolver from his boot, aiming it at Sumner's head. *.32 caliber Saturday night special,* thought Sumner. *What a putz.* "I need this junk," insisted Sumner.

"Gimme that shit. I'm not fucking around here," stammered Monte.

"Put that fuckin' gun away," screeched Jeannie as she pushed past Monte and climbed into the passenger seat.

"I'm serious," demanded Monte. "I want that shit back."

"Sorry, man, but I need this more than you." Sumner jammed the bug in reverse and began backing out of the parking space.

"Gimme that shit back. I'll shoot," screamed Monte who was out of control as he brandished the pistol in the air. Sumner shook his head as he placed the car in gear and proceeded out of the parking lot, watching Monte's temper tantrum in the rearview mirror.

"That shit's dead and stinkin," that was Jeannie's automatic assessment of anything she found unpleasant. "You got balls," admired Jeannie. "I think he was ready to shoot."

"That was Monte McCueston?"

"Sure was, he's a real bad ass."

"Yeah—well, I reviewed his file in detail," explained Sumner. "He's a major hype, dope dealer, and a big time snitch, but he's no killer." Snitch is what the dopers call what the police refer to as Confidential Informants or CIs, and while this was precisely what Jeannie was, she did not consider herself a snitch, but rather a "working girl" getting the best deal she could manage.

§

Sumner dropped Jeannie off at her aunt's home on the east side of town. "I'll pick you up tomorrow at 10:00 and we will hit that place again."

"You're going back in there?!" Jeannie was incredulous.

"Hell, yes," replied Sumner. "The only one who won't sell to me now is McCueston." She stood, looking in the window of the vehicle shaking her head.

"You sure got balls," mused Jeannie. "Either that or you're just plum out of your mind."

"A little of both," Sumner chuckled as he drove off.

CHAPTER 41

At an underground parking garage below an office building on Saratoga Avenue, Sumner handed Sergeant Farnsworth the evidence and his report. Farnsworth quickly scanned the report, then suddenly threw his hands in the air and shouted, "Hallelujah, you finally got that son of a bitch." He gave Sumner a good natured punch on the shoulder and explained. "McCueston snitched for us for several years while at the same time he was the biggest dealer going. He managed to burn every undercover we had while using his position as a CI to avoid prosecution," Farnsworth lamented, "and now you got that son of a bitch."

"Well, there won't be a second buy, he's totally spooked," said Sumner.

"This will be good enough," stated Farnsworth. "And when they load that prick on the bus to Vacaville, I'm going to be standing at the window with a cup of coffee and a Danish waving bye, bye."

Vacaville is the California Department of Corrections Medical Facility. Standard procedure is for all convicted felons to be transported from the county jail to Vacaville where they spend ninety days undergoing extensive medical and psychological examination before being sent to the particular prison where they will serve their sentence. The Santa Clara County deputies would remove the sentenced felons from their cells at

3:00 a.m. each Thursday morning and relocate them to a holding cell near the drunk tank on the ground floor of the jail where they await transportation. At exactly 5:00 a.m. every Thursday morning the deputies would then load the prisoners onto a bus for "the joint run," that is transportation to Vacaville.

"Here's an idea," Farnsworth offered. "Tomorrow morning why don't you go into the methadone clinic and ask the staff about getting on the program. The dopers will see you go in and come out and will think you are on the program and a real doper." Sergeant Farnsworth was very experienced and one of the most successful undercovers in the history of SJPD Narcotics. Sumner had great respect for him but this suggestion crossed the line.

"Are you out of your mind?!" he asked incredulously. "The staff there will know I'm not a hype and they'll get spooked and then spook all the crooks."

"How will they know you're not a hype?" questioned Nails. "Just tell them you been strung out for about six months and you're looking to get clean. They're not going to check your arms or anything. They'll probably fill out a form and ask you to come back."

"I don't know, this could backfire," Sumner squirmed.

"It'll work great," assured Nails. "Give it some thought."

§

Sumner picked up Jeannie at 10:00 A.M. As they drove down the road, she asked "Are you going back to the clinic?"

"Absolutely," replied Sumner.

"You don't have to do this," she stated. "There are a lot of other places I can take you."

"The clinic it is," said Sumner. "I've got a plan."

§

All eyes were on Sumner as they drove into the bustling clinic parking lot. Sumner scanned the mob, but Monte McCueston was curiously absent. Sumner pulled into the parking space in front of the entrance and stopped. "Wait here," he ordered as he exited the vehicle heading for the front door of the clinic. As he entered, he noticed a receptionist behind a desk and several people sitting in a waiting area. Down the hall he observed technicians in white coats passing in and out of the hallway. The receptionist gave Sumner a skeptical appraisal.

"Can I help you?"

"I wanted to talk to someone about getting on the program," mumbled Sumner, looking at the floor and giving no eye contact.

The receptionist turned to a passing technician and asked "Eldon, will you help this gentleman?"

"Certainly, right this way." The tech motioned to an open door down the hall.

"What can I do for you?" asked an affable Eldon.

"Well, I seem to have gotten myself strung out the last few months. It's getting worse and I really want to get clean."

"Have you been sentenced by the court to enter the program?"

"No."

"Have you been referred by any agency?" Eldon continued.

"No."

"Well, I am sorry, but we only treat people who have been sentenced or referred by a legitimate agency. We do not take walk in cases," explained Eldon apologetically. "You might try dropping in at Cryscalis and see if they can accommodate you."

"That's cool," replied Sumner. "I appreciate your time." As he rose from the chair, he asked for a drink of water. Eldon showed him to a water cooler at the end of the hall. Sumner dispensed a cup and filled it with water.

Clear plastic two ounce cups, thought Sumner. *The exact same cups they use to dispense the methadone.* Sumner walked down the hall and out the front door as he finished his water. Jeannie Tye stepped in front of Sumner, looking pensively at the cup.

"Did they treat you?" she asked with undisguised incredulity.

Sumner smiled elusively as he asked "Who's got the bag?"

"Jeri over there, but be careful…she gots the syphilis," Jeannie cautioned. "This is Les," Jeannie said.

"Oh, Monte's friend," Jeri chuckled through cheeks stuffed full.

"Well, fuck him," snapped Sumner. "You don't set someone free and then try to take it back." Jeri, an attractive woman in her mid-thirties smiled at Sumner as she nodded agreement. She showed evidence of tertiary syphilis in the oozing unhealed sores on her arms, a consequence of her primary occupation as a prostitute.

"What do you need?" asked Jeri.

"Two bags," replied Sumner.

"Are you going to shoot over?" asked Jeri, looking at the empty cup in Sumner's hand. *I'll be,* thought Sumner. *Nails was right, it worked like a charm. She thinks I'm going shoot heroin right after taking methadone…well, It is rumored to create a much more enhanced "rush" from the injection of the heroin into the vein— So much for the methadone keeping them off heroin.*

"Yeah," replied Sumner dumbly. Jeri then spit two rolled balloons containing quarter spoons of heroin from her mouth into Sumner's hand.

"Put it in your mouth," Jeri cautioned.

"Like hell," said Sumner slipping the balloons into his right boot. "See you tomorrow." He took Jeannie by the arm and headed toward the car.

"What the hell was that all about," asked Sumner.

"She keeps the balloons in her mouth," explained Jeannie. "If the bulls come, she just swallows the balloons and the evidence is gone. She wanted you to do the same."

"Really," marveled Sumner.

"Yeah, then she goes home and dumps on newspaper until she passes out her dope," Jeannie said.

Amazing, thought Sumner. *Nasty, but amazing.* "Where was Monte today?"

"He's afraid of you. He's telling everyone you're a cop."

"And they believe him?"

"Some do, some don't, some are just paranoid. But you stood up to him with a gun at your head. And they may be dopers but they respect that."

Sumner dropped Jeannie at her aunt's handing her fifty dollars for the day's work.

"See you at ten tomorrow," said Sumner as he drove off.

CHAPTER 42

The law of "Un-Intended Consequences" applies to
police work every bit as much as it does to life itself.
There are times when a "bad break" can be a blessing
rather than a curse. You just have to be prepared.

Sumner's physical training schedule was set in stone. Each Tuesday, Thursday, and Saturday at exactly 12:05 PM he met with his workout partner Dr. Wayne Meyer at the Fitness Center on Blossom Hill Road. Dr. Meyer was a local dentist and fitness enthusiast with whom Sumner had been training for several years. Dr. Meyer scheduled no patients between noon and 1:30 on Tuesdays and Thursdays so that he could exercise with Sumner and punctuality was imperative. On Tuesdays and Thursdays they would start with a 1 ½ mile run, then sit ups, pull ups, chest, shoulders, arms and back, followed by leg training then a quick a sauna ending with a shower. This got Dr. Meyer back to his office just as the next patient was climbing into the chair.

On Saturday's, however, they met at the track at Santa Teresa High School with six or eight of the other Fitness Center regulars. Every Saturday they would each attempt a new "PR" or personal record. They would time themselves on the two mile, one mile, quarter mile, and 100 yard dash. The records and the date set would be recorded on a chalkboard on the wall at the Fitness Center.

Sumner was sporting a new pair of Addidas running shoes. He had treated himself to this sinful luxury with money from an overtime check he received for the many hours spent on the Mexican Bob" case. He was anticipating setting a good time on the two and one mile runs. It had been raining earlier in the week but the track was now dry. Ideal conditions except for a few ruts in the track where some kids had ridden their bicycles while the surface was wet. *Watch out for the ruts,* Sumner made a mental note. The two mile run went as expected. Sumner knocked four seconds off his best time, a new personal record. Conditions were perfect and Sumner was feeling a little smug. He anticipated another PR as he started out on his one mile run. He broke out ahead of the pack second only to Dr. Meyer. Sumner drafted behind "Doc," attempting to keep the Doc's lung busting pace. As they rounded the far turn, Sumner felt his ankle fold over as his left foot came down on one of the ruts. With a sickening, crunch, his ankle gave way and he fell to the ground.

§

At Regional Medical Center of San Jose's Emergency Department, X-rays confirmed a fracture of the left ankle. Regional's ED was named Best Emergency Department in the region; and Sumner was determined to get back on two legs as soon as nature would allow. He couldn't risk second best skills. The treatment was swift and professional. Sumner's foot and leg were encased in a cast to just below the knee. The attending physician fitted Sumner with crutches and strict instructions not to apply any weight on that leg for the first three weeks. At the end of that time the doctor said he would add a walker to the cast. Sumner did a slow burn at being treated like a child, even if this was the doctor's meager attempt at humor.

§

"What are you doing?" Sumner's wife asked with a deep scowl.
"Getting ready for work," he responded defensively.
"You have a broken ankle, you can't go to work," she protested.

"So?" Sumner shrugged.

"You're a police officer. You can't go work with a broken leg," she begged in now near hysteria. Ted's job had been a festering point of contention, almost from the outset of their marriage. He tried his best to minimize his wife's fears by leaving the dangers at the office. But there were times when the risks were transparent.

"I'm a narcotics officer," Sumner pointed out. "It will be great for my cover."

"You can't do this, it's too dangerous," she pleaded.

"Karen, I'm not going to have this fight with you," Sumner said stoically. "This is what I do." Sumner hobbled toward the stairs on his crutches.

"Then go do it," she screamed with tears streaming from her eyes, "and I hope you do get killed this time."

§

Karen's parting words burned in his memory as he drove off to pick up his CI. *She didn't mean what she said,* he reasoned, but there was part of him that wasn't so sure. While her words cut deeply, he had to shake it off and get into character. It was a matter of life and death that he remain clear headed and mentally tough for the coming day's work.

Operating a clutch with a throbbing ankle wrapped in a cast was a bitch. By the time he arrived at Jeannie's, she was waiting outside.

"Back to the clinic?" asked Jeannie as she climbed into the passenger seat.

"Yup," Sumner snapped.

§

Sumner found a spot near the front door of the clinic and parked. As he climbed out of the car he pulled his crutches from the backseat.

"OK, I gotta ask, …What the hell happened to you?" asked Jeannie.

"I broke it working out."

"Dumb ass," she summed up the situation in her usual caring manner.

He hobbled up the steps toward the front door of the clinic. "Where are you going?" asked Jeannie.

"Inside. I'll be right back."

"What happened to you?" asked the female technician who had been talking with the receptionist.

"I fell," replied Sumner sheepishly. "Can I get a drink of water?"

"End of the hall," the receptionist pointed with her chin. He worked his way to the water cooler where he poured a cup of water and slowly drank it. He then hobbled back down the hall and out the front door into the parking lot, drinking the last bit of water in the cup. He scanned the area without moving his head and spotted Jeannie talking with a man and woman across the parking lot. They were watching Sumner closely as he discarded the clear plastic cup and made his way over.

"This guy's no cop," stated the short Hispanic man to his red-headed female companion. "He's got a broken leg, and cops don't work if they got even a hangnail," he stated as though it was a well established fact.

"This is Raul and Shirley," Jeannie offered by way of introduction. *Raul Guerra and Shirley Rodriguez,* Sumner reasoned. *Big time dealers.*

"Can you believe that?" mused Raul. "Monte thinks this guy's a cop."

"Monte is a wack job… suffering from paranoid delusions," snarled Sumner.

"Besides, this guy's on the program," observed Raul.

Farnsworth is a genius, thought Sumner. *That crazy idea of his is working beautifully.*

"You holding?" asked Jeannie.

"What do you need?" asked Raul looking around.

"Two bags," Sumner said quietly, holding out thirty dollars. Raul jerked his hands back and up as if the money was contaminated.

"Whoa, whoa, whoa…hand the money to Jeannie," directed Raul. Sumner complied as Raul continued to Jeannie, "Now hand it to Shirley." Jeannie did as directed. Raul then handed the two balloons to Shirley, who handed them to Jeannie, who handed them to Sumner.

"How do I get a hold of you if this is good shit?" asked Sumner. Raul scribbled a phone number on a piece of paper and handed it to Sumner.

"Take care of that leg," said Raul as Sumner and Jeannie headed toward the car.

"OK, what was that all about?" asked Sumner as they drove out of the parking lot.

"He thinks he didn't sell you anything," said Jeannie. "He took the money from Shirley and gave her the dope," she explained, "He never sold you anything."

"And he believes that nonsense?" Sumner asked in disbelief.

"It's not true?" asked an obviously stunned Jeannie.

"It is not true. All he has done is put you and Shirley into the chain of evidence. I got a buy on each of them... and you," chided Sumner.

"That shit's dead and stinkin," protested Jeannie. "I ain't never sold no dope."

Sumner broke into laughter. "You are a confidential informant. You have immunity," explained Sumner.

"Well, I ain't touching no more dope!" informed Jeannie.

Damn she's easy to rile, thought Sumner. *No wonder Taylor uses drugs.*

§

Following the required meeting with Sergeant Farnsworth, where he submitted his reports and turned over evidence, Sumner headed home to elevate his throbbing ankle and enjoy some self prescribed medication in the form of a glass of Wild Turkey Kentucky Bourbon.

He slept in the next morning to rest his painful ankle that had continued to swell in the cast. When he woke about 11:00 a.m., he called to check in with Sgt. Farnsworth.

"The Boss wants you to come in," advised Nails.

"That's risky," Sumner cautioned. "I'm awfully easy to spot on these crutches."

"Doesn't matter, the Boss wants a direct debriefing on this Old Man Richard thing."

O-K...That's, that, Sumner realized. "What time?"

"Five o'clock."

"See you then," Sumner hung up.

CHAPTER 43

The garage at the annex on Pedro Street was two blocks from headquarters. Sumner drove slowly past watching carefully for any signs of surveillance. Satisfied there wasn't, he pulled his non-descript Volkswagen Beetle into the parking garage. This small house was owned by the City. The Narcotics Unit used it as a covert site away from the Police Administration Building where officers could meet with confidential informants or other at risk individuals.

Now comes the difficult part, thought Sumner. He dreaded both the exposure and the pain he was about to endure, but he had no choice. He would have to cross the street to PAB and work his way around to the elevator that led to the third floor Detective Bureau where the Narcotic Unit was housed. It was a long walk on crutches, not to mention the fact that each time he lowered his injured foot below the level of his heart it felt like hot lava was pouring into his leg. *The direct approach is probably the best,* thought Sumner as he headed straight across Mission Street toward the front lobby entrance to PAB. Whether the direct route was the best choice or not, it was the only choice his pain wracked leg would allow him to choose. He approached the steps leading up to the lobby. Sumner then, suddenly, re-directed his crutches to the right and headed toward the police garage. Then he moved along the side of the PAB on a much less traveled path to the detective's elevator.

The elevator jerked to a stop and the door slid open. Sumner glanced both ways to the limit of his vision from the back of the elevator, and then took a painful step forward. The door closed behind him. As he peered down the hall of the Detective Bureau, he noticed an officer with a man in custody on his way to the Robbery Unit. Sumner stepped back into the nook of the elevator doorway and waited for the elevator to return. As the elevator door opened, Detective Sergeant Dennis Bush stepped out. Bush had been Sumner's supervisor one shift while assigned to patrol several years back.

"Dennis, take me into custody and walk me to Narco," Sumner asked in a horse whisper.

"Sure," agreed Bush grabbing Sumner by the scruff of the neck and marching him down the hall to Narcotics.

§

As they barged their way into the Narcotic Unit, everyone in the room looked up in open mouthed surprise. Sergeant Bush manhandled Sumner into one of the interrogation rooms.

"I believe this belongs to you," Bush said, with a wry smile to a bewildered Lt. Bertotti.

"What was that all about?" asked Bertotti as he entered the interrogation room. "There were prisoners in the hallway. I didn't want it to look like I work here."

"Good thinking," nodded Bertotti "We're just waiting for Booth and Bercelli."

§

Sumner hobbled clumsily into the commander's office. He spilled his coffee as he struggled to maneuver on his crutches. Cursing his immobility under his breath, he settled into a chair at the end of Bertotti's desk. With a groan, he lifted his casted foot up onto the desk. Bertotti shot Sumner a look of disapproving disdain.

"I'm sorry, Boss, but this thing throbs when I don't have it elevated."

Bertotti rolled his eyes in begrudging, but temporary, approval.

"Why do we need Booth and Bercelli?"

"Farnsworth, Booth, and Bercelli have all worked the Old Man Richard case at some time over the years," replied the Boss. "I'm hoping that they might be able to offer some insight."

Insight on how to screw up, thought Sumner. *These guys all worked the case and failed and they would probably love to see me fail.* Sumner had no illusions as to the intensity of the competition in the field of law enforcement, particularly in special operations like Narcotics. Every time one of these guys took a step, you could hear the slosh of surplus testosterone.

The three sergeants entered Bertotti's office, cup of coffee in hand. Bertotti and Farnsworth lit cigarettes.

I hope we finish this before I suffocate, Sumner thought.

"What is your in?" Sergeant Booth began the meeting.

"Jeannie Tye says that Jeri Steinlie is going into business with Old Man Richard," Sumner reported. "I've already copped from her. I figure with the right enticement I can work her into Richard."

"She's a hype with a $400 a day habit," snapped Booth. "Why would he trust her?"

"I think that's exactly why the Old Man trusts her," answered Sumner. "She won't touch speed. He knows she'll keep her nose out of the bag. Also she's a $15 a trick hooker," added Sumner. "That's a lot of Johns to service everyday to feed her habit. Richard knows she's desperate for a better source of income to support that habit."

The Boss and his sergeants looked at each other, shrugged, and gave a grudging nod of approval.

"Looks like you get a couple ounce buys and then set up a pound buy bust," said Nails as he blew three perfect smoke rings, then exhaled the remaining smoke out his nostrils. They all nodded in agreement.

Amazing, thought Sumner. *They have been trying that exact procedure on this guy for the last 30 years and have never gotten anywhere. And now all they can come up with is the same old, by the book narcotic plan. And even if it does bring down Richard, we won't even touch his organization.*

"We are going to have to let some money walk on this caper," stated Bertotti. "We may want to bring in the state."

"Nooooo," moaned Sumner.

All four looked at him as though he had sworn in church.

"You aren't thinking about working this operation without cover?" asked an astonished Bertotti.

"I most certainly am," shot back Sumner.

The sergeants grumbled their disapproval and shook their heads in adamant opposition.

"This guy is extremely dangerous," cautioned Bercelli. "You've done some incredible things, but don't let your success cloud your judgment."

"We could bring in T-Bone Smith. You guys look like brothers," offered Bertotti.

"Boss, for thirty years this guy has been able to smell a rat and smoke out every undercover we've sent at him," reasoned Sumner. "Hell, the Bulls can't even catch him holding. He cancels appointments, changes meeting places, and pulls no shows until someone on the cover team exposes himself," reminded Sumner. "You brought me into Narco to work deep undercover, and in that capacity I can move fast and adjust when he jukes right or left. I can't move a cover team that easily. Someone will get careless or screw up and expose me, and then I will be in deep trouble... or dead."

Bertotti looked at his sergeants for feedback. Farnsworth blew another smoke ring, then shrugged his shoulders in bemused neutrality

Booth allowed himself a slight affirmative nod.

"I don't like it," insisted Bercelli. "This operation is dangerous and that asshole isn't worth the life of one cop."

"I have no intentions of sacrificing my life," assured Sumner, "but this will never work unless I have the flexibility to move fast and go deep."

Bertotti sat in silent contemplation for several minutes. "All right," came the Boss's response, "make the contact, get an initial buy if the opportunity presents itself, and after that we will meet again and reevaluate the situation."

Farnsworth and Booth left the room, and Bercelli stood and closed the office door behind them. Then Bercelli, a veteran undercover, turned to Sumner, and in undisguised agitation pointed his finger two inches from Sumner's nose warning, "This is going to be like nothing you've done before, nothing you've ever experienced."

Sumner nodded in agreement.

"Don't patronize me," snapped Bercelli. "This guy has been successful all these years because he knows his market…he never does business outside the black community. I don't know what you have up your sleeve, but you will need to have your wits about you at all times and never drop your guard around this guy or his people. And promise me," Bercelli implored, "if you sense anything is wrong, that you will get the hell out of there."

Sumner, touched by this display of sincere concern, nodded, looked over at the Boss, then back at Bercelli and nodded again. "I promise."

"Want to join us for a beer?" asked the Boss. It was just after 7:30 P.M.

"Naw, I got some work to do… I'm going to use the Bat phone."

Sumner engaged the recording device attached to the phone and dialed the number on the piece of paper Raul had given him at the clinic a few days prior.

"Yeah?" answered the voice at the other end of the line.

"It's Les," said Sumner.

"Who?" asked Raul.

"Broken leg Les," explained Sumner.

"Oh, yeah," said Raul. "Wasssup?"

"You holding?" asked Sumner.

"Come on over," offered Raul.

Sumner got the address and hung up the phone. He then removed the tape cartridge on which the conversation had been recorded, marked the label with the date, time, name of the suspect, and his initials and badge number. *Not much, but better than nothing*, thought Sumner as he placed the tape in an envelope and dropped it through the slot of the evidence locker.

§

Sumner arrived at the address he'd been given an apartment building on San Jose's west side. He lumbered down the long hall to the apartment at the far end and knocked softly on the door. The door opened slightly as Raul peered out, evaluating his visitor.

"Come on in," said Raul opening the door just wide enough for Sumner to navigate his crutches through. *Shooting gallery,* Sumner realized as his blood ran cold. He looked quickly around, cataloguing each of the nine people present in the apartment. A shooting gallery was an undercover officer's worst nightmare. It was a place where the dealer insists that the heroin be injected before the purchaser leaves. This requirement reassures the dealer that the customer was in fact a user of heroin and prevented the customer from possibly being arrested by the narcs for possession of the heroin that had just been purchased at that location.

Time stopped while everyone in the room evaluated each other. Sumner made a quick assessment of those present. The hypes did the same, looking him over intently.

"This guy's a narc," came the automatic assertion from one of the addicts preparing his hypodermic. There was no shortage of paranoia in the drug world.

"He's no narc," assured Raul. "Look at him, and besides, he's on the program."

"You got a rig," asked Raul, anticipating that Sumner would be injecting the heroin he would purchase while on the premises.

"Shit, I left it at the crib," explained Sumner. "I didn't want to be holding it when I went to the clinic. You got one I can use?"

Raul glowered in undisguised displeasure. No addict liked to loan his hypodermic. Needles become increasingly dull with each use and it was always possible that the guest shooter might contaminate the hypodermic with hepatitis, syphilis, or some other communicable disease.

"I'm sorry, man, I'll just get down when I get home," Sumner offered as an alternative.

Raul ruminated for a moment, and then removed two quarter spoon balloons from an urn on his kitchen counter, handing them to Sumner. "You're cool," said Raul as he took the $30 Sumner handed him.

Sumner split as fast as his crutches could propel him. Sweat formed on his brow as he realized that he had just escaped one of those dangerous situations all undercovers dread, and about which Sergeant Bercelli had recently and pointedly cautioned him. *That's enough for tonight,* Sumner reasoned.

CHAPTER 44

Jeannie was waiting on the curb when Sumner pulled up at precisely 10:00 A.M. the next morning.

"Jeri wants to know what this is about," Jeannie launched without so much as a good morning.

"I'm going to tell her," replied Sumner. They arrived at the house where Jeri lived with her grandmother that was located on, appropriately enough, Richard Ave.

"What's this all about?" asked Jeri.

"We have an opportunity for all of us to make a lot of money," advised Sumner. He went on to explain that Curly Williams, the cooker for the Hell's Angels, had been arrested. Without Curly the Angels had all the chemicals necessary to manufacture methamphetamines, but no chemist who knew how to accomplish the complicated, and dangerous, process. Consequently the Hell's Angels were without their primary source of income. "I talked to Patrick Thornton. He said the Angles will take all the meth Old Man Richard can supply," announced Sumner.

"Richard won't do business with the Hell's Angles," snorted Jeri. "They're too treacherous, and besides, they hate blacks."

"And that's our opening and our opportunity," said Sumner. "He only has to do business with me. I'll act as the conduit to the Angels."

Jeri contemplated the situation for a moment, then shrugging her shoulders and chirped "I'll see what he says."

§

"Jeri said Old Man Richard wants to meet you today," Jeannie said without preamble as she climbed into the car the next morning.

"Great," said Sumner as he drove toward Jeri's grandmother's home. He felt the adrenaline rush that always preceded his forays into harm's way. They picked up Jeri and headed north toward Palo Alto.

"He'll meet us at the Colonial Coffee Shop on El Camino Real," advised Jeri.

§

The Colonial was sparsely occupied as they took a booth near the window and ordered breakfast. Sumner sipped his coffee while Jeannie and Jeri jabbered about matters long gone. Patrons came and went. Surveying the room, Sumner noted a couple of Hispanics with spattered coveralls, obviously painters, three young men who could only be mechanics, judging from the grease on their hands, an elderly black couple—the old man hunched over, the woman sitting tall and rail thin, they were obviously retired—but no Old Man Richard.

After about an hour Sumner asked "Is he going to show?"

"Maybe not," replied Jeri. "Let's give him a little more time."

When, after another half hour, he had not arrived, Sumner suggested that they depart and that Jeri reschedule the meeting. *This is how the guy works,* thought Sumner. *He no shows, changes locations, and waits for people to reveal themselves.*

§

The next day Sumner picked up Jeannie, then Jeri, and headed back toward Palo Alto.

"He wants us to meet him in the parking lot on the west side of Stanford Stadium," advised Jeri.

Parking lot? thought Sumner. *There's no parking lot at Stanford Stadium. It's just a grove of eucalyptus trees.*

They arrived at Stanford Stadium twenty-five minutes later. A car would pass by from time to time. A grounds crew arrived in a pickup truck and went to work on the extensive shrubbery surrounding the walls of the stadium. A grey Buick pulled up across way at the entrance to Stanford University's Sunken Gardens baseball park, but nobody exited the vehicle. After an hour Sumner made the decision to leave and have Jeri schedule another meeting.

§

For the next three days the routine repeated itself. Sumner picked up Jeri and proceeded to a designated location to meet with Old Man Richard, but to no avail. Each time Richard would either call Jeri and move the location of the meeting to a place where he would not show, or he would just fail to appear. Sumner's patience was wearing thin, but he reminded himself that this is not uncommon with high level distributors of narcotics. It was also the reason that he had been adamant with his superiors that a task force approach would never get close to the Old Man. He would have has people watching every one of the aborted meetings; they would have been watching for evidence that the meetings were covered by law enforcement. He could bring his impatience under control; he was determined to accomplish a meeting.

§

Days passed. Then, when Sumner was about to despair, they picked up Jeri, once again "Where to today?" asked Sumner as Jeri climbed into his vehicle.

"Richard's house," replied Jeri. Sumner's jaw nearly dropped into his lap. "Why is he suddenly so trusting?" asked Sumner.

"I guess you checked out."

§

At Jeri's direction, they took the freeway and exited Hwy 101 at University Ave. Jeri navigated them into the seedy ghetto of East Palo Alto.

Amazing that this poverty stricken slum could exist so close to all that opulent wealth just the other side of 101, Sumner pondered. He steered the car down a dead end street guided by Jeri.

"That's his house," Jeri said. "Park here."

Well he sure doesn't live like a big time drug kingpin, thought Sumner. On the other side of the homes along the street was nearly fifty yards of swampy wetlands leading out to the San Francisco Bay.

Clever, at least he doesn't have to worry about any sneaking up on him, observed Sumner.

Jeri knocked, and the door was opened by a tall black woman in her sixties wearing a white print dress, something like what June Cleaver might have worn back in the 60s. *Interesting! The woman from the Colonial Coffee Shop,* Sumner observed.

"Come in," she said curtly while opening the door. The house was modestly furnished, and Sumner detected the faint smell of stewed tomatoes or maybe spaghetti sauce cooking. She directed them into a large room where a slender grey haired black man sat on a sofa with a coffee table in front of him. He was dressed in grey slacks, a yellow shirt and green cardigan sweater looking like he had just stepped off the golf course.

"This is Richard," said Jeri as the man stood to shake hands with Sumner. Richard said nothing and sat down as the woman stepped up, standing at the end of the sofa. Sumner noticed that the house was uncomfortably cool— not much more than sixty degrees, yet the woman was not wearing a sweater or coat. *Maybe she's menopausal and suffering from hot flashes,* thought Sumner.

"Why do you want to do this?" she asked with a tone of revulsion. Sumner raised his eyebrows in inquisitive surprise.

"To make money."

"Why would you want to have anything to do with those animals?" she hissed with undisguised disgust.

"Well, they aren't exactly my favorite people, but they do have money and a very large customer base," explained Sumner. "But your speed has a reputation for being substandard and I need to convince them that you can reliably supply quality shit."

She looked at Richard, who nodded approval. The woman then opened a box resembling a cigar case sitting on the coffee table.

"There ain't no free samples," she scolded. "That will be $2000," she said as she handed Sumner two one-ounce plastic bags of white powder.

"You won't have to ever get anywhere near those people," promised Sumner as he took the drugs.

§

They drove back to San Jose and Sumner inwardly heaved a huge sigh. "Now I have to get this shit to the Angels who can make a financial decision. Jeri, give me your phone number in case I need to get a hold of you quickly."

Jeri dutifully complied as Sumner pulled up in front of her grandmother's home.

"I'll get a hold you tomorrow or the day after," Sumner promised as he drove off.

CHAPTER 45

S ergeant Farnsworth met Sumner in the parking lot of the Valley Fair mall. There he accepted Sumner's report and evidence.

"I need an expedited purity report from the crime lab on that dope," advised Sumner.

"I'll take care of it," promised Farnsworth. "Amazing," he marveled, "after thirty years Old Man Richard has finally been done."

"Well, maybe the bad economy made him a little more willing to do a deal." *It was almost too easy,* Sumner mused, *Why do I still have a very uneasy feeling?*

"Let's go grab a beer at the Fog Horn," offered Farnsworth.

The Fog Horn was a local establishment frequented by San Jose Police detectives and a favorite of the narcotics crew.

"I'm not ready to celebrate yet. I won't be able to relax until this operation is history."

§

"The Boss wants you to see if you can get another ounce buy without Jeannie present;" Farnsworth delivered the demand as though he were asking Sumner to bring in a dozen donuts, "That way if anything goes wrong or she goes sideways we can just prosecute that case."

"I'll get on it." *Damn! I don't like this!* Sumner cursed silently to himself.

CHAPTER 46

Friday afternoon, at last! Sumner was ready to celebrate. The day had finally arrived and the cast was about to be removed from his left leg. He entered the treatment room and lifted his leg up onto the table. The doctor cocked his ear, gave the cast a playful thump as though testing a watermelon, nodded smugly, as if to say "Yep, it's ripe," and proceeded to cut away the plaster. To Sumner, the cast had become his personal ball and chain. As the doctor split the cast open Sumner looked at what was left of his leg. Atrophy had taken half the muscle mass.

That's going to take a while to build back up, Sumner decided. "What are my limitations, Doc?"

"Pain will be your guide. Just don't overdo it for a few weeks."

§

"Are you going to go work out today?" asked Sumner's wife.

"Yes, Karen, just like I do every Saturday.

"What time?" she snipped.

"One o'clock, just like every Saturday."

"Why do you have to be at the track at one? You can't run. Why don't you just meet them at the gym at two?" she demanded.

"Karen, they are depending on me to time them on their runs. Then we go to the gym, just like every Saturday."

"Well, I want to go shopping."

Just like you do every Saturday, Sumner thought. "Fine, just please be home by 12:45."

Karen was unable or unwilling to grasp the fact that keeping physically fit was as much a part of the job of a police officer as going to the shooting range, attending legal training classes, and showing up for work on time. Each Saturday this same conversation would occur. Each Saturday she would return home five minutes later until she finally arrived at 1:15 at which point Sumner would become angry and an unpleasant argument would occur, but the result of which would be that she would arrive home the next weekend at 12:45 to relieve Sumner from the task of looking after the children.

§

Saturday night. Sumner bit into a slice of orange and glanced at his watch. *Nine p.m. Yeah, good time to get this next buy done,* he thought. He phoned Jeri at her grandmother's. "Jeri, let the Old Man know I need another ounce tonight."

"What for?"

"For the Angel's. They have some other people who want to try it."

"Why?" she asked again.

"I think they're getting ready to make the buy. My guess is they want a consensus on a purchasing decision. That's my hope anyway."

"Why do they need so many people to make a decision?"

"How the hell do I know? Maybe they're a democratic people."

"I'll call him. What time are you going to pick me up?"

Here comes the trump card. "Jeri, I'm on my motorcycle...you don't really want to ride up there in this cold on the back of a motorcycle."

"OK, I'll call."

"Tell him I am on my way. I'll be there in about an hour."

§

It was just after 10:00 when Sumner arrived. The neighborhood was quiet except for some classic jazz escaping from a house down the street. He positioned his Triumph 750 Tiger motorcycle on the sidewalk in front of the house and faced it toward the exit to the dead end. As he approached the door, he was troubled that the house was dark. He rang the doorbell. The door opened a crack, revealing only the right side of a young man's face.

"Come on in, man."

Sumner entered, and the door closed behind him. He looked around, sensing tension in the air cloaked in a veil of sinister evil. Old Man Richard was sitting on the sofa. Five other black men were standing about as if he was holding court.

The young man who had answered the door placed his hand on Sumner's shoulder. "Have a seat," he said gesturing to a chair across the coffee table from the Old Man. The chair had not been there during Sumner's previous visit.

Sumner stepped to the chair. The men watched him intently as he took his seat. Without a word they moved to the side. Sumner sat across from the Old Man. *I'm sensing this is one of those situations Bercelli was talking about where I ought to get out,* Sumner quickly analyzed his situation. Lying on the coffee table in front of Richard was a napkin; and on that napkin was a fully drawn hypodermic needle.

"You're gonna want to try this shit before you lay it off on any Angels," explained

Richard. "Go ahead and give it a try."

Hot shot, Sumner reasoned. *Something has gone wrong and they are going to hot shot me.* "Hot shotting" was a common way for players in the supply of illicit drugs to dispose of unwanted individuals. They prepare a hypodermic with a very large overdose and then add a large dose of something to which the victim is not addicted. Even if the police do become interested in the death of a drug addict, the toxicology reports just show a high concentration of drugs in the system.

"Not a good idea," dodged Sumner. "I'm on a bike and I gotta meet my old lady. She doesn't like it when I get high without her."

"Oh man, now if you gonna be supplying the Angels with Richard's dope and bein' Richard got a reputation for selling shitty dope, you're

gonna want to know fur sure that the Old Man is bringing kick ass stuff."
Richard stared at Sumner, his eyes piercing.

The jig is up, Sumner realized… *now what?*

Richard, without taking his eyes off of Sumner or even blinking, stated slowly and deliberately "I think you better shoot this dope."

Sumner's heart was racing, *who needs speed.* He stared back, never taking his eyes off the legendary Old Man Richard. "Not…a fucking… chance," came Sumner's reply.

Sumner felt the barrel of a gun slam against the back of his head. "I knew it, I knew it. I told Richard don't trust this white boy, he's snitching." The almost gleeful assertion came from the young man holding the gun to Sumner's head.

"Who you snitchin for?" asked Richard.

"I'm not snitching. I came here in good faith to do business with a man I thought was reputable."

Muffled laughter came from the other men. "You settin' me up for the Angels to rip off; or you workin' for the police?"

"Neither."

"It don't matter, it don't matter," sang the man with the gun as he jumped up and down like an excited school kid. "Let me kill him, Richard. Let me do it now." The other men nodded in approval.

"We not gonna shoot him here in my living room," scolded Richard. "Mrs. Hendricks would have my hide if we make a big mess right here."

"Then let's put him in the bathtub and I'll kill him there," pleaded the gunman.

"What do we do with the body?" asked one of the other men.

"We can cut it up with my chainsaw in the bathtub and dump the pieces in the garbage disposal," offered another man.

"Whoa, those fish in the bay gonna be eatin' good tomorrow," sang another man as they all laughed and snickered.

Sumner, a realist, was resigned to his fate. He prayed. Not for himself but for the well being of his young son, his infant daughter, and his wife who would awaken the following morning to find that she is a widow. And he prayed desperately that he would not be remembered by law enforcement as a reckless showboat who got himself needlessly killed because he thought he did not need anyone's help and could do it all himself. He could not bear the thought that his name would become a euphemism for how not to conduct an undercover operation. *What will it feel like*, he thought to himself, *when the bullet crashes into my skull? What will be the level of pain? What if I am still alive when they start cutting me up with the chain saw.* He never thought that when his demise came he would have so much time to contemplate the details of his fate. He was by now, completely unraveled emotionally and the life force was rapidly draining from him. *Damn, so this is how it ends.*

Suddenly Sumner was struck with an inspiration. *Worth a try, nothing to loose*, he thought, *after all, what the hell does a dead man have to loose.* "Gentlemen, I hate to break up your good time, but I am afraid we have run out of time."

"Yeah, you damn sure run out of time," came a response from one of the men.

"You are right about me being a narc, but I'm no snitch," said Sumner. "I am a detective with the San Jose Police Department."

"Shit!" came the collective reply as Sumner felt the swagger slip from his tormentors. San Jose's Police Department had a reputation for being the youngest, highest educated, most professional and "whitest" law enforcement agency on the west coast.

"My cover strike team is in position and will be taking this place down in four minutes," Sumner warned.

"He's lying!" screamed the young man with the gun slamming the barrel again into the back of Sumner's head.

How the hell did he know? Sumner thought. He could sense a hint of fear in the air. *Time to pour it on...all or nothing.* "You think I'm lying sonny?" Sumner challenged. "Go ahead and fire a shot into the floor and see how quick you get everyone in this room dead. I hand picked everyone on this strike team...all southern boys," Sumner continued to push. "If I don't walk out of here in the next three minutes, they will make sure everyone leaves feet first."

"He's lying. I know he's lying," insisted the gunman.

Sumner aimed his piercing blue eyed gaze directly into the eyes of Old Man Richard. Sumner could feel the rising alarm among the men, but he could also sense despair. *They don't know what to do,* Sumner realized. *You've got to give them a viable option.* "Richard, you haven't done anything illegal, you haven't supplied me with any dope," Sumner instructed. "Flush everything you've got in the house, get rid of all the stuff any of you are holding and you might survive this night." He could feel the psychological advantage swinging his way. "I'll walk slow and give you time to clean the place, but that's all I can do. The SWAT Team is coming in one minute."

Old Man Richard stared into the clear blue eyes of the Police Detective…and Richard blinked first. "Get," ordered Richard "And walk slo-o-w." *A death sentence reprieve. Sumner felt a faint pulse of life begin to return.*

Sumner could feel in the men a collective hope rising that they might get out of this situation unscathed. He stood and turned to the twenty-some young man with the pistol. "You better get rid of that gun, sonny. If it's here when I get back, I'm going to stuff it up your ass," Sumner promised. The tables had turned and his confidence grew now that he was in control and might even live to tell about all this.

"Fuck you!" replied the gunman. The bravado was betrayed by the beads of sweat above the kid's quivering upper lip.

Sumner walked slowly out of the house and down the driveway to his waiting motorcycle. His heart was now racing and his breathing accelerated. He inserted the ignition key and pressed the starter…nothing. *Damn, this is a hell of a time for the battery to go dead.* He climbed up on the bike and jumped on the kick starter…nothing. In growing desperation he dismounted the bike and started pushing the 400 pound motorcycle down the street. His left ankle ignited in a firestorm of searing pain as he pushed with every bit of strength he could summon. He then jumped onto the bike and popped the clutch in an attempt to get the engine started, but the bike merely skidded to a halt. He engaged the clutch and again started down the street pushing the motorcycle with almost inhuman strength fueled by fear. He jumped on the bike and popped the clutch once again. This time the engine roared to life. He hit the throttle and the front wheel of Triumph Tiger rose off the pavement as he barreled down the street.

He didn't stop until he reached the gas station at Hwy 101 and University Avenue where he found a telephone booth. He inserted a dime and dialed Lt. Bertotti's home number. "Boss," Sumner panted, "this whole operation just came apart."

"Are you all right?" asked Bertotti.

"Just barely," explained Sumner. "I'm not sure if they made me or were just paranoid, but they were all set for a snuff. I had to reveal my identity to get out alive."

"We better go ahead and take him down tonight," reckoned Bertotti. "He might be a flight risk. I'll contact San Mateo County SO," said Bertotti. "Give me your location." East Palo Alto is an unincorporated town located in San Mateo County and is in the jurisdiction of the Sheriff's Department. Eleven minutes later a San Mateo Sheriff's marked unit pulled up. A young sergeant dressed out in SWAT gear exited the vehicle.

"San Jose?" he asked.

Sumner nodded.

"It would have been nice if we had known you were operating in our jurisdiction." The sergeant's statement was a thinly veiled chastisement of Sumner's violation of interdepartmental protocol.

"Sorry," offered Sumner, not sorry at all. "This came together rather quickly. Where is your team?"

"Already deployed."

These guys are good, Sumner thought to himself.

"Any particular reason you need to be present?" asked the sergeant. "The troops are getting anxious."

"No," said Sumner, "have at it."

"You have a green light," said the sergeant into his microphone.

"Let's go," he motioned to Sumner. Sumner moved his motorcycle into the service bay of the gas station and piled in with the deputy.

When they arrived the residence had already been taken down and secured by the San Mateo County Sheriff's Department SWAT Team.

"The place is clean as a whistle," reported the team leader. "The only person we found home was him."

Sumner looked over at Old Man Richard who was sitting on his sofa, smug expression on his face. "I figured the place would be sterilized," said Sumner. "Go ahead and take him in, sales of a controlled substance and conspiracy to commit murder." The smugness vanished from Richard's face, replaced by astonishment. "You're going down," was all the explanation Sumner offered.

Upon completion of the affidavit for setting of bail and supplying the San Mateo County deputy who had been assigned as case officer with all the information necessary to complete the booking of Old Man Richard, Sumner prepared to leave.

"We'll file through the DA in Santa Clara County on Monday and arrange for arraignment proceedings up here." Sumner then started his motorcycle and saddled up for the long, cold ride home.

He pulled his bike into the garage, then undressed, hanging his undercover clothes on a hook next to his work bench, then showered in the downstairs bathroom. As he washed, he became acutely aware of the painful knots on the back of his head inflicted by the loudmouthed gunman. *I sure would like to meet up with that little twerp again,* he mused as he gingerly scrubbed his long hair.

He proceeded upstairs and climbed into bed. His wife slid over and wrapped her arms around his torso and laid her head gently on his left arm. Though she has been distancing herself emotionally, this night the safe return of her husband provided the security and peace of mind that would allow her to now sleep deeply. He took a deep breath and closed his eyes. *Damn, my head hurts.*

§

Subsequent investigations and interrogations revealed that over the years Old Man Richard had brought up trusted lieutenants who initially handled the risky work of transporting the drugs and dealing directly with the customers. But over time, these middle management subordinates had gradually taken over all of the day to day operations of organization. They initiated and began to rigidly enforce a strict business modes operandi, violations of which were ruthlessly retaliated against. As the organization prospered, and order and smooth operations were maintained, Richard became more and more a figurehead. Recently, he had decided that he was ready to retire to southern Arizona. He enlisted the services of Jeri Steinle in a dangerous plan to create a side business out from under the watchful eyes of his organizational operatives. His plan was that this shadow operation would provide sufficient personal income to enable him to retire from the business and live comfortably in Arizona. When Jeri came to the Old Man with Sumner's plan to supply the Hell's Angels, the temptation for a quick windfall was more than the tired old man could resist. Ultimately, Sumner's success in bringing down the legendary drug kingpin had been a matter of timing and luck.

But the organization's bosses had learned of the Old Man's independent enterprise and were determined to put a stop to it. In a meeting sprinkled with impassioned racism, they were able to convince the Old Man that the Hell's Angels could not be trusted under any circumstances and were no doubt setting him up to rip him off. They convinced him that if they could eliminate the white boy, all contact with the outlaw motorcycle gang would be extinguished. The fact that Sumner showed up that night on a motorcycle only served to validate these theories.

With information gained during extensive interrogations of Old Man Richard, over the next six months his lieutenants were, one by one, brought down and much of his organization dismantled by officers of the San Jose Police, Santa Clara, and San Mateo County Narcotic Task Forces, San Francisco and Oakland PDs. But ultimately the insidious far reaching tentacles of his distribution processes had entangled and infested societal elements far removed from the Old Man and would find new sources of supply as they continued to grow and thrive on the back of the American publics' seemingly insatiable appetite for drugs.

In a negotiated plea of guilty, Old Man Richard's cooperation with the police was factored into a reduced sentence of three to five years in the state penitentiary. As part of the conditions of his cooperation, his long time companion Mrs. Hendricks was also given a reduced sentence of one to three years in the state penitentiary.

After thirty years, the book on Old Man Richard organization had finally been closed.

CHAPTER 47

"The Boss wants you to come in at 5:00 tonight," Sergeant Farnsworth's voice seemed a little too smug on the phone, and in Sumner's experience that always spelled trouble. "We have a new snitch he wants you to work."

"Who?"

"He's not a crook, no record," Farnsworth explained. "It seems one of his buddies got overdosed and he wants to give up the crooks."

"Great, an avenging angel," moaned Sumner. "The last time you had me work one of those, he was a born again Christian who took me into a shooting gallery and then tried to convert all the hypes while I was coping from the connection. We both nearly got shot."

"This guy carries some weight, looks like he might be able to bring down some big players. He knows Scott Dillingham and the people who supply him."

Scott Dillingham, thought Sumner. *He lives across the street from the SWAT Commander, Captain Brown, in the affluent Willow Glen area of town. The snake deals right out of his parents' house...a cagey player. Captain Brown comes up to NARCO almost daily complaining about all the dopers coming into his neighborhood.*

"I'll be there at five," Informed Sumner as he hung up the phone.

Sumner cleaned himself carefully as he headed for PAB (Police Administration Building). Cleaning oneself is the process used by an undercover to make certain that he is not being followed. One of the more

252

effective techniques Sumner employed that day was to stop at a busy intersection and wait until the flow of traffic approached from the left, then pull out into the lane just in front of the oncoming vehicles leaving the "tail" stuck at the intersection. This would usually be followed by a series of right hand turns to make sure any possible tail was shaken.

§

As Sumner entered the elevator to the Detective Bureau where the Narcotics Division is located, he was joined by Buckley and Smythe, two of the Street Enforcement Team officers. The Enforcement Team made all the arrests for the other teams and served search warrants and arrest addicts or hypes who are out in public under the influence of heroin. The hypes were then interrogated to extract any useful information and if they prove reliable, they were often recruited as confidential informants to be worked by the Buy Teams.

"How does the hallway look?" Sumner hung back as the elevator door opened.

"We better take you into custody just in case," Smythe responded as he handcuffed Sumner's hands behind his back.

This is becoming monotonous, Sumner groused.

Buckley then grabbed Sumner by the scruff of the neck and all three proceeded from the elevator to the Narcotic Unit. Upon reaching Narcotics Sumner was then placed into an interrogation room where the handcuffs were removed. A smiling Lt. Bertotti entered the room joking, "Did you manage to get yourself arrested again?"

"I just can't seem to stay out of trouble, Boss."

"Leave the cuffs on, Lew, and take him down to Robbery," instructed Bertotti to Officer Smythe. "Sergeant Molosky wants him for a line up on that 211 that occurred this afternoon."

"Right."

Smythe reapplied the cuffs and walked Sumner in custody to the line up room where he was placed on display with four other suspects. The group was viewed by witnesses through a two-way mirror. Once the line-up was completed, Sumner was taken by Smythe back to Narcotics.

"How did it go?" asked Bertotti.

"All of the witnesses picked out Sumner as the perpetrator," laughed Smythe.

"Moonlighting again Sumner? I guess we get credit for clearing that bank robbery pinch," howled Buckley as the room erupted in laughter.

"Yeah, you guys are a couple of real crime fighters," snickered Sumner. "Now get these handcuffs off me. They're cutting off my circulation."

"Come on, you got work to do," chided Sergeant Farnsworth as he directed Sumner into the first interrogation room. "This is Officer Sumner. He will be directing the investigation," said Farnsworth. "This is Robert McCrory."

Sumner shook hands with the new CI. He was a short man about 5'6" and maybe a 150 pounds with long brown hair. For a man of his stature, he possessed an unusual air of confidence and self assurance. As Sumner sat at the table next to McCrory, Farnsworth exited the room.

"So what is it that brings you here?" Sumner studied the CI through hooded eyes.

"A friend of mine's brother was a user. These guys hot shoted him and left him to die. I told his brother I was going to bring them down—that's why I am here." McCrory was nervous, but he looked Sumner directly in the eyes and didn't hesitate with his answer.

"OK, and how are you going to explain me?" asked Sumner.

"You're a buddy of mine, we grew up together," he began with his well thought out cover. "You just got out of the Army; that will explain your build, you were over in Nam and had a rough time in combat, plus you got some bad acid," (LSD) "that really screwed up your head. That way you won't have to talk so much," McCrory explained.

Sumner shook his head once. "These cases will be much easier to prosecute if I talk more and you talk less. You really don't want to have to testify in court in front of these people after all this is over."

"I don't care," snapped McCrory. "They killed my friend's brother."

Sumner frowned. Bravado had a way of disappearing when things got rough. The last thing he needed was a CI with a chip on his shoulder and little or no control of his emotions.

"OK, I'll bring these people down for you, but first you are going to have to do something for me."

"What's that?"

"Scott Dillingham." Sumner stated flatly.

"That's easy," assured McCrory. "I can take you into Scott tonight. Why do you want him?"

"Let's just say he is bringing a bad element into a nice neighborhood," Sumner replied. "He goes down along with his line of supply."

"That's going to be tricky," McCrory was suddenly more cautious. "He gets his junk from Patrick Thornton and his crank from Charlie James, and they're both Angels and badass sons of bitches."

"They gotta go down," Sumner was cold as ice.

The door opened and Sergeant Farnsworth stepped in. "Let me talk to you for a minute," he pointed his chin at Sumner. They both left the room and joined Bertotti in the Boss's office. "We completed the back ground on the guys he wants to give up," the Boss explained. "They're heavy-duty."

"Butch Swearengen and Weston Campi," Farnsworth explained, "are both ex cons, both ANS," (American Nazi Society) "and both have a long record of violent crimes."

"Butch Swearengen," Sumner mused. "I wrestled him in high school. I was the 121 pounder for James Lick High and he was 121 for Andrew Hill High."

"Who won?"

"I lost on points," Sumner confessed. "About two years ago I stopped him for a traffic violation and issued him a citation. He didn't remember me."

"Well let's hope he doesn't remember you now," said Farnsworth. "These two are about as stable as nitro glycerin. You watch your ass."

"You're going armed on this operation," ordered the Boss.

"Sometimes that's not so advisable," reasoned Sumner.

"AT ALL TIMES!" commanded Bertotti.

"Sir," Sumner instinctively responded to the direct order. "The new snitch is going to take me into Dillingham tonight. It seems he gets his dope from Patrick Thornton and Charlie James."

"Four assholes who are known or suspected murderers," marveled Farnsworth. "You're playing with the big boys now; every bit as danger-ous as Old Man Richard. Make sure you are frosty at all times. Don't get sloppy, don't get lazy, and don't let your guard down."

"Well, this isn't exactly the assignment I would have chosen," Sumner admitted. "Hey, don't you have any cases where you need me to infiltrate a gang of outlaw Playboy Bunnies?"

"Get to work. Be careful and check in with Farnsworth morning and evening!" the Boss commanded.

"Aye aye, sir!" Sumner saluted.

"Smart ass," Bertotti muttered to himself and turned to the stack of papers on his desk.

CHAPTER 48

Sumner and McCrory arrived at the Dillingham home at approximately 7:30 p.m.. Dillingham's mother answered the door with an expression of irritation and disappointment across her face.

"Scott!" she yelled over her shoulder. Scott Dillingham, a young man in his early 20s sauntered to the door, his eyelids at half mast.

The 5-50 shuffle, he's loaded right in front of his parents. The 5-50 shuffles is a distinctive gate walked by those under the influence of heroin. 5-50 refers to Section 11550 of the California Health and Safety Code which makes it a misdemeanor to be under the influence of a narcotic.

"Don't be long, dinner is almost ready," his mother ordered.

"I'm not hungry," shot back Scott.

Dillingham shook hands with McCrory. "This is Les," McCrory gestured to Sumner who shook hands.

"Come on in," offered Dillingham.

The three proceeded to Scott's bedroom where he closed the door and turned on his stereo loud enough to cover conversation from anyone outside the room.

"You holding?" inquired McCrory.

"What do you need?" mumbled Dillingham.

"Junk, four bags."

"I gotta have it delivered," replied Dillingham, picking up the telephone. "You like Quaaludes?" he asked Sumner handing him a pill. "Try this."

257

Quaaludes or methaqualone was a prescription drug used in the treatment of anxiety. Methaqualone is a central nervous system depressant causing an effect similar to barbiturates. Sumner palmed the pill and then slipped it in his pocket.

Twenty minutes later Scott's mother called from the front door. Scott left the bedroom and returned with a short, swarthy, black haired, young man with the nervous look of a hype.

"Who's this?" the new arrival demanded, looking as though he might bolt. "That's Robert, that's Les," replied Dillingham. "They're cool, bust out the goods."

The supplier nervously produced the four rolled balloons. Sumner held out his hand taking possession of the items in exchange for which he handed over a $100 bill.

"A Ben," slurred Dillingham, referring to the image of Benjamin Franklin on the face of the one hundred dollar bill. "I love Bens. You got something for me Gus?" he asked.

Gus, thought Sumner— *Argusto Lujan; Heroin dealer and all around crook.*

Lujan tossed a rolled balloon to Dillingham.

"How do I get a hold of you to get a refill?" asked Sumner.

Lujan looked around nervously as Dillingham prepared a hypodermic.

"Just call Scott," said a jittery Lujan.

"Scott's not always around," replied Sumner. "Besides, he lives with his parents and I need to be able to get what I need when I need it."

Lujan scribbled a phone number on a piece of paper he found lying on Dillingham's desk and handed it to Sumner. "Just be cool when you call. Aren't you going to try this?"

"Not right now and not here," replied Sumner.

"It's just a little too weird with Scott's parents down the hall," added McCrory. "We'll see you tomorrow," said McCrory as he and Sumner headed for the door.

Good intervention by the CI. Sumner drove McCrory to his one bedroom apartment on North First Street, less than a mile from the Police Department. "See you tomorrow at 10:00 a.m."

"Tomorrow," replied McCrory as he exited the vehicle.

CHAPTER 49

Later that evening as Sumner sat at his kitchen table writing his crime report, he thought back on the evenings events and how Dillingham had been such an elusive drug dealer. Several times the Narcotics Unit had tried to cold insert undercover operatives into his circle of activity with no success. The Street Enforcement Team had worked the area arresting numerous dopers leaving Dillingham's home, but none of them could be persuaded to give him up. Then with seeming effortlessness this informant who was not a drug user or a habitual criminal waltzes Sumner into Dillingham's confidence where he was able to make two felony cases on him and one on career criminal Argusto Lujan. Strange how events turn.

Sumner locked his report and the dope in his gun safe in order to preserve the ever crucial chain of evidence and retired to the sofa to read a few chapters of Bram Stoker's *Dracula* before going upstairs to bed. San Jose was experiencing a rare thunder and lighting storm that evening. *The perfect setting to enjoy a Gothic horror movie,* Sumner thought. *Let's see, Johnathan Harker was in some real trouble when we left off.*

§

Sumner picked up Robert McCrory at 10:00 a.m. As they proceeded to Dillingham's, Sumner informed his CI that he would need him to make an excuse to leave after they made contact with Scott.

"Why?" asked McCrory.

"I am going to get Scott to take me to Thornton today," Sumner replied.

"I should be there, man. I got your back," McCrory advised. *He's got my back huh? The first thing we were taught as undercover operatives was no matter how fond you become of your informant, never forget that they are not police officers. They are not trained or conditioned to deal with danger like a police officer and will usually take off at the first sign of trouble.*

"Robert," Sumner reminded, "these prosecutions will go much smoother if you don't have to testify in court."

"I don't care. I'm not afraid."

"It's not about being afraid," Sumner explained. "Prosecutions proceed much more smoothly if we don't have to synchronize our testimony. It eliminates the possibility that we might contradict each other while being examined by a scumbag attorney. It's the way we do things in law enforcement."

Scott answered the door wearing nothing but his boxer shorts. *It's 10:30 in the morning and this guys already loaded.* "Come on in," said Scott. "I been jonzen for three days and I haven't eaten anything. I need to shoot some more junk to kill the hunger pains." *Haven't eaten and haven't bathed.*

"I need to score a piece," Sumner said.

"What do you need that much dope for?"

"Some of my buddies got strung out in Nam. They started popping H to relieve the anxiety of combat and they got hooked. They got no connection here, so I figure I can do them a favor supplying good quality stuff and make a few bucks," Sumner laid out his cover.

"I've got to trip for it," Scott said.

"Cool, I'll come with you."

"We can't all go," Scott complained. "I'll get my ass kicked."

"I got other things I gotta do. You guys can just drop me off at the mall," offered McCrory. "I'll catch up with you tonight."

Sumner drove to the Valley Fair Shopping Mall where he dropped off McCrory, handing him a $100 bill. He then proceeded, at the direction of Dillingham, to an apartment complex off of the Lawrence Expressway just inside the neighboring city of Santa Clara. They proceeded to a locked entrance where Dillingham pressed the intercom button for apartment 24.

"Who the fuck is it?" The voice over the box was agitated

"Scott..." the intercom clicked off. "And Les," Dillingham continued.

"That's not going to fool him," Sumner chided.

The lock to the entrance door clicked open and Sumner and Dillingham entered and proceeded down the hall toward apartment 24. Suddenly the door to the apartment swung open and the satanic person of Patrick Thornton stepped into the hallway stark naked and wielding a long barrel .22 revolver.

"Why are you interrupting me while I'm fucking my old lady...and who the fuck is that?" screamed Thornton pointing the pistol at Sumner.

"That's Les. I told you..."

"You didn't tell me anything, you lying little prick," yelled Thornton as he brandished the pistol toward Dillingham. "Who the fuck are you and what do you want?" demanded Thornton, pointing the revolver at Sumner's forehead.

"I'm just along for the ride, here to do some business," Sumner explained raising his hands.

"What kind of business?" Thornton demanded.

"This kind of business," offered Sumner pulling a roll of $100 bills partway out of his pants pocket.

Thornton's eyes bored into Sumner's face as he methodically examined every feature, searching punctiliously for any sign of treachery. Sumner met his gaze and looked into the soulless black eyes of the pathological killer. *Black eyes, the stories about him are true. He has black eyes, you can't see his pupils. They probably turned black when sold his soul to the devil.*

"You packing?" demanded Thornton.

"What difference does that make?"

"Don't get smart with me asshole," Thornton jammed the barrel of the pistol into Sumner's forehead. "Are you packing?"

If I don't answer this investigation is over and so perhaps is my life.

"Yeah, I'm packing," Sumner shot back. "I've been back from Nam for less than a month. I carry a whole year's pay on me. I keep a piece on me all the time, when I eat, when I shit, hell I even shower with it," Sumner hissed. "I'm packing."

"Give it to me," Thornton demanded.

"What!"

"You heard me, asshole. Hand me your gun right now."

Let's see, I'm standing in the hallway of this building with a naked psychopathic murderer, an enforcer for an outlaw motorcycle gang and a drug addict holding a gun to my head and all he wants is my weapon, what could possibly go wrong. What the hell, they didn't bring me up to Narcotics to play it safe. Let's see where things go.

Sumner reached slowly under his shirt into the elastic waistband where he concealed his Walther PPK semiautomatic pistol. He pulled it slowly out holding the weapon between his index finger and thumb. Thornton grabbed the pistol with his left hand and stepped back into the doorway, closely examining the weapon.

"Outstanding," exclaimed Thornton. "Come on in and close the door."

"You army guys always carry the best hardware," Thornton explained. "If you ever think you got a cop on your hands, demand to see his gun. The cops only carry Smith and Wesson 357 magnum revolvers, nothing else. This ain't no cop's gun. This is primo firepower." Thornton handed the pistol back to Sumner.

Incredible, Sumner marveled. *Using his own cockeyed deductive reasoning this psychopath has thoroughly validated my cover.*

"What do you need?" With his suspicions allayed Thornton was now ready to conduct business, obviously intrigued by the money Sumner had flashed.

"Junk, a piece," Sumner replied.

"What do you need that much for?"

Sumner imparted his story about his army buddies and how he wanted to serve as a reliable source of safe heroin for them and to make some money.

"Hummm, a piece should get you started," Thornton surmised. "If it works out we can talk about quantities later. Now listen, I know these guys are your buddies but don't let anyone get his nose in the bag. You demand payment at the time of delivery. If you start giving credit, you'll never get paid."

Thornton went to the kitchen and removed a plastic bag containing a light brown powder. "Keep this in the refrigerator, but never in the freezer and never leave it laying out, it'll loose potency," he tutored. "You get a large jar of peanut butter and take the shit out of the middle of the jar. You keep the junk in the peanut butter jar in the fridge. If you ever get searched, the bulls will look in the fridge but they never open the jars and containers. It's some kind of rule they have. And if they use a dog, the mutt won't be able to smell the junk because it will be covered by the smell of the peanut butter."

Remarkable. This murderer outlaw is reveling in his role as a teacher, tutor and mentor. He is actually giving me a crash course in Drug Business 101, Sumner sniggered to himself.

"How do I get a hold of you?" Sumner asked.

"I will get a hold of you. Day after tomorrow at noon," replied Thornton.

Sumner wrote down the phone number for the Bat Phone, on the inside of a matchbook cover and handed it to Thornton.

Sumner counted out $1000 and handed the money to Thornton in exchange for the ounce of heroin. Sumner lifted the plastic bag of powder to his nose. "Smells like peanut butter," Sumner laughed. Thornton let out a howl as he clapped Sumner on the back.

As Sumner and Dillingham walked to the door, Thornton placed his hand on Sumner's shoulder in a good natured show of concern saying "You be careful, soldier boy. If you come across any fine weaponry like you got, let me know. I'm always in the market."

Remarkable, Sumner thought sarcastically, *how a psychopathic killer can exude so much charm.*

CHAPTER 50

There are many details that are better left out of a crime report. Handing his weapon over to a psychopathic killer is one of them. *So much for the advisability of going armed at all times.* With that thought, Sumner handed his reports and evidence to Sergeant Bercelli.

"Where's Nails?" Sumner asked.

"He had court," replied Sergeant Bercelli as he scanned the Crime Report. "You had Patrick Thornton holding a gun to your head!" exclaimed a visibly agitated Bercelli. "Are you nuts?"

"Well, that's just the way the buy went down," Sumner explained. "I didn't expect to be greeted at the door by a naked, gun wielding, crazy man."

"Look, you're not working for me. Nails is in charge of your operations, but you're in with some very dangerous people," Bercelli protested. "You've done some great work, but you're still relatively new at this and situations with people like Thornton can get out of hand very quickly. You should be working with cover."

"Sergeant, I appreciate your concern, but what the hell could cover have done for me this morning? Situations have got to be worked out on the spot. That's why quick thinking officers make the best undercovers."

"You better hope your quick thinking doesn't fail you at a critical time," Bercelli warned as he exited Sumner's vehicle and entered his unmarked police unit.

CHAPTER 51

Sumner returned home where he parked the police undercover vehicle in his garage and mounted his motorcycle. *Great day for a ride.*

As he arrived at Dillingham's, he observed Scott standing in the driveway talking with a blond haired young man on a new Harley Davidson motorcycle. Sumner pulled up next to the Harley. "Nice bike," Sumner said.

"Thanks," replied the rider. "This is Mike Dallas," Scott introduced Sumner. "I gotta go. I'll catch you guys later," Dillingham climbed into the passenger seat of a new Chevrolet Monte Carlo that had just pulled up and was being driven by an attractive young lady.

"What the hell," said Sumner as the vehicle pulled away. "I need to score."

"What do you need?" asked Dallas.

"A spoon," replied Sumner. "Scott knew I was coming and said he would have the junk ready," said a bewildered Sumner.

"His dick is thinking for him right now," said Dallas. "Let's take a putt and I'll see what I can do for you."

Where the hell are you taking me? Sumner thought. *Better not ask too many questions.*

"I'm with you," said Sumner as he fired up his bike and followed Dallas as he accelerated to over sixty miles an hour down the residential street.

Ten minutes later they arrived at a residence on the corner of Settle Ave. and Minnesota. Built in the 1930s, these Santa Clara homes had basements. Because San Jose sits on the floor of a valley that sits on a vast aqua reservoir, most basements eventually flooded. Dallas lived in the basement of this home in rooms he rented from the owner, who was a widow who occupied the ground level where she also operated a hair salon.

"Nice set up," said Sumner as he entered the living area.

"Who is this?" demanded a diminutive young woman.

"This is Les," replied Dallas. "He's a friend of Scott's."

"What's he doing here?"

"He's just going to score and then we're leaving."

"What do you know about this man?" she doggedly continued. "He could be a policeman for all you know."

"He's a friend of Scott's and he's a nice guy," replied Dallas as he handed Sumner four rolled balloons. "He'll shoot the stuff right here in front of you if that would make you feel better."

"Mikey, you don't know anything about this man. If you are going to sell him anything, I want to see him shoot it right here."

"Who is she?" inquired Sumner as he handed three $20 bills to Dallas.

"My girlfriend."

"Is she your old lady?"

"I care about him," snapped the woman.

"Just shoot the dope and that will make her happy," reasoned Dallas, handing Sumner a hypodermic.

"Not a chance, for all I know she's a cop and she's trying to set me up," Sumner used his well worn excuse. "I'm not shootin' in front of some crazy bitch. I'm getting the fuck out of here. I'll see you later. Maybe we can go for a ride." Sumner hastily departed.

"I hope you're happy, bitch!" echoed Dallas' voice from the residence as Sumner fired up his motorcycle.

Sumner turned his bike right onto eastbound Hamilton Avenue and began accelerating past 30 miles per hour as a vehicle from the super-market parking lot on the right approached the entrance to the roadway. He made eye contact with the female driver as she slowed to a near stop and then suddenly accelerated onto the roadway, smashing into Sumner's bike just behind the front wheel. As Sumner and the motorcycle careened out of control into the path of oncoming traffic, he prepared for impact. He reflexively used his falling skills, to protect his vitals, landing on his left hip striking down on the pavement with the palms and forearms of both hands coming to a stop in front of oncoming traffic. The driver of the lead vehicle in the oncoming lane brought his vehicle to a screeching halt, the bumper just inches from Sumner's head.

Sumner slowly reached over and shut off his still running motorcycle. Then he gingerly stood up, examining the palms of both hands. What, a moment before, had been healthy skin was now road hamburger, embedded with broken glass and tiny rocks. He looked over at the driver who had struck him and held up his bleeding hands for her to see. The woman looked in obvious terror and suddenly accelerated away from the accident scene. *Idiot,* Sumner thought.

The driver of the lead vehicle, who's alert action had prevented Sumner from becoming road kill stepped out of his vehicle in obvious concern. A curly red haired, freckle faced young man of about twenty years. "Man, that was intense. I got her license number for you."

"Yeah, I got it too." Sumner attempted to lift his bike back onto to two wheels and was treated to a shooting pain in each wrist. *Great, both wrists broken.*

"Let me help you with that man," offered the driver. "Are you sure you don't want me to call an ambulance?"

"Naw," Sumner shrugged. "Thanks for the help though." Sumner climbed onto his motorcycle and painfully, rode home, parking the bike in the garage. He then entered the house from the garage into the laundry room where his wife was folding laundry.

"Are you home for the day?" she asked as Sumner concealed his hands.

"No, I just need to get the car," explained Sumner as he squeezed past and into the hallway. He then proceeded into the kitchen where he removed the keys to his undercover vehicle from a hook on the side of the cabinets. *Damn,* Sumner noticed that he had left a trail of blood on the floor. He grabbed a couple of paper towels and wetted them at the kitchen faucet then proceeded to clean up the floor. He then stopped at the downstairs bathroom and washed off his injured, bleeding hands under the warm running water. It felt like hot lava was being poured onto his palms. *I gotta get to a doctor.*

"See you in a while," said Sumner as he exited out the front door.

§

"What happened to you?" asked the nurse as Sumner limped into the city infirmary holding up his hands in an attempt to slow the bleeding.

"I had a little accident."

The nurse took him into a treatment room where she filled a bowl with warm water and a powder substance. She placed Sumner's hands in the liquid, palms up as the doctor entered with a scalpel and tweezers. "Nasty," observed the doctor as he began the tedious task of removing pieces of rock and glass from the wounded hands. "How did this happen?"

Sumner described the accident and the manner and force with which he landed. "That kid driving the oncoming vehicle ought to get a medal," mused the doctor. "Get X-ray ready," he directed the nurse. "Both wrists and left leg and hip."

Sergeant Dreyer entered the room shaking his head. "Mexican Bob and Old Man Richard couldn't take you out, but a young mother with a baby in the car laid you low," he laughed.

"She had a baby in the car and she was driving like that?"

"Yeah, she took off because she thought you were some crazed biker," Dreyer explained. "She was afraid you were going to harm her and the baby."

"I understand," said Sumner "I guess I was not showing my most congenial side at that moment. But damn that hurt."

Dreyer filled out the injury report as the nurse took X-rays.

"Both wrists broken," advised the doctor. "We can't cast them because of the flesh wounds so we will splint them with inflatable splints. You'll have to soak the hands in a solution of warm water and a packet of this," he held up the same substance that the nurse had deposited in the bowl into which she had placed Sumner's hands. "Change the dressing twice a day after soaking the hands, then apply Neosporin, clean bandages and reapply the splints."

"What about my left leg?" asked Sumner.

"Bruised up real good but no fractures."

"Thanks, doc," said Sumner as he and Dreyer walked slowly across the street from the City Health Building, past the Communications Building to PAB. As they arrived at the Narcotics Unit, the Boss called them into his office.

"Bercelli is a little concerned about your encounter with Thornton," explained Bertotti. "He has had dealings with Thornton when he was in the cars and he says he's a wild card—completely unpredictable and quite violent."

"Boss, I don't know what else I could have done except maybe make a move for the gun, which may or may not have been successful," Sumner explained. "One way or the other, that would have been the end of the investigation, but instead we have a solid case on the guy and I'm still standing here."

"Entirely due to luck in the opinion of Bercelli," the Boss pointed out.

"The guy is wild and violent and usually armed. And I'm playing it very low key and non-threatening. He's real interested in guns and getting more of them. Another buy off him and we can hand it off to the Majors Team to see what they can make of it. He's calling here tomorrow at noon. I can set up the buy for tomorrow evening."

"You're going covered this time," ordered the Boss.

"Not a good idea. This guy can smell pork," Sumner protested.

"This is not negotiable."

§

Sumner's wife was furious. "I told you that motorcycles are dangerous. My cousin was killed riding one. I never wanted you to get that thing. Now look at you!"

"Karen, I just need some help applying the bandages. I can't manage it by myself," pleaded Sumner.

"Well, you're just going to have to do it alone. I'm not going to help you kill yourself," she burst into tears as she exited the kitchen.

Sumner fumbled with the bandages, finally getting them to cover his raw hands and then gently reapplied the splints. *This is going to be one painful recovery.*

The phone rang. Sumner fumbled the receiver to his ear. It was Sergeant Farnsworth checking on his injuries. "Do you want to shine Thornton on tomorrow and take a mental health sick day to decompress?"

"Naw. The Boss wants me to go covered on the next buy from Thornton. I'm not used to the additional worry of coordinating with cover and with a wild man like him, I'm a little uneasy. I want to get this next buy done."

"All right, see you tomorrow morning," said Farnsworth. "Get some rest."

Sumner could not sleep. His wrists throbbed with pain and his hands were on fire. He tried to read, but could not concentrate with the nagging pain. He poured a shot of Jack Daniels and turned on "The Tonight Show" with Johnny Carson just in time for the monologue. The pain in his upper extremities began to subside. He poured another shot and sat on the sofa, chuckling at the stream of jokes on the TV. As he finished his third shot, he realized he was sitting in the family room, alone, laughing like an idiot at a TV comedian. *Aw, this is no good, I gotta go to bed.*

CHAPTER 52

Sumner woke at 6:00 a.m. with a dry mouth, feeling feverish, hands and wrists pulsating with pain. *This is going to be a long day.* He walked downstairs, poured a cup of coffee, and downed four Tylenol. He then walked out to the garage to examine his motorcycle for the first time since the accident. *Gas tank smashed bent frame, shattered front fork and front wheel rim crushed. How the hell did I make it home.* He then proceeded upstairs where he drew a hot bath where he could soak and bathe without getting his bandages wet.

He arrived at the Narcotic Unit at 8:06 a.m. "He must have fallen out of bed," joked Bertotti. "The only time I've ever seen him up this early is just before he went to bed."

"Ha, ha. You try sleeping with two broken wrists and no meat left on your palms. How is this going to go down? Thornton is real spooky and my ass is going to be hanging out there," Sumner reasoned. "One false move, one screw up by cover, and my kids will be orphans and you boneheads will be heroes for taking out a psychopathic cop killer."

"Grab a cup and come into my office," ordered Bertotti gesturing to Farnsworth.

The Boss settled into his chair as Sumner and Farnsworth pulled seats up to the other side of the desk. "You seem a little edgy," Bertotti said. "Is there anything we should know?"

"Well, the fact that I can't feed myself, wipe my own ass, or hold a gun is a little more than annoying. That, and that I will be dealing with a murderer while worrying about a blown cover has me a little on edge, yeah. And the pain is not helping things either."

"The cover is to assure your safety, not stir you up."

"I'm just not used to coordinating with cover. I wasn't ever trained in that, You brought me up here to work deep undercover where I am able to adjust to circumstances as they change moment by moment and that's what I have been doing the last two years."

"Well, you're not in condition to adjust to anything right now," pointed out Bertotti. "So here is what we'll do. You establish the location for the buy. Give yourself at least one hour, tell him you have to arrange a ride due to your injuries. We'll position Randy Cardini from SWAT well back with the .308, Buckley and Smythe a little closer with the scoped AR and Nails will drive you in," Bertotti proposed.

"Cardini doesn't know the first thing about undercover operations," Sumner explained. "What if he gets jumpy and let's one fly?"

"Then you can be sure the round will hit Thornton right between the eyes," assured Bertotti. "He's one of the best shots in the world."

"OK, I'll make the arrangements as soon as he calls."

"And loosen up, everything will go down like clockwork," coaxed the Boss. "Hey didn't they give you anything for the pain?"

"Jack Daniels," advised Sumner. "All it did was give me a sour stomach and a headache this morning."

"Overmedicating will do that," Bertotti laughed.

"Come on," ordered Farnsworth. "We need to get you fitted with a wire."

"A wire? I've never worked with a wire," Sumner protested. "I am going to be so hinky this guy won't come within a mile of me."

Farnsworth led Sumner next door to Crime Scene Investigations Unit where Sergeant Aubry Parrot assessed the situation. "What we'll do is put the transmitter and microphone inside an empty cigarette pack, run the wire out the back of the pack, through a hole we'll punch in your shirt and tape the wire up over your shoulder. The cigarette pack with the transmitter will be in your right front shirt pocket."

Sumner removed his heavy flannel long sleeve shirt and handed it to Parrot. This is the type of shirt preferred by heroin addicts for its ability to conceal needle marks on the arms.

"And what if he asks me for a cigarette?" Sumner cracked.

§

The Bat Phone rang at exactly 12:01 p.m. Sumner pressed the on button to the recording device attached to the telephone as Farnsworth picked up receiver and held it to Sumner's ear.

"Les?"

"Patrick, you're the man of the hour."

"Huh?"

"Your product has been well received by the consumers," Sumner smoozed.

"Good, that's good," replied Thornton. "You ready for more?"

"Another piece and I should be good until the middle of next week," Sumner informed. "I won't bother you until about Wednesday."

"Five-thirty tonight, the Safeway parking lot at Bascom and Hamilton."

"No problem," answered Sumner. "I'll need to get a ride. I crashed my bike yesterday and both my hands are in casts. I can't drive."

"You did what?"

"Some bitch pulled out on me and knocked me off my bike into on coming traffic. I nearly bought the farm."

"I told you to be careful. Especially riding a bike. Damned idiots just don't watch," Thornton replied. "So who's driving you?"

"One of my army buddies."

"So here's how it will happen," Thornton laid out the plan. "I'll be in my white van. I'll park in the middle of the parking lot. Have your guy park at least fifty feet away on the north side of my van. I'll be on the south side. Nobody sees me."

"Understood." Farnsworth hung up the phone, removed the tape cartridge from the recorder, and marked the date and case number on the cartridge. Sumner then fumbled the pen between his throbbing fingers and marked his initials and badge number on the cartridge. Farnsworth then placed the cartridge in an evidence envelope and deposited it into the evidence locker just outside the soundproof room where the bat phone was located. They then proceeded to the Boss's office where Sumner briefed everyone on the upcoming operation.

"That works very well for us," said Cardini. "Five-thirty is gathering darkness and gives me a little better concealment."

"The only problem I see is that parking lot is just across the city limits in Campbell," Bertotti pointed out. "We may have a jurisdictional problem if anything goes down."

"Let's hope it doesn't," Sumner offered. "You know he is going to have cover of his own."

"No doubt," Farnsworth agreed.

"I'll notify Campbell that we will be operating in that area as an FYI and that we will require no assistance," said Bertotti.

§

Farnsworth slowly pulled the vehicle into the parking lot. Sumner glanced in both directions, trying to spot Thornton's cover. Then, with a thrust of his chin he indicated the location of Thornton's beat up white van near the center of the parking lot. Farnsworth parked fifty feet north of the van as instructed. Sumner exited the vehicle and approached the south side of the van walking slowly with an obvious limp.

"So you got all smashed up, eh?" Thornton asked in his gravelly voice.

"Pretty much."

"Looks like you're in a bit of pain."

"Just a bit."

"So the product was well received?" inquired Thornton.

"Oh hell yeah," Sumner replied. "And I'm telling you this is a sweet set up. These guys are all former GIs getting a regular check from the government. No problems with payment."

"Cool," smiled Thornton.

Sumner reached for the roll of $100 bills that Farnsworth had placed in the left front pocket of his flannel shirt, but because of his bandages was unable to remove the cash. "Grab the dinaro would you," he said to Thornton gesturing with his chin to the left front shirt pocket.

Thornton stepped forward and nonchalantly reached into Sumner's right front shirt pocket where the body transmitter and microphone were placed inside the empty Marlboro cigarette box. *Damn, if he discovers the transmitter…*

As Thornton took hold of the cigarette pack and began to lift it from its place, Sumner turned slightly to the right gesturing again to the left. "Wrong pocket," Sumner said casually.

Thornton's lifeless black eyes bored into Sumner's. *What the hell is he thinking? Stay cool, don't get edgy…*

"The dough is in the other pocket."

Thornton stared as cold and emotionless as a black widow might at the prey stuck in its web. *Oh god, here we go…*

Suddenly, Thornton's face leapt to life with animation and comprehension. "Oh," he said. *Is he really that dense or is he just uptight?* Thornton released his grip on the cigarette pack and removed his hand, then reached into the left pocket and removed the roll of bills, replacing it with a clear plastic bag containing the heroin.

He's spacey. He's either a little bit loaded or paranoid or a bit of both. Time to change the focus of attention.

"I don't know if you're in the market for this kind of quantity, but my pilot buddy is sitting on a load of state of the art weaponry," Sumner dangled the bait. "I think he'd be willing to deal on the price."

"What kind of stuff?"

"I think it's mostly M-16s and some army issue pistols," Sumner offered. "Maybe some AKs."

"I'm definitely interested," Thornton said with obviously rising excitement.

"I'll set up a meeting," Sumner suggested. "Call me Monday at noon."

"Yeah, yeah, let's set that up," clamored Thornton with all the subtlety of a salivating dog at supper time. "Monday, I'll call you."

"Cool. I gotta go, I'm in a lot of pain."

"Monday man. I'll call you at noon Monday."

Sumner hobbled back to the vehicle where Sergeant Farnsworth was waiting. Farnsworth looked into Sumner's face, searching for an indication of success. Sumner let a wry smile slip. Farnsworth nodded approvingly.

Sumner finished booking the contraband into the evidence locker and submitted his report to Sergeant Farnsworth. "I'm glad that's finished," he said.

"Quittin' time," announced the Boss walking from his office. "I'm buying at the Fog Horn." The Fog Horn Restaurant and Bar was another favorite off duty hang out for San Jose Police Detectives.

"I gotta get home," pleaded Sumner. "I'm still in a lot of pain."

"That's why you need some medicine," replied Bertotti.

"OK, I'll come over for one."

"One at a time," joked Narcotic Officer Stewart.

Sumner piled into the corner booth of the dimly lit tavern followed by the Boss, Nails, Dreyer, Jones, Buckley and Smythe. He rested his throbbing hands against the frosty glass of beer, finally getting some relief from the ever present pain. *Ahh, that feels good.*

"Did you know that a recent study by the Rand Corporation shows unequivocally that when the police put assholes in jail, the crime rate goes down," announced Bertotti. "I'm going to apply for a grant, and commencing Monday we're going to start putting assholes in jail."

"Here's to putting assholes in jail," toasted Dreyer holding up his glass of beer. Each of the officers clinked glasses and drank to putting assholes in jail.

Sumner finished off the contents of his glass and stood. "I gotta get going."

Bertotti pushed Sumner back into his seat. "You can't go. It's your turn to buy a round."

"Yeah," agreed everyone at the table.

Sumner reluctantly sat back down and signaled the waitress that the table was ready for a refill.

Sumner arrived home just after midnight, feeling the best that he had in several days. He went to bed and enjoyed a rejuvenating good night's sleep.

CHAPTER 53

"What's the game plan?" Jonesy's countenance suddenly went from his jovial self to intent. This was the focus that had kept Jonesy alive as a combat helicopter pilot in Viet Nam through the course of over 600 missions.

"We're handing it off to Majors," explained Bertotti (The Major Violators Team of the Narcotics Unit). "I want to see how far you can take this."

"How has it been laid out?" inquired Jones.

"Thornton is dying to get his hands on some high powered weapons. I'm not exactly sure if it's a fetish. He's trying impress someone or he actually has an outlet for the stuff," Sumner explained. "The cover is you were a pilot in Viet Nam during the Cambodian invasion and you were able to smuggle out some M-16s, pistols, and maybe some AK-47s. You're sitting on the stuff and want to unload it."

"This operation is going to come to an abrupt conclusion when I don't supply the weapons," Jonesy pointed out the flaw in the cover.

"I did indicate that you want to off the whole inventory. I figured that will smoke out any heavy players he's connected to. He doesn't have the cash or the wherewithal to handle a caper like this alone."

"Yeah, but this cover has limited range. When I bring this down, your operation needs to be completed, cause it's all going to be over with these people right then."

"Let me go ahead and set up the meeting and see how it plays out. If it doesn't look like you can make it work with that cover, I can tell him you got spooked and don't want to deal."

"All right. Set up the meeting at Muni Airport out by the south hangars. I'll taxi up in my plane. That should help legitimize the cover."

Sumner took the call from Thornton and made the arrangements for the meeting. Bertotti picked up the phone and called the MERGE Commander, Captain William Brown, who was in charge of all SWAT deployments. Bertolli explained the situation and requested sniper cover. Brown surmised that three snipers positioned with a triangulation of fire would be sufficient. "The meeting is set for 4:00 p.m. You've got two hours to deploy," Bertotti said and hung up.

§

Sumner arrived at 3:50 p.m. at the southern hangars where the civil aircraft was parked. He stood at the edge of the tarmac and looked across buildings, searching for any sign of the SWAT officers. *Nowhere to be seen. These guys are good.*

"What the hell is going on? Who the fuck is this?" asked Sumner nervously. Though he had anticipated that Thornton would be accompanied by someone else, he feigned the appropriate and expected paranoia.

"Everything is cool, man. This is my partner," explained Thornton.

"You didn't say anything about bringing a partner."

"From now on you can just assume that Charlie is in on everything we do."

Charlie James…it just doesn't get any better than this.

"Where is your connection?"

"He'll be right here. He just landed."

Sumner stepped close and put his arm across Thornton's shoulders and spoke in hushed tones. "Patrick, maybe you can help me. My customer base is growing, but some of these guys coming back from Nam like to speed. I heard they would jump start just before going into battle and they still like it. But I got no connection."

Thornton turned to face Sumner with a smile that spread across his face. "And you were getting all paranoid about my partner. Well, it just so happens that Speedy James here is 'the' connection for primo crank. Charlie," he said to his partner "we got a man here with a solid income stream and people who need just what you got."

"Cool," replied James, shrugging his shoulders. "I'll give you a call tomorrow and we can do some business."

Just then Jonesy taxied up in his single engine plane. Thornton and James looked on intently as he brought the plane to a stop, shut down the engine, and exited. Sumner made the introductions and Jones got right down to business.

"So you want to purchase armament? How are you going to pay for it?"

"How do we know what you got?" asked Thornton.

Jones walked over to the plane, gesturing for all to follow. He opened the door and moved the seat forward where a blanket lay across the backseat. He removed the blanket revealing two Colt M-16 rifles and two Smith and Wesson Model 59 high capacity semiautomatic pistols. Their eyes widened as they reached for the weapons. "Go ahead," said Jones "touch them, feel them...get your fingerprints all over them."

Thornton and James pulled their hands back abruptly. Suddenly Thornton stuck his thumbs under his armpits and began to walk in a circle flapping his arms like wings and making sounds like a turkey. *This guy is completely out of his mind.*

"Hey, Foghorn Leghorn," Jonesy snapped. "How you going to pay for quality merchandise like this?"

Thornton stopped his insane gyrations and turned to Jones. "I'm thinking we can trade dope for it."

"Not a chance," came Jones. "There are 250 pieces in this load. $35,000 cash for all of it. You got that kind of financing?"

"As a matter of fact...you ever hear of a little organization called," Thornton suddenly dropped his head below his shoulders cocking it to the side and lowering his voice to a Satanic pitch, "the Hell's Angels?"

"You got my attention."

"But they're going to want to meet you and examine the merchandise."

"That's cool. Set it up through Les," Jones replied.

CHAPTER 54

"Charlie is on the phone," informed undercover officer Danny Guzman.

Sumner jumped from his chair and entered the sound-proof Bat phone room. "Yeah," Sumner said into the phone.

"You want to do some business?" came the coarse voice of Charlie James.

"Sure do. I need an OZ to start. You think that is about right?"

"That should get you started," James replied.

"How should I package that stuff? What are people expecting?"

For purposes of prosecution in court later Sumner needed to get him to talk about drugs while being recorded demonstrating knowledge and culpability.

"You put it into dime bags; usually a measured quarter spoon," James explained. "Haven't you done this before?"

"Not with crank. I only been peddling junk."

"Get some of those little plastic bags or you can even fold it in bindles like coke," James explained with some irritation.

"Cool, thanks." *Perfect, just perfect; Thank you, Mr. James.*

"Chef's Kitchen on the Alameda, one hour."

"See you there." Sumner hung up the phone and took the tape cartridge from the recording device attached to the phone. After marking and booking the tape, he placed a new tape in the recorder, which turns on automatically when the phone is answered.

Sumner left the Police Administration Building through the basement and crossed the street to the Narcotic annex on Pedro Street where his undercover vehicle was parked. He drove to the Chef's Kitchen coffee shop, a popular eatery with the local criminal element, and entered the establishment where he took a booth near the window.

Charlie James arrived five minutes later accompanied by what appeared from the distance to be a stunning auburn haired woman. "Speedy" James, five foot eight or nine, 140 pounds, black stringy hair, and a Saturnine countenance only surpassed in reprobated depravity by Thornton himself. *So what the hell is a woman like that doing with him?*

"Who's that?" asked Sumner indicating the woman.

"That's my old lady Sheri."

"Nice to meet you, Sheri." Up close Sumner could see the tell tail signs of years of drug abuse written across the woman's face. Dry pallid skin, brittle hair, and the inevitable blackened and decaying teeth. *She was once a very attractive woman…what a waste.*

"Are you sure you know what the hell you're doing with all this?" asked the visibly dubious James. "Do you even know what this shit is all about?"

"I'm helping out some of my army buddies," Sumner explained. "They used this stuff over in Nam to hop up before battle. They liked the ride and want more now that they are home. I figure I can make a few bucks and take care of them."

"This stuff is probably a little stronger than what they're use to, so be careful," James stared intently. "And don't I know you from somewhere?"

Ahh there it is. All paranoid drug addicts eventually get to that question. It is a standard to flush out snitches and rookie undercover officers.

"Maybe. Were you at Camp Red Devil near the DMZ?"

James stared with a blank expression that bespoke an envelope with no address. "I was with the 1st ID in support of the 5th Mechanized." His cretinous stare descended further into the depths of ignorance. "Were you on Mountain High, Clinched Fist, Bird Down, Phantom Lake, Skinny

Dip...any of those operations?" *He hasn't got a clue. Even the draft wouldn't touch this piece of human refuse.* "Well that's were I been the last year and a half. Maybe we haven't ever met."

James's countenance shifted suddenly to one of coherence. "Maybe not. You just look familiar."

Sumner felt James's hand under the table. He reached to receive an ounce bag of white powder. *Speed, crank, meth-amphetamines.* Sumner handed back $1000 in the form of a roll of $100 bills. *Slick, nobody saw a thing. Even if we were caught on camera nobody would be able to tell what just transpired. This guy is good.*

§

Sumner left the coffee shop and entered his vehicle heading south on the Alameda to Race Street where he stopped at the Race Street Fish and Poultry for a soda and some deep fried clam strips. Race Street Fish and Poultry was located next door to the south bay offices of the California State Parole Board. There were ex-cons in and out of the building all day long meeting with their parole agent, and the fish store provided an ideal setting to meet other criminals.

Sumner got his order and took a seat at a table located outside on the sidewalk. *Deep fried clams strips with malt vinegar, what a lunch.*

"You got a light?" the inquiry came from a tall skinny young man with straight brown hair. Sumner handed him a book of matches. "You here to see your PO?" he asked.

"Just got done," Sumner replied.

"Sucks, doesn't it?"

"It's a hell of lot better than being inside," Sumner answered.

"Where'd you do your time?"

"Look," Sumner snapped, "I don't know you and you're asking some pretty personal questions, so why don't you just move on."

"OK, OK, don't get jumpy. I'm just killing a little time. I'm Dave Allen," he said, holding out his hand to shake.

"Les," said Sumner laconically, deferring to shake.

"How's the weather?" asked Allen in the cryptic criminal code which in fact meant "Are there any drugs available?"

"Dry, very dry," answered Sumner, indicating that there are no drugs available.

"You don't happen to know where I can score a quantity of acid do you?"

"You're about a week late," Sumner answered. "My source got rolled up. He won't be out for another two years."

"Ouch, tough break," Allen schmoozed. "Well, you wouldn't be interested in a quantity of purple by any chance?"

"I told you, my source got rolled up. Of course I'd be interested."

"You got a ride?"

"Right over there," gestured Sumner.

"It's going to cost you. Ten percent of the bag."

"Five," growled Sumner. "Let's go."

At Allen's direction, Sumner drove to a condominium complex on Judith Drive off Blossom Hill Road on San Jose's south side. Sumner parked on the street in front of 719.

"Give me $250. I'll be right back."

"Like hell," Sumner snarled. "I hand over that cash to you and I'll never see you again. We go together."

"I can't do that," Allen protested.

"That's the only way this is going to happen," Sumner explained. "If this guy is on the level, you're out, but you take half the bag today."

Allen's eyes widened at the prospect of a grubstake of half a quantity of acid just for the introduction to his supplier. "Let's go," chirped Allen.

The door was answered by a medium height, blond haired man in his early twenties. A heavy odor fresh marijuana waffled from the residence.

"Who's this?" the man demanded. "Why didn't you call first?"

"This is Les. We have the same PO," Allen explained. "He's in need of a quantity."

The young man looked Sumner up and down with undisguised chariness.

"He's OK," Allen assured. "We've run together for a long time. He's cool."

"Just don't ever come over here without calling first," warned the young man. "And don't ever bring anyone over here that I don't know." He opened the door to allow entry.

"I'm sorry about that, man. I thought he had already greased things. I didn't know he'd dummied out. …Totally un-cool. My apologies man," Sumner effused.

"Awww, that's cool. Mark," he extended his hand.

"Les," Sumner shook his hand. "What's all this shit?" Sumner inquired about the pots of liquid and bricks of marijuana on the living room floor.

"Making hash oil," Mark explained. "You can put a few drops on a regular cigarette and smoke it like a joint. The bulls will never detect it."

"No shit," Sumner marveled. "Amazing. Can I get some of that when it's ready?"

"Here, let me know how you like it," said Mark, handing Sumner a small vial of a brown oily substance.

"We need a quantity of the purple haze," Allen interjected.

"$200," announced Mark. Sumner shot a dirty look at Allen who shrunk in obvious guilt at being caught high balling the deal.

Sumner produced the cash and indicated for Mark to hand the merchandise to Allen. Allen opened the plastic bag and began to count out fifty tablets.

Mark glanced quizzically at Sumner. "We're partners on this deal."

Allen finished counting out fifty tablets and handed the bag to Sumner. *Thank you very much. Two buys for the price of one.*

"So, do you make this stuff yourself?" asked Sumner.

"Naw, this is quality stuff. I get it from a chemist we call the Professor."

"Wow. See you again," said Sumner. "Oh, you want me to call first?"

"Sure," answered Mark writing the phone number on a piece of paper.

CHAPTER 55

"Y ou're up early," ribbed Nails. "Got a guilty conscience?"

"Lots to do today," said Sumner, handing his reports and evidence out the car window to his Sergeant seated in his car.

"That was a pretty good day's work yesterday. The Boss thinks you can do things like that anytime."

"Great, do I get a bonus?"

"Only the satisfaction of knowing that you have served your city with distinction," joked Farnsworth. "We broke down your daily report last night. David Allen is an ex-con, burglar, and small time dope dealer. But his older brother is Andreas Petersen, a real heavyweight. He did time in Oregon for kidnapping, robbery, and attempted murder. It seems he kidnapped a Gemco store manager from his home, took him to the store at gunpoint, made him open the safe and cleaned it out, then took the manager out on a remote road, shot him and left him for dead."

"He's a real saint," Sumner mused.

"Well, he's out of prison and living in San Jose. Be cautious if you run across him."

"I am always cautious."

"The other guy is Mark Stithe. He's a real up and comer. Very smooth. We haven't been able to get anywhere near him."

"Well, now you got him."

"He gets his LSD from an actual chemist they call the Professor. He apparently used to be a college chemistry professor, but we don't have many details, just unverified intel."

"I will, as always, find out what I can. I'll get another buy off Charlie James tomorrow and then we can hand that thing entirely off to Jonesy and the Majors."

"McCrory called yesterday, wants to know why he hasn't seen you lately."

"Yeah, I'm going to meet with him later today. I just got busy with all the other stuff."

"The Boss wants to see some action on Swearengen and Campi."

"Tell him I'm on it."

"Looks like your hands are feeling better."

"The doc took the splints off, but I still can't workout or lift anything heavy. The road rash is a lot better though. I went to the range the other day and could actually shoot accurately."

"Well, watch yourself out there and keep your head out of your ass if you run across Petersen," warned Farnsworth.

§

Sumner drove to the apartment building where he had dropped off Dave Allen the previous day. He pulled into a vacant lot next to the apartments on Merrill Drive off Camden Avenue and parked. He then proceeded to the carport area where Allen was working on the engine of his 1968 Buick. Allen looked up with a start. His face then broke into a broad smile.

"Hey, man, what's going on?"

"Nada," Sumner replied. "Just chillin until the action starts."

"You got something going?"

"Not until later today, thought I'd see what you were up to."

"Give me a ride over to my mother's. I got to pick up a spark plug puller."

"Let's go."

§

At Allen's direction, Sumner drove to a residence located about a mile away on Dartmouth Drive across from Dartmouth Middle School. There were three adult males standing on the front lawn as they pulled up. Allen alighted from the vehicle and greeted all three, then turned to Sumner.

"This is my brother Andreas."

Sumner shook his hand. *He doesn't look like much. Five foot six, 135 pounds, glasses, high squeaky voice.*

"Wes," Said Allen.

Sumner shook the hand of Weston Campi. *Tall, athletic build, deep voice, long straight brown hair, quite formidable. Well this fortuitous encounter will make insertion into that case much simpler when the time comes.*

"And this is Brandon, the Crystal King." *Medium height and build, long coarse hair.*

"Shut up, Dave," warned Brandon punching Allen on the shoulder.

"What? He's all right. We've done hundreds of deals together. We have the same PO."

Andreas' eyes rolled. "You haven't done a hundred deals in your whole life, you poop butt. What the hell do you want?"

"The spark plug puller."

"You still trying to get that piece of shit to run?" asked Andreas, turning toward the garage.

Sumner and Allen followed Andreas into the garage as Wes and Brandon departed. Upon entering the garage Sumner noticed a double bed mattress made up on the floor, a dresser against the wall, and small television on the dresser.

"You live in here?" asked Sumner.

"It's better than living inside with my mother. It's just till I get back on my feet. I got a few things cooking." He handed Allen the spark plug puller.

"No, it's cool," Sumner replied. It's better than some of the shithole places I had to live in when I was in the army."

Andreas eyed Sumner warily. "What are you on parole for?"

Sumner rolled his eyes back. "Non support...ok." Failure to pay spousal support was the standard answer given by ex-cons who generally didn't like to discuss their record.

"Of course," Andreas smirked, laughing to himself.

"Of course." *He knows the drill.*

Sumner and Allen departed and returned to the carport where Allen went to work on his vehicle.

"What's the story with your brother?" Sumner inquired.

"He's a fucking genius. I've never met anyone as smart as him. But don't get on his bad side. He can be very dangerous."

"He says he's got something cooking. You think it's anything we can get in on?"

"Naw, you and I do drugs…he's into things like taking down banks and armored cars and shit like that."

"I dunno, bigger risk, bigger score. Keep me informed, I may want in."

"I'll let Andreas know, but it's entirely up to him."

"What's Wes's deal?"

"Absolute fucking badass. Completely out of his mind. His parents left him a house that's right behind the Willow Glen businesses on Lincoln Avenue. Big Victorian. He's into some heavy shit. Nobody to mess with."

"What about Brandon?"

"You sure are curious," Allen replied warily.

"Just bored. Thought I'd sharpen my interpersonal skills by learning about those people with whom I am engaging in social intercourse."

Allen looked up quickly with a mixed expression of bewilderment and disdain. His face then slowly cracked into a huge smile as he unleashed bellicose peels of uproarious laughter. "Well, la de-da …aren't you society's child." As he continued in uncontrollable laughter, Sumner joined in for a good belly laugh.

"I gotta get going," Sumner said. "I'll catch up with you later."

§

Sumner drove to the Valley Fair Shopping Center parking lot where he had previously arranged to meet with Confidential Informant Robert

McCrory. McCrory was waiting near the entrance to Macy's Department store.

"Let's grab something to eat," Sumner said as he pulled up. McCrory climbed in and Sumner drove down the street to the Doggie Diner for a hot dog with onions and a soda.

"I met Campi this morning."

"How, where?"

"Just by chance. Passing intro. It will be much easier now when you take me in."

"Well, it's time for you to meet Butch Swearengen," McCrory warned. "I told him I would be bringing you by his place this evening."

"And?"

"He said no fucking way! He said not to bring you by until he can check you out. But you're going to have meet him sometime."

"Tonight's not good," Sumner pondered. "Can you put it off till tomorrow evening?"

"There's nothing to put off! He doesn't want to meet you!"

"Good. Then we'll go by tomorrow night when he isn't expecting anything. Far less chance of getting our heads shot off."

"Yeah…great," McCrory shook his head.

Sumner drove McCrory back to Macy's and dropped him off. "See you here tomorrow about 5:00."

3:30 PM. Time for a squeeze play. Sumner drove back to Allen's apartment. Dave was sitting at the top of the stairs, smoking a joint, hands covered with grease from his day's work.

"Dave, I've got a deal going down in an hour and a half. I found out the guy is totally into crystal. You gotta help me find Brandon so I can score some to gift to this guy to schmooze my way in."

"He just lives three doors down from my mother. Come on, we'll go over right now."

Keep talking. Information overload. Don't let him ask any questions or start to think. Just keep talking. "This deal could be big, Dave. If it works out the way I hope, I'll bring you in on it. We could be farting in silk underwear."

§

Sumner pulled up in front of the house Allen indicated. As they exited the vehicle, Brandon came to the front door. "How much crystal you holding?" Allen demanded. "This man has business and he needs drugs to smooth the deal."

"I've got eight joints is all," Brandon explained. "But it's rocket fuel."

"Rocket fuel?" Sumner looked perplexed.

Allen looked at Sumner with an expression of satisfaction that he would now have the opportunity to be the teacher. "Rocket fuel is when you dissolve the PCP in vodka and then sprinkle it on marijuana instead of parsley," he explained. "It will fuck your head up to the max."

"Haven't you got a gram?" Sumner asked Brandon. "This guy is big time."

"I never hold more than a gram at a time."

"Well, who do you get your grams from?"

"Andreas!" answered Brandon and Allen simultaneously.

Andreas. And that will be a case for another day. He must be approached with a little more caution than is required with a light weight like Brandon.

"Alright, I'll take all the KJ you got."

Sumner kept talking on the drive back to Allen's apartment. Finally Dave got a word in edgewise. "Why didn't you want to just go score a gram from Andreas?"

"You said he was nobody to cross. He just met me today and might be a little uncomfortable around me. I figure if this works out tonight, you can grease the way for me later."

"Good thinking. He probably would have freaked anyway."

"Gotta go. See ya."

Sumner drove to a phone booth where he called in his daily report while it was still fresh in his mind. He then called Sergeant Farnsworth to check in and update him on the day's activities.

"Dammit, be careful around Petersen. I've been reading the details of his robbery/attempted murder case. He's cold blooded."

"Well, he sure ain't much to look at. If he was a trout, I'd have to throw him back."

"Yeah, well with a gun in his hand, he's a real big man. And he's not afraid to use it." "You calling it a day?"

"I'm going to get another buy on Stithe. Then I'll call it a night."

"Call me when you're finished," ordered Nails.

§

"Mark? It's Les," Sumner spoke into the handset of the pay phone.

"Yeah, man, what do you need?" asked Stithe.

"Well, I don't know if you can help me, but my buddy and I are going to the drive-in with a couple of honeys...and, well...they want some coke."

"How much do you need?"

Sumner spoke as if conversing with someone outside the phone booth. "How much do we need? Well, ask them. Just a minute Mark," he said into the receiver. "A quarter ounce? A QUARTER OUNCE?! Shit." Sumner spoke back into the receiver. "Mark, it looks like we need a quarter ounce."

Stithe chortled into the phone. "You got a couple of real coke whores there. Come on over. I got you covered."

Sumner drove to the Judith Drive condominium and parked around the corner. He then walked to the residence of Mark Stithe and knocked softly on the door.

Stithe opened the door and gestured for Sumner to enter. "I'm sorry, man. I don't know if this is your thing or not, but these chicks are hot and they want coke, and I didn't know who else to call," Sumner rambled.

Stithe laughed out loud. "No problem man. Anything you want, you come to me."

"No shit? Anything."

"Except heroin. I don't mess with that stuff."

"Right on! Me neither."

Stithe dangled a plastic bag filled with white powder in front of Sumner's face. "Five hundred...I hope they're worth it."

Sumner handed over five $100 bills. "Oh, they're worth it. You should see the body on mine."

"Good luck man," Stithe closed the door behind Sumner.

Now I will call it a night.

CHAPTER 56

"I just got the call from Speedy James," Sumner informed Farnsworth. "The Dew Drop in at 3:00." The Dew Drop Inn was a small bar located on the edge of a residential neighborhood just across the San Jose border in the city of Campbell.

"That's a favorite hangout for the Hell's Angels," Farnsworth pondered. "Anything smell fishy to you?"

"No, but I will be careful. I want to get this done and hand it off to the Majors."

"Just don't get sloppy. You want cover?"

Sumner was suddenly seized by feelings of mortality. For an instant, his confidence vanished. He doubted his abilities and felt wholly inadequate to the task. *What the hell is wrong with me? If anyone needs cover, it's that emaciated little asshole.* "No, I'll be fine."

"Get your ass back here when you're done. I need you to help me finish the report officially closing out this investigation so we can hand it off."

"10-4," Sumner answered.

Farnsworth's face went ashen. "You better loose that shit right now!" Using police radio codes while engaged in an undercover operation is a quick way to get killed.

"Sorry," Sumner explained. "It just popped out."

Farnsworth's eyes burrowed into Sumner's with an intensity that be-spoke the gravity of what he was about to say. "From this moment forward, nothing just pops out. You don't open your mouth until you have carefully considered exactly what you are about to say. Think about the ramifications of every fucking word you are about to utter. You've come a long way. Don't get yourself killed when you are about to bring this thing across the finish line."

"Sorry. I don't know what happened. I'm totally focused. That will never happen again."

"For your sake I hope it doesn't."

What the hell is wrong with me? I never make mistakes like that. Focus, man, focus.

§

Sumner drove to the Dew Drop Inn on Woodard Road in Campbell and pulled into the parking lot. Across the street, and three doors down was 385, was the home his parents lived in when he was born.

He spotted James near the front door of the tavern talking with two men. James glanced in Sumner's direction and gestured for him to come over. *Shit, that's just what I need to complicate things.*

James shook hands with Sumner and proceeded to introduce his companions. "This is Dan," Sumner shook the hand of "Dirty Dan Bannister, Sergeant at Arms for the Hell's Angels. "And this is Larry," Layton Greene Jr; Secretary of the Hell's Angels. *Greene' father had been one of my sergeants when I was a deputy in the jail. Well, Speedy does not traffic with light-weights. Now what???*

"We got to do some business," James informed his companions. "I'll be with you in a second." *Thank god he didn't invite me in. The last place I want to be is undercover in the company of a bunch of drunk Hell's Angels.*

James walked slowly toward Sumner's vehicle. "They want to inspect that hardware your buddy has for sale."

"He's off flying somewhere. I'll pin him down when he gets back next week."

James casually slipped a plastic bag containing methamphetamine into Sumner's hand. *This guy is slick.* Sumner reciprocated with ten $100 dollar bills. James then opened Sumner's car door for him. "How is this stuff working out?"

"It has been very well received."

"Good, very good. Let me know when you need more. And get that fucking meeting set up."

"Will do." Sumner pulled out onto Woodard Road heading toward Union Avenue as he heaved a heavy sigh of relief. *Uneventful, good…no, great.*

CHAPTER 57

Confidential informant McCrory was waiting when Sumner pulled up in front of Pete's Steak House on North First Street across from the county welfare office.

"So what's the plan? Sumner asked.

"Well, it's your call. Swearengen told me not to bring you over."

"Then I guess he'll just get an early Christmas surprise."

"Whatever, man. He's going to be pissed at me, but he is going to be totally out of his mind paranoid about you."

"Let's go see what we get."

§

Sumner drove, at McCrory's direction, to a small residence on Coastland Drive between Curtner Avenue and Bird Avenue. These were spec homes built prior to World War II and the subsequent housing development boom.

"This is where Tommy died." McCrory's explanation was tinged with anger. He was referring to his friend's younger brother who choked to death as a result of an overdose of heroin. That tragedy was the reason that drove McCrory to enlist as a confidential informant for the San Jose Police Narcotic Unit.

"Is this Swearengen's pad?"

"Not all the time. Some chick he sees. He shacks up with her some of the time but made himself scarce when that all happened."

"How did the girlfriend explain to the cops the dead body in her living room?"

"She said that she had had a party for some friends. She said some people showed up that she did not know but were friends of some of her guests. She told them that after everyone left she noticed this guy passed out at the end of the coffee table. She said she thought he was just drunk but when she tried to get him to leave she couldn't wake him up. That's when she realized he had OD-eed."

"And the cops bought that story?"

"Apparently you guys don't get too interested in an overdose by a known addict," McCrory sneered sarcastically.

True enough.

Sumner and McCrory approached the front door and knocked. No response. McCrory knocked again. After a brief period, the door slowly opened. Sumner could see the right side of Butch Swearengen's face peaking around the door. Swearengen swung the door open and turned his back, walking into the living room of the residence. McCrory looked to Sumner for direction. Sumner shrugged his shoulders and entered the residence.

Sumner stood five feet from Swearengen, who still stood with his back to the two men. Suddenly, without warning, Swearengen swung around bringing a semiautomatic pistol to bear. *32 Auto, Saturday night special. What an amateur.*

"What the fuck man? I told you not to bring anyone over here, you little fuck," screamed Swearengen, eyes bloodshot and bugging out like a wild beast.

"Everything's cool," assured McCrory. "This is Les. He's my partner."

"I don't give a fuck *who* he is. I told you never to bring anyone over here," screeched Swearengen, swinging the pistol back and forth between Sumner and McCrory.

"Hey, man, I appreciate that you're cautious, but I'm just here to do a little business," Sumner tried to calm the increasingly hysterical man. By now in his career Sumner had become immune to the paranoid response of drug dealers that he encountered uninvited.

"Shut...the...fuck...up...asshole," screamed Swearengen, face red with frenzied madness as he brought the pistol up to Sumner's head and holding it with his wrist bent poked the barrel into Sumner forehead as he pronounced each syllable of his command.

This is getting to be a habit, fumed Sumner, fighting his own growing rage.

"Fuck this...," Swearengen raged, "I've had enough. You're both dead!"

At that instant, Sumner dropped into a crouch below the muzzle of the pistol as both of his hands shot up with blinding speed, grabbing the barrel of the pistol, bending it rapidly back as it discharged into the ceiling, prying it from the hands of Butch Swearengen.

Swearengen's expression changed from one of crazed anger to sudden abject terror as he reeled backwards away from the gun wielding Sumner. "Please man...don't shoot. I was just trying to get a little respect for my privacy. I wasn't going to shoot anyone. Please man."

Sumner pointed the gun at the cowering Swearengen. "I just got back from a year and a half in combat. I'm tired of being shot at and having guns stuck in my face. So please don't do that again."

Swearengen's face was now covered with tears as his shaking hands wiped his red eyes. "I'm sorry man, no problem. Would you please just set the gun down?"

Sumner tossed the gun onto the coffee table. "I'm here because I heard you got the best junk around and I need to take care of my buddies."

"I know, I know," explained the still hyperventilating Swearengen. "Robert laid the whole thing out to me."

"Then why the fuck did you pull a rod on me?"

"Like I told Robert, I wanted time to check you out. And he needs to respect my crib."

"Well, here I am. What do you want to know?"

"Nothing, man, nothing. I already checked you out," stammered Swearengen. "You're cool."

"Oh, for the love of god, man," Sumner railed. "Then what was all this crap all about?" demanded Sumner as he tapped his forehead where the barrel of the gun had struck him. Then he turned away in disgust.

"It's about respect." The answer was almost a whine.

"Really?" asked Sumner indignantly as he whirled back to face Swearengen who had rearmed himself with the pistol and was again pointing it at Sumner.

"That's right, asshole."

"Well, then, teach me some respect," challenged Sumner as he walked slowly toward Swearengen. "Give me a lesson in manners."

Swearengen's hand convulsed as he desperately tried to pull the trigger, but unfortunately for him the weapon was jammed. The shadow of uncontrollable fear again swept across Swearengen's face as Sumner slowly placed his hand on the barrel of the pistol and pried it gently from Swearengen's shaking hands. He then jacked the slide, discharging the jammed round, and fired a shot into the ceiling.

"I was holding the slide when you fired the first round," Sumner explained. A semiautomatic will always jam when the action of the slide is interrupted... dickhead."

Sumner then turned to McCrory. "You're friend here has tried to shoot me...twice. I think it's my turn to shoot him. What do you think?"

"No, man, don't shoot him. He's cool. He was just a little upset with me for bringing you here when he told me not to."

"Yeah. I'm cool. I didn't mean anything."

"Shut the fuck up, you little weasel. You just tried to shoot me. And I told you I'm tired of people trying to shoot me. I want to shoot somebody."

As McCrory pleaded on behalf of Swearengen, Sumner detected the wafting smell of human feces. *He shit his pants. The badass Butch Swearengen really is a "bad" ass now.* Sumner was amused. *Aw what the hell am I laughing at? This guy just tried to kill me.*

Sumner removed the magazine from the pistol and jacked out the chambered round. Placing the bullets in his pocket, he then field stripped the pistol and placed the components of the disassembled weapon on the coffee table.

"Come on, Robert," Sumner called. "We'll come back when Mr. Butch is feeling more hospitable."

§

As they drove off, McCrory rolled down the window and hung out his head. "I thought we were both dead. Stop the car. I'm going to be sick."

Sumner turned onto Pine Avenue and pulled up at River Glen Park. McCrory stepped from the vehicle and began to vomit onto the lawn. When he finished puking, he reentered the vehicle and Sumner drove on.

"Feel better now?" Sumner asked.

"How the fuck did you know the gun was jammed?!"

"That's the kind of stuff they teach you in the Army," Sumner explained. "It doesn't take much interruption of the action of the slide to prevent the next round from seating properly. When I grabbed the gun from Butch and it went off, I felt the slide barely move. I knew it hadn't cycled. Lucky thing it was only a popgun of a 32 or we would have had the whole neighborhood calling the cops."

"Shit…shit, shit, shit, shit, shit," groused McCrory. "And where did you learn to move like that?"

"Robert, all the cops know how to move like that," explained Sumner thinking that it couldn't hurt to unleash a little fear into the criminal community. "I better get you something to eat and take you home."

When he arrived home, Sumner speculated on the advisability of describing the evening's events in his report. If the report makes its way to certain powers that be, it may be decided that Swearengen is too much a danger to the public to be left at large, and they may decide to have him arrested and prosecute on this case, which would bring the entire investigation, including Jonesy's, to an abrupt halt. On the other hand, two firearm rounds had been discharged. One, by Sumner intentionally. *Better write a painstakingly thorough and detailed report.*

CHAPTER 58

"The Boss wants you in here, now!" Farnsworth demanded.

"I'll be there at two, after my workout."

"Now, God-Dammit."

He's not fooling around. The Boss must be pissed. So much for writing detailed reports.

Sumner responded directly to PAB, this time parking his vehicle in the area reserved for the Street Enforcement Team near the Patrol Unit entrance, and hurried up to the Narcotic Unit.

Bertotti, standing at the door to his office, indicated for Sumner to get his ass inside. "Nails!" Bertotti yelled.

As Sergeant Farnsworth entered the office, Bertotti slammed the door and wheeled toward Sumner. "Who the fuck do you think you are...the Lone Ranger?"

"I don't get it. Thornton pulls a gun on me. I play it cool and you get pissed. Swearengen pulls a gun on me and I cop a move and you get pissed. I don't know what the hell you want me to do."

"Don't give me that crap. You gave a loaded gun back to a suspected murderer. What kind of a cowboy trick is that?"

"The gun was jammed."

"You couldn't know that for sure. That was pretty damned dumb! No, it was stupid, and exceedingly irresponsible—irresponsible to the Department, to the Unit, and to your family. You think I want to have to be the one to tell your wife that her kids are orphans and she is a widow because her idiot husband got himself killed showboating like some kind of god-damned Wild West show cowboy?" The veins in Bertotti's forehead and neck were bulging, and his face was flushed. Sumner had seen his Boss angry before, but never red faced with fury.

"Boss, I felt the slide stall when the gun went off. I knew it had not seated another round."

"Yeah, well, did you know for sure when you handed him the damn pistol that he did not know how to clear a jam? Huh, Einstein?"

I guess that was pretty arrogant assuming that he was that ignorant.

Knowing he would be unable to formulate an explanation that would be acceptable to the Boss, Sumner stood red faced and contrite.

"Well, at least everything worked out OK," Sumner finally offered.

Bertotti looked up from his desk as his anger turned to rage. *Maybe I shouldn't have said anything.* The Boss stood and charged around the desk to confront Sumner directly. "What did you say? Exactly what did you say?"

Sumner shrugged his shoulder and looked at the floor.

"Give me your badge," Bertotti screamed.

"But I don't carry a badge when I'm working."

"Give me your goddamned badge!" screamed the Boss, spit flying from his mouth onto Sumner's face. "You're going home. For three days. You're going home for the next three days and you are going to spend time with your wife and kids, and you're going to think about the conse-quences of actions like what you pulled last night."

"What about these investigations?"

Bertotti turned as he was returning to his chair and the rage began to boil up again. Farnsworth grabbed Sumner by the arm and pulled him through the doorway as the Boss charged, stopping just short of the exit. "Home! Make sure that asshole goes home," he yelled at Nails.

"You really do not know when to shut up, do you?" Farnsworth said to Sumner.

"I'm rolling, what the hell am I supposed to do?" Sumner replied.

"Here's what you are going to do. Just exactly what the Boss told you to do. That's what you're going to do. Go home, unwind, take it easy, play with your kids, make love to your wife, get drunk, watch reruns of 'The Three Stooges,' and think about how close you came to losing it all."

"My wife won't make love to me while I'm dirty," Sumner whined. Dirty was the designation given members of the detective bureau who have grown long hair and beards in order to conduct undercover operations. Sumner's wife detested this departure from the clean cut college boy she had married.

Farnsworth stopped and grabbed Sumner by his jacket lapels and pulled him up on his toes and looked him in the eye nose to nose. "You just can't get your head out of your ass, can you? You don't see the big picture. Either that or you are biggest smartass we have ever had on this department," Farnsworth hissed through clinched teeth. "You are the first San Jose Officer to ever work unsupervised deep undercover in the history of this department. The Boss sold the Chief on this program and on you personally as the operative, although how I can't imagine. If you get yourself killed pulling these idiot cowboy tricks, it will end the program, probably end any officer conducted undercover operations by this department ever again, and it will most certainly end the Boss's career." Farnsworth released his grip on Sumner's jacket, and Sumner settled back onto his feet. "So quit being such an asshole and go home and get your head straight." Farnsworth turned in disgust and headed back to the Narcotic Unit.

Red faced, Sumner shook his head and headed down the hall toward the elevator. The crowd of detectives from the Burglary Unit who had gathered to observe the disturbance dispersed.

Sumner stopped at the pay phone just outside PAB and dropped a dime. *There was only one thing to do when everything is going to shit.* Schmidt, his partner from his Uniform Division days, answered the phone. He had obviously been sleeping. "Bar call. Bruni's Tap Room."

"Thirty minutes," answered Schmidt groggily.

CHAPTER 59

Sumner slid into the Naugahyde-lined booth at Bruni's and sat in silence just looking at the wet rings the waiting beers had made on the tabletop. As the muscles in his shoulders began to relax, he made a sarcastic toast, downed a brew, and engaged his old partner in some jovial conversation about the good old days. Soon it seemed as though it was only a few weeks ago when they were working patrol tearing up the Eastside on midnight shift. They had a few more drinks and reminisced about some of the spectacular cases they had made. Then they had a few more drinks. Several other officers arrived, and a rollicking good time was had by all.

Sumner arrived home about midnight, feeling much better about matters. He opened another beer and sat down to watch television. "The Thing," about a creature from another world starring James Arness as the creature was just coming on. *Great movie.*

§

"Hey, man, haven't seen you in a while," Dave Allen greeted Sumner looking up from the engine of his Buick.

"I was just laying low for a few days," Sumner explained.

"After the shit that went down with Swearengen, I'm not surprised. What the hell were you doing trying to buy heroin?" asked Allen.

304 · *Sumner and Crenshaw*

"Just trying to take care of some of my buddies and make a little money on the side."

"Butch is wrapped about as tight as a mashed potato sandwich," Dave explained.

"How did you hear about it?"

"His old lady was in the kitchen and heard the whole thing," Allen explained. "Butch was so humiliated by how you handled him that he beat the shit out of her after you left. She came to Wes to get some money to leave town. She's had enough of Butch."

"Yeah, well, I've had about enough of Butch myself. I'm still trying to put this other caper together. You talk to Andreas about getting some grams?"

"He said no problem. You can get all you want from Brandon."

"Except, Brandon is high balling me. I'd like to eliminate the middleman."

"That's what *you* are...a middleman," Allen cracked.

"Yeah, so I know what rip offs middlemen are."

They both laughed. "After he gets to know you a little better, he'll probably deal direct."

"Do you know where Brandon is? I need to pick up a gram for tonight?"

"I'll go over there with you," Dave offered.

When they arrived on Dartmouth Drive, Sumner noticed Petersen and Campi on the front lawn of Petersen's mother's house, talking with an adult female. "Ah, my sister's home," Allen remarked.

"Home? Where's she been?" Sumner inquired.

"Locked up."

Sumner parked across the street by the school and approached the house where he was greeted at the front door by Brandon. Allen proceeded down the street to his mother's house while Sumner concluded the transaction with Brandon. Upon completion of the purchase, Sumner walked slowly and cautiously down the street to join Allen.

As Sumner approached, he observed Campi watching him closely. The smile on Campi's face grew wider as Sumner got closer. Suddenly he grabbed Sumner around the neck and hugged him roughly. "You believe this guy? Making poor Butch shit his pants. We're going to call this guy Exlax," Campi laughed as Petersen shook his head.

"He shouldn't be sticking guns in people's faces. Didn't his mama teach him any manners?" Sumner asked.

"He's a little rough around the edges. Likes to intimidate people," Campi explained. "I guess he misjudged his target this time. Hey, he wants to know if you can stop by and show him how to put his gun back together." Campi and Petersen howled with laughter as Allen clapped Sumner on the back.

"Well, I got no hard feelings," Sumner attempted to schmooze.

"I'm not sure Butch feels the same way. He was pretty embarrassed."

"As long as he doesn't stick a gun in my face, we'll be fine."

"He won't do that again. This time he'll stick it in the back of your head and pull the trigger. I'd watch out if I were you."

"Thanks for the advice," Sumner said. "So I guess he is not going to be a reliable source of junk for me."

"No, I don't think so. What do you want with that shit, anyway?"

Sumner laid out the story about his friends getting hooked while serving in Viet Nam. "I figured I could make a little money supplying them with safe dope and keep them out of trouble."

Campi stared into Sumner's eyes. "Come by and see me tonight. Nine o'clock."

§

Sumner arrived at Campi's house at 8:57 p.m. It was located off an alley behind the upscale Willow Glen businesses located on Lincoln Avenue. A large Victorian built in the 1890s when Willow Glen was a separate city located southwest of San Jose and separated by a bog of willow trees and artesian wells that sprung up regularly. The City of Willow Glen had since been completely surrounded by the ever growing San Jose, and in 1938 was finally annexed as part of the City of San Jose. Willow Glen, however, had retained its unique identity as an affluent interurban community nestled completely within the San Jose city limits.

Sumner knocked on the door. The door was opened by Dave Allen's sister. *This is interesting.* "I'm here to see Wes," Sumner explained.

"Come on in, Exlax," called Campi from the kitchen.

Sumner followed Allen's sister into the kitchen. Wes was seated at the kitchen table, a bowl of light brown power, a scale, plastic bags, and colored balloons before him. "How much do you figure you're going to need here?"

"I figured an OZ to get started. Make sure they like it and are going to buy more before I invest a lot of money."

Campi measured out a quantity of the power into a plastic bag and placed it on the scale.

"One ounce." Campi handed him the bag as a smirk crawled across his face. "I just can't get over old Butch crapping his pants. You must have really put the fear of god in him." Campi shook his head as he looked down while stifling a laugh.

Sumner paid him and got up to leave. He turned to the woman. "You're Dave's sister."

"Half sister," was her husky voiced response.

"Les," Sumner extended his hand.

"Mary. Nice to meet you."

"Thanks, Wes, I'll get back to you." Sumner departed.

How could that go so smooth and Swearengen was such a disaster?

§

"Looks like the time off didn't hurt. Nice clean buy off of a heavyweight supplier, no theatrics," Farnsworth finished reading Sumner's report.

"Yeah, just think what I could do if you guys would send me to Hawaii for a week or two."

"Do you think you're going to be able to get a buy on Petersen?"

"I dunno. He's paranoid as hell and very cautious. Give me a couple of weeks."

"Take your time. Jonesy is up and running on his operation, so we got a while before they'll be ready to wrap it up."

"Is the Boss still pissed?"

"He's pretty much over it. Just don't …"

"Understood," Sumner acknowledged. "But that incident is what got me right into Campi."

"Yeah, well, find another way from now on." Farnsworth put his car into gear and drove off.

CHAPTER 60

"The purity report from the county crime lab confirms a three percent heroin composition," reported Bertotti.

A little weak. Well, that will give me a topic to discuss with him.

"Thanks, Boss, that's what I needed to know." Sumner hung up the pay phone, climbed into his vehicle and headed toward Allen's. *I need a little more G-2 on Campi.*

§

Dave Allen answered the door to his apartment, eyes red, the smell of marijuana drifting out the door. *He's stoned.*

"Come on in, man," offered Allen swinging the door wide. "You want to smoke some dope?"

"Sure." Sumner sat down on the sofa and took a drag off the joint that Allen handed him being careful not to let any of the intoxicating smoke into his lungs. "So what's the deal with Wes?"

"What do you mean?"

"The junk he sold me was weak. Some of the guys are complaining. They think I stepped on it before I sold it to them to make more money... I don't need that grief."

"Did you say anything to Wes?"

"No. I wanted to talk to you first. I don't know anything about him. And after what happened with Butch, I don't want to go tell the guy that he's selling shitty dope."

"Wes is nobody to fuck with. He runs a smooth operation. Lots of dope, lots of stolen property. He fences expensive jewelry, credit cards, furs…even stock certificates. He has a small army of rip offs who work the rich people homes in Willow Glen, Los Gatos, and Almaden. The dope is all delivered by his soldiers. Nobody comes to his house. It's all delivered, so no heat comes down on Wes or his crib."

"He had me pick up the dope at his house."

Allen's head snapped around. "That is very unusual. He generally won't let anyone around his house between 7:00 and 9:00 and then midnight to one. That's when his soldiers pick up the dope for delivery and bring back the stolen goods. He must trust you."

"Well, I'll talk to him tomorrow." Sumner left. *Maybe I'll have a look at the comings and goings occurring at Mr. Campi's.*

§

Sumner drove to the parking lot behind the Garden Theatre. It was located next to Campi's house. He parked on the far side of the lot next to the fence under a low hanging willow tree. He was hidden by darkness of the early fall evening. *All lights out. It looks like nobody's home.*

Sumner watched for about a half an hour. He stretched and reached for his keys. *Nothing happening …Might as well get going.* Suddenly he noticed movement near the front porch. Then, out of the gloom, another shadowy figure appeared. Over the next fifteen minutes, no less than a dozen individuals approached the house from out of the darkness, entered the pitch black house and left within minutes. No vehicles, no headlights, no noise. Unless someone knew what they were looking for, nobody would be aware of the evening's activities at the Campi household. *Interesting! Might as well see how this plays out.* Sumner remained on stakeout, watching the residence. *No lights, no movement.*

Just after midnight he detected movement again near the front of the house. As they had before, people quietly and stealthily entered the house and after a few minutes left just as inconspicuously. *He certainly has them well trained. No noise, nothing to upset the neighbors or draw suspicion. Smooth.*

Around one in the morning, the kitchen light came on for about fifteen minutes and then went out. An hour later the bedroom light upstairs came on for five minutes then went out, leaving only the eerie blue glow of the television. Weston had apparently retired for the evening. *Time to call it a night.*

Sumner drove home and entered his garage through the side door inside the gate to the backyard. There, in the garage, he undressed, placing his undercover clothing on hangers. Then he hung them on a nail on the side of his workbench. The clothes smelled bad from the cigarettes and marijuana to which he was exposed in the course of his daily activities. While a certain level of uncleanliness was expected, a daily washing and a springtime fresh odor would draw suspicion. Besides that, many of the dopers with whom he came in contact were suffering from hepatitis and syphilis. There was no way he would allow his family to be exposed to any of that sort of thing. He entered the house through the laundry room and stepped into the shower in the downstairs bathroom where he washed thoroughly. He threw on his robe and went to the kitchen and poured a glass of milk. After a couple of swallows, he grabbed the phone to call in his daily report.

Once his report was complete, he wearily climbed the stairs. Quietly, he adjusted the covers on each of his sleeping children, and then he succumbed to the call of his own bed and instantly fell into a deep sleep.

§

"You're going to do what?!" demanded Sumner's wife in dismayed shock.

"We're going to swim under the Golden Gate Bridge," replied Sumner casually.

"You're going to swim across the bay?!"

"Just the entrance-from San Francisco to the Marin side under the bridge."

"Are you out of your mind? Who's doing this with you?"

"Doc, Mike, Gene, and the other guys from the gym. It's a San Francisco Dolphin Club event. They do it every year. There will be about 100 people."

"You've gone completely mad. You are certifiably crazy. Don't you know you could get killed out there?"

"If it were that dangerous, they wouldn't hold this event every year. They have poop out boats to pick up the stragglers when the tide changes."

"When are you doing this craziness?"

"Tomorrow. They're picking me up at 6:00 a.m."

"You're nuts." She threw up her hands as she stomped out of the kitchen, shaking her head in disbelief. "My children have a lunatic for a father."

Sumner shook his head in bewilderment as he tried to comprehend his wife's reaction. As he exited the house, he could feel his mood shift from anticipation to self doubt.

§

He drove to the residence of Andreas Petersen and parked on the street. When he reached the door that led to the garage that served as Andreas' bedroom, he knocked three times.

"Who's there?" came the sleepy request.

"Les," answered Sumner.

A minute passed. "Come on in."

As Sumner entered, he observed Petersen in the semi-darkness standing next to the dresser clothed in only a tee shirt and boxer shorts.

"What do you need, man?"

"I'm looking for Wes. Do you know where he might be?"

"What do you want him for?" asked Petersen, obviously suspicious.

"We did some business the other day. The product was a little weak and I got some complaints. I want to find out if he can fix that."

Petersen mused for a moment. "Wes will be here in about a half an hour. You can wait if you want."

"That's cool, if you don't mind. You want some coffee? I'll go get it."

"Yeah, great," Petersen's answer had overtones of increased suspicion. Sumner left and returned ten minutes later with two black coffees. He knocked on the door.

"Who is it?"

"Les."

Ten, then fifteen seconds of silence. "Come on in."

Sumner opened the door with his shoulder and entered to find Petersen standing near the head of the bed, obviously concealing something behind his back. Sumner placed Petersen's coffee on the dresser. "I hope you like it black." As he turned back he noticed Andreas placing something under the pillow on the bed. *Pistol, revolver, heavy frame, 38 or 357.* Sumner proceeded to indifferently take a seat in one of three bean bag chairs on the floor at the foot of the bed. "So Dave tells me you did some time for a caper up in Oregon," Sumner inquired. "What was that all about?"

Petersen shook his head in mock disbelief. "Nonsupport. Same as you man." They both laughed.

"But in all seriousness," Sumner offered conversationally, "I would like to get Brandon out of the way. He's highballing me on the price of those grams."

"Well, that's working OK for right now," Petersen sidestepped the issue.

"Well, it's not working so well for my pocketbook," Sumner groused.

"What, you don't want to help out a struggling young businessman?"

"I don't intend to singlehandedly put his kids through college."

There was a knock at the door and Weston Campi barged in without waiting for acknowledgement. He started with surprise when he spotted Sumner.

"Hey, Exlax, how they hanging?" he extended his hand.

"All the way to the floor." Sumner crunched his hand with an intimidating grip.

Petersen stepped forward with smug nonchalance. "This man has a little problem with the product you provided a few days ago." It was a fat pitch down the middle of the strike zone. Peterson was obviously anticipating an entertaining reaction.

Wes's head snapped toward Sumner. "What's the problem?"

"The consumers have complained that it was weak," Sumner explained.

"Weak? What the hell, you didn't step on it, did you?"

"Hell no, I don't even know how to do that. They just complained that it was a bit off. Can you fix that?"

Campi stared at Sumner, intently searching for any indication of deception. Then his expression softened. "Well, we have to take good care of our soldier boys. Come by my place tonight at 9:00. Well fix it up."

"That's cool. I really appreciate that," Sumner smiled.

"Not a problem."

§

Sumner made his excuses and drove to the Valley Fair Shopping Center. There he picked up confidential informant Robert McCrory who waited impatiently in front of the entrance to Macy's Department Store.

"So what do you think? Should be give Swearengen a try?" Sumner inquired.

"It's up to you. But I wouldn't get my hopes up."

"What, you don't think he likes me?"

McCrory responded with a crooked smile. "If he won't sell to you, I'll take you to one of his outlets. She'll supply you."

"Who is it?"

"Some nutty bitch who just got out of a mental institution."

Sumner parked in front of the residence that had been the scene of the previous unpleasantness with Butch. The two men marched up to the front door and knocked. Then they rang the bell, waited for a moment and then knocked again. *He is either not home, not living here or simply does not want to see us.*

"Come on," Robert motioned with a jut of his jaw. "I'll take us in the back door."

He directed Sumner to drive to a four-plex of condominiums on Branham Lane. Sumner parked and they walked to the stairway in the rear of the building that led to the only upstairs unit. McCrory knocked on the door. After a half minute, the door opened part way, and a woman peaked around the edge.

"This is Les. He needs to do some business."

She opened the door and stepped back. They entered as she closed the door and turned. *Allen's half sister, Mary.*

She looked warily at Sumner, then asked "Why do you need to score from me? You're dealing directly with Wes."

Sumner sat on the sofa, looked her directly in her eyes and spoke earnestly. "I'm trying to take care of the needs of some of my army buddies who got a little strung out in combat. If they're looking to me as their sole source of supply, I need to have multiple sources. After what happened with Butch a couple of weeks ago, I don't know if I can count on Wes. Butch may talk him into cutting me off just for spite."

"You really scared the shit out of Butch."

"Literally," interjected McCrory.

"You know I get my junk from Wes."

"Yeah, and you know where Wes and Butch get their junk," Sumner explained. "We get things going and I steer all the business to you, then we bypass them and go straight to the man."

"He would never trust me." She stated matter-of-factly. "He knows I'm an addict."

"When we're moving enough product to make it worth his while, you'll introduce me," Sumner coaxed. "He deals directly with the money; money talks and you get 25 percent of the profit right off the top."

Mary sat, nodding her head, struggling to process the information. "That sounds good, but what about Butch and Wes?"

"Do you think they give a shit about you?" Sumner snarled. "They would throw you away like a used rubber."

Mary nodded in agreement. "How much do you need tonight?"

"A piece."

"I don't have that much," She explained. "I've got a quarter ounce."

"I'll take that and score the rest I need tonight from Wes," Sumner instructed. "You lay out to Wes that you are making a little money dealing on the side and buy a half ounce. See how he reacts. If he has no bitches, we'll take it from there." Sumner paid for the quarter ounce and handed her another $500 to purchase the dope from Campi. "I don't like cutting into another man's business, but we have an opportunity to make some money here and I've got to make sure I've got a reliable source for my friends."

Sumner and McCrory stood to leave. "And don't get your nose too far into that half ounce bag," Sumner warned. "I'll be by to pick it up tomorrow."

§

Sumner arrived at Campi's just after nine p.m. Wes opened the front door and waved Sumner in. As he stepped into the living room, Butch Swearengen entered from the kitchen.

"Now both of you be cool," ordered Campi.

Swearengen scowled at Sumner with the expression of scolded child. At Campi's direction Sumner followed him into the kitchen.

"How much stronger do you want this shit?"

"I don't know. They just said it was weak."

"Well, what do you want, twice as strong, three times, what?"

"I don't know. Two guys said it was all right, but that they didn't get a rush," Sumner explained. "Does that help?"

Campi nodded affirmatively. He removed a plastic bag from the refrigerator and handed it to Sumner. "Try this."

"Nobody's going to OD are they? These guys are my friends. We went through some shit together. I don't want anyone getting hurt."

"Awww," taunted Swearengen. "Are the big bad soldier boys going to get sick?"

"Shut the fuck up," ordered Campi. "This is just a little stronger than the normal street dope," he explained to Sumner. "I think they'll be happy with it."

"Cool," Sumner counted out the cash.

"Ahhh, that will be an extra hundred for the enhancement."

"No problem," Sumner said, then handed over an additional one hundred dollar bill.

He headed for the door, but Swearengen blocked his path, staring at

Sumner out of the corner of his eyes like a mad dog. Sumner stopped and waited for Butch to move out of the way. Swearengen stood his ground and began to breathe more heavily as the muscles in his jaw and neck tightened. *It's showtime. And I would so very much love to kick this prick's ass, but I gotta stay focused.* Sumner's right hand snapped quickly forward lightly striking Swearengen in the testicles with the second knuckles of his four fingers. Swearengen involuntarily buckled over, clutching his crotch with both hands as Sumner stepped indifferently around him and left the house. As the door closed behind him, Sumner could hear Campi's raucous laugh as he began to lecture Butch on the inadvisability of messing with certain people.

Sumner headed home where he completed his crime reports and locked them and his evidence in his gun safe. He retired early to bed in anticipation of the strenuous day to come.

CHAPTER 61

"The bay is about ten degrees colder than the ocean," explained Doc Meyer. "It is because of the snow runoff from the Sierras."

"I'm wearing a wetsuit," Sumner declared.

"No you can't. You'll look like a pussy," all in the car protested.

"The Polar Bear and Dolphin Club guys just swim in Speedos," Gene explained. "If any of us doesn't swim in just a Speedo, we all look like sissies."

It was grey and foggy as they gathered beneath the Golden Gate Bridge in front of Fort Point to begin the annual swim to Marin. *I'm half frozen already.*

At the sound of the whistle, approximately 100 swimmers dove into the frigid San Francisco Bay and began stroking toward the north. At approximately 300 feet from shore, Sumner realized that this was perhaps the coldest he had ever been. As he continued swimming, the tide slowly moved the swimmers to the ocean side of the bridge. *Half way across. A little back stroke to rest the shoulders.* Sumner looked up at the bridge and patch of blue sky that shown through the parting clouds. A seagull hovered near the south tower of the bridge. *Breathtakingly beautiful.*

As he turned back over onto his stomach and began swimming, he saw something move swiftly past him. *Oh shit!* Before he could position himself defensively, a harbor seal surfaced five feet to his right. Sumner let out the breath he had been holding, relieved that it was not a shark. He continued swimming as the seal swam along next to him, darting forward and crisscrossing in front of him. All of a sudden, the seal began to bark. *What the hell is that all about. This is a great white shark spawning ground. Great whites eat harbor seals and this asshole is sounding the dinner bell.* Sumner splashed at the seal to try to get him to shut up. "Get out of here. Shut the hell up!" The damn seal just kept barking. Sumner kept swimming. The current had now taken the swimmers about fifty yards past the bridge. Shore about 100 yards away. Sumner doubled his effort. *Thank god that damn seal is gone.*

As Sumner exited the water, he looked back. Several of the swimmers who were only about halfway across were being picked up by the poop out boats before the tide fully changed and the current accelerated through the narrows and swept them out to sea. One swimmer had drifted well past the bridge and was headed toward the point that jutted out just to the west. The fog had lifted, the sky was blue, and a brisk wind had kicked up. Sumner shivered involuntarily as he searched around for his workout partners. It suddenly dawned on him that he was mortal. *This effort played no essential role in my life; which I just risked for no reason at all. I will never do anything like this again.*

CHAPTER 62

Sumner parked in the Princeton Plaza parking lot and entered the video arcade located on the premises. Unexpectedly he encountered Mark Stithe playing video games and socializing with the local high school kids off campus during their lunch hour.

"What's the haps dude?" inquired Stithe.

"Just checking the scene," Sumner replied. "Qué pasa?"

"I'm looking after the customer base, that's all."

"These poopbutts?"

"These are rich kids. They have money and want what I can provide."

"I see…cool."

Sumner looked on with disgust as Stithe concluded a transaction with a Pioneer High School football player. The students then dispersed from the premises as the noon hour faded.

"So what else is happening?" Sumner inquired.

"I've got to go shopping…give me a ride," Stithe requested.

"No problem. Let's go," Sumner replied.

As he pulled out of the parking lot Sumner asked "Where to?"

"280 to DeAnza," Stithe replied.

"What are we after?" inquired Sumner.

"Stuff," responded Stithe.

Sumner followed directions from Stithe that led them to a remote location in the Rancho Rinconada area of the west side of the valley beyond the San Jose City limits. They arrived at an old home built in the late 1800's located off the main road that lead to the Kaiser Permanente Plant at the base of the foothills.

"Wait here," ordered Stithe as he exited the vehicle.

"Not a chance," replied Sumner as he followed the drug dealer.

As they arrived on the porch of the old home Sumner noticed a half dozen younger individuals sitting around a sofa as a bearded older man in his mid to late forties was speaking. Suddenly the man went silent as he noticed Stithe and Sumner.

"Hello?" he called.

His audience turned in unison to see the cause of their mentors sudden distraction.

"Mark!" called out an attractive young blond girl as she rose to greet the new arrivals. She kissed Stithe somewhat passionately on the mouth as she opened the screen door. "Who's this?" she asked, gesturing to Sumner.

"My partner Les, everything is cool," he replied.

The girl looked pensively back at the older man who, after a few seconds of contemplation nodded his approval. "Come on in," she invited, opening the screen door wider.

"Professor, glad to see you," Mark effused reaching to shake the hand of the elder man.

"Mark…who's your friend?"

"This is Les," he stated gesturing to Sumner. "He's a bit of a pharmacist himself." "Les, this is the Professor."

The Professor??? Could this really be the famous Professor? Sumner reached to shake his hand. *If this is the actual Professor we might be able to bring down the whole LSD trade in this town today.*

"So what's the haps?" Sumner asked.

"Primo pot," answered the Professor.

Pot? I thought this guy was all about LSD.

"Pot?" Sumner asked.

"The Professor grows the best pot in the world," a young admirer admonished. "He grows it in water without dirt."

"It's called hydroponics," interjected the Professor. "It enables me to infuse the plants with nourishments that are much more healthful and give you a better high."

"Wow, cool," Sumner feigned interest. "So can I score a couple lids?" *Might as well make a case one way or the other* he thought.

The Professor looked at his audience pensively. Sumner produced a roll of bills and began to peal off twenties. The Professor became suddenly interested at the appearance of cash and removed two plastic baggies filled with his primo pot from an ice cooler at his feet. Handing the marijuana to Sumner he received the cash from the officer.

"Thanks. I was really looking for something to trip on," Sumner said.

The Professor locked on Sumner's gaze, then looked slowly toward Stithe. Mark shrugged his shoulders and looked away.

"Maybe I can help you," he replied. "Have Mark give me a call next week."

"I need something tomorrow," Sumner pressed for a sale.

The Professor nodded his head as he turned away in silent contemplation. "Well, I won't have anything for a few days. Get with Mark and maybe we'll do some business next week."

"So where do you teach?" Sumner asked.

"DeAnza College."

"Cool, what discipline?"

"Chemistry."

Damn…he fits the profile…this may be the actual Professor of LSD fame.

"Chemistry? That was a tough subject. I didn't do well in Chemistry," Sumner replied.

"It's not for everyone."

"So you're a chemist. Do you make the acid yourself?" Sumner probed.

The Professor looked warily at Sumner. "Who said anything about acid?"

The Professor walked past Sumner and Stithe and out the front through the screen door. "Call me Monday," he said to Stithe. "If this guy is legit and well funded we might do some business."

As the Professor departed Sumner made a comprehensive study of the identifying characteristics of the man in order to later identify him should another meeting not come about. Mark Stithe apologized to the attractive blond girl for not having informed her that he would be coming by with another person with whom she was not acquainted.

"That's all right. He seems cool," she replied smiling at Sumner.

"Yeah, but I didn't know the Professor was going to be here."

"He seemed all right with it," she assured.

"OK, as long as everyone is cool," Stithe sighed.

§

Monday came and went. Sumner was never able to get Mark Stithe to commit to setting up a meeting with the Professor. Ultimately it was time to round up the drug dealers who had been the targets of this series of investigations and it had become abundantly clear that Sumner was not going to get another face to face encounter with the Professor before the mass arrests took place. One buy of marijuana would have to suffice. Perhaps Major Violators would be able to extract some vital intelligence after the arrests.

Lacking any information as to his place of residence, it was necessary for the Narcotic Unit Street Enforcement Team to arrest the Professor, on the authority of a Grand Jury Indictment obtained by Sumner, during his class time at De Anza College. The apprehension took place in front of his student body. The bearded professor was arrested, cuffed and lead away to the awaiting patrol car in front of his astonished class. Predictably, the College was enraged by the seeming callousness of the San Jose Police Department. Complaints were lodged, irate phone calls made; all of which brought collective smiles to the faces of the San Jose Police brass who were always pleased when a crime of such moral depravity as providing minors with drugs became high profile.

During the trial of The Professor, his wily attorney avoided alienating the jury. Instead of following the standard defense line of attacking the integrity and honesty of the undercover police officer, which tends to put juries off, he simply contended that Office Sumner had innocently committed a mistake in identifying his client as the individual from whom he had purchased the marijuana. Unfortunately for the Professor this defense was thoroughly demolished during cross examination by the District Attorney. Sumner first pointed out the distinctive identifying morphological characteristics of the Professor. He then read the meticulously detailed description of the suspect from his Criminal Report written on the day of the incident months earlier. Coincidentally one of the Administration of Justice classes that Sumner had taken during his time at San Jose State University had been "Criminal Identification" taught by a former FBI Forensics expert. Sumner, intrigued by the subject, bore down on his studies and had received an "A" in the class. The detail with which he had identified the Professor convinced the jury beyond a reasonable doubt that the this was indeed the man who had sold the marijuana to the undercover police officer.

The Professor was ultimately convicted of "sales of marijuana and sales of marijuana to a minor", but it was never definitively established as to weather this individual was, in fact, the notorious "Professor" of LSD fame. When it came to recreational drugs like LSD, restriction of supply had no noticeable affect on the crime rate in the same way that a shortage Heroin or Cocaine did. Disruption in the supply of those two underworld staples tended to cause a veritable crime wave as prices invariably rose as demand remained. Therefore it was impossible to determine if the arrest of this particular Professor had in anyway crippled the LSD trade in San Jose.

CHAPTER 63

"I talked to the man," explained Mary Petersen. "If you need that much, he said he'll give it to you uncut and you can step on it."

"No problem," Sumner assured. "When can you get the stuff?"

"Tonight."

"Where are we trippin' to?"

"You can't go with me."

"I go where the money goes."

"You're going to get me shot."

"Don't worry about it. Money talks. See you tonight."

§

Sumner drove to Dartmouth Drive and parked at the corner. The street looked deserted. He slowly approached and parked in front of Petersen's house. He took a stack of $20 bills and one $100 bill from his pocket and grasped it in his left hand. He then approached the door to the garage and knocked with his left hand.

"Who is it?" asked Petersen.

"Les," Sumner replied.

"Come on in."

Sumner slowly pushed the door open, with his left hand flaunting the cash. "I'm looking for Brandon; do you know where he is?"

As Sumner stepped into the garage, he fumbled the cash and dropped it on the floor. As he slowly picked up the bills one by one, he remarked to Andreas that he needed three grams of PCP but could not find Brandon.

"I don't know where he is. You still gifting that shit?"

"Actually I'm selling it. The guy is redistributing some it. He likes your stuff."

Petersen warily eyed the bills in Sumner's hand. *If he was a dog he'd be salivating.*

"You wouldn't happen to be able to cut loose with four or five grams would you," Sumner asked whimsically.

"Shi-i-it…all right," said Petersen as he removed a five pound coffee can from behind a shelf of tools. "Four or five?"

"Five if you've got them."

Sumner received the drugs as he handed the cash to the eager Andreas.

"Thanks, man. I'll see you later," remarked Sumner casually.

"Yeah, later," replied Petersen as Sumner exited.

§

"The city can't bankroll this sum," Bertotti explained. "We need to use the state's money. They're going to want in."

"I'm not even in," replied Sumner. "I don't know how this is going to go down."

"Rondal McGuire, a cagey old fox…the county has hit his place twice," Bertotti sighed. "Both times his high priced attorney got the search warrants suppressed."

"Look, Boss, my operation is pretty much done. We've got grand jury indictments on everyone except Swearengen, but his parole officer is willing to violate him based on my reports, which will put him away for five years. Why don't we buy-bust on this guy?" Sumner suggested. "That way the state will get a piece of the action and they'll get their money back to boot."

"Let's check with Jonesy and see how this is going to affect his operation," Bertotti replied.

Sumner went to get a cup of coffee from the pot located in the room that housed the Crime Scene Unit at the rear of the Narcotic Unit. The crime scene crew was screwing around with a new polygraph machine that they had just received. They had hooked up the electrodes to a potted rubber tree plant located next to the door.

"Hey, Sumner, watch this," called Sergeant Leroy. He walked up to the plant and violently tore leaf from a limb of the plant then exited the room.

"Now watch," said Sergeant Parrot, indicating to the graph as Sergeant Leroy sent first Detective Newton into the room. No change on the readings. Then detective Boone. No change. Then Leroy walked back in and toward the plant. The readings when wild. *Amazing, the plant recognized Leroy.*

"Sumner, get your ass in here," called Bertotti. "It's a go for tonight."

"I'll set it up for 9:00."

"MERGE," (the SJPD SWAT Team) "will be ready to start executing the warrants and indictments at 0500 tomorrow," Bertotti advised.

"We have 173 indictments and 44 warrants. Then there are six parole searches to be conducted," Sumner informed.

"It's going to be very busy around here the next few days," Farnsworth sighed.

"I'm headed over to the DA's Office to get a search warrant for McGuire's pad," Sumner explained. "It will make the search much more legal."

§

Assistant District Attorney John Meuser finished reading Sumner's affidavit and heaved a long sign. "This guy has been quite active...would you like to search?"

"Most assuredly," replied Sumner. "But the catch is we need it endorsed for night service."

Meuser looked up from his desk. "Are there any exigent circumstances that would necessitate night service?"

"We will be conducting a purchase of a large supply of uncut heroin by an unwitting informant, followed by an immediate arrest to recover the funds, which are substantial."

Meuser nodded his head thoughtfully. He called for a stenographer as he wrote two sentences on his legal pad, which he then handed to the steno asking in a polite Texas accent "Will you please prepare that immediately?"

"Not a whole lot there," Sumner observed in some dismay.

"Enough," assured Meuser. "An attached copy of your affidavit will provide all the substantiation required. Better for the judge to see what you have to say than for him to have to decipher what I say you said."

Brilliant, this guy is brilliant.

The search warrant was ready in less than ten minutes.

"Take this to Judge Markham. I'll call over and tell him you are on your way."

Sumner was back at the Narcotics Unit by 4:45 with a signed search warrant.

"Night service?" asked Bertotti incredulously. "You got this endorsed for night service?" "How the hell does he do that?" the Boss asked, as much to himself as to Sergeant Breuner, who walked with the Boss to his office.

§

Sumner allowed himself a satisfied smile as he hung up the Bat Phone. He had just successfully taped his conversation with Mary Petersen. It was the final preparation for the evening's transaction. He marked and booked the tape, then hurried to the Chief's conference room where Sergeant Farnsworth was conducting the briefing of the officers who would be taking part in the bust. The San Jose Police Narcotic Unit, as well as the State Bureau of Narcotic Enforcement, would be compromising every undercover officer in their respective organizations to assure complete surprise on this operation. It was necessary to get the arresting officers as close as possible just prior to the bust. This could only be accomplished by undercovers. They would need to hit the target with speed and precision to secure the suspects and evidence while uniformed officers quickly establish a perimeter around the target. It was essential that no unauthorized persons cross into the designated scene. Once the search was completed, it was necessary that the officers be able to leave by a route that did not expose them to the eyes of curious onlookers or overlooked and unrecognized accomplices.

"As soon as Sumner has the unwitting informant and the evidence in hand, he will proceed to the parking lot of Los Gatos GMC where Buckley and Smythe will take the informant/suspect into custody," Sergeant Farnsworth directed. "As soon as they have her, they will give the green light. As soon as you have the green light, move quickly…this guy is slippery."

Sumner proceeded to the Crime Scene Investigations Unit where he was fitted out with a body transmitter by Sergeant Aubry Parrot. He then headed to the Boss's office to sign for the money being provided by the State Bureau of Narcotic Enforcement for the purchase of the heroin. Sumner counted out the stacks of money.

"That's $20,000.00 you owe that state if anything goes wrong," advised State Agent Bob Lucas.

"Then you guys better make sure you don't screw up and spook the crook," Sumner replied dryly.

§

Sumner keyed the microphone of the police radio concealed in the glove box of his undercover vehicle. "32-28, I am 10-97 at the residence of the unwitting informant," he announced. "This will be my last transmission. ETA to primary target ten minutes." Sumner placed the microphone back in the glove box and carefully locked the glove box door.

Mary Petersen met Sumner at the front door to her residence and they proceeded to Sumner's vehicle. She was visibly nervous and slightly agitated.

"You all right?" asked Sumner.

"Just a little nervous. I don't want anything to go wrong."

"Relax, nothing's going to go wrong," assured Sumner as he put the car in gear and proceed down the road.

"32-12 and 32-16 are 10-8 in route to the primary target," the police radio traffic suddenly blared into the vehicle. *Geezz, I forgot to turn the police radio off.*

"What the hell is that?!" demanded Mary.

"I'll be dammed if I know," replied Sumner innocently. *What the hell now?*

"32-12, 10-4. 32-18 is in position."

"It sounds like the cops!" exclaimed Mary in near panic.

"32-18 what is your 10-12?"

"Across the street from the primary."

How the hell am I going to talk my way out of this one?

"32-01 and 32-06 are 10-8 in route to primary target." *Just great. Lt. Bertotti and Sergeant Dreyer are on the air and I'm busy screwing up the biggest case of the year. Damn, damn, damn.*

An idea suddenly ignited in Sumner's mind. He grabbed the tuning dial of the car's radio and turned it back and forth. "32-01, 10-4."

"I don't know why but the cop's radios are bleeding on my car radio. It's on all the stations."

"I don't like this. It's a bad sign," protested Mary Petersen.

"No," said Sumner pensively. "No, it's a good sign. We know where they are and what they're doing. This is great!"

"How is this great?"

"Something happened—some atmospheric thing," Sumner shrugged. "It's causing the police radio transmissions to blow out all the radio broadcasts." Sumner made up his story as he went along. "We can hear everything they're doing. All we have to do is stay away from where they are." *And pray like hell that none of those knuckleheads announces his location.*

They arrived at the office of Rondal McGuire, located in a two story building off Los Gatos Blvd behind a bar called Otto's Garden Room. Sumner noticed the undercover vehicles parked at the bar as he drove down the long driveway to the ground level parking located under the two stories of offices above and parked the car.

"Let's go," Sumner quipped.

"You can't go in with me," she protested.

"There is no way I'm letting twenty thousand dollars out of my sight."

§

"What's he doing?" Buckley asked his partner Officer Smythe as they monitored the now in range body transmitter Sumner was wearing.

"We better let the Boss know that he's changed the game plan."

"He's doing what?!" screamed Bertotti. "Continue to monitor. Advise of any other changes to the plan." Bertotti slammed the microphone on the dash of the vehicle.

"That goddamn cowboy is going in," Bertotti screamed at Dreyer. "I'm going to kick his ass clear over the top of his pointed head. How dare he change the plan! How dare he expose himself to that kind of danger." Bertotti was shaking with anger.

"Boss, he's doing exactly what you brought him into Narco to do," Dreyer attempted to reassure his Lieutenant. "He's intelligent, he's daring, and he's resourceful. Those were the very attributes you were looking for in this operation and that's why you staffed it with him," he reminded the Boss. "Now he's exercising his best on the spot judgment. Obviously he sees something we don't and he thinks he can construct a better case by doing it this way."

"His ass is transferred back to patrol tomorrow morning," Bertotti groused. "No, no...the school crossing guard detail. Yeah, let him use his 'best judgment' there."

"Sure, Boss, tomorrow morning," Dreyer patronized.

§

Mary Petersen knocked on the office door. An intercom crackled, "Come in."

Sumner and Petersen opened the heavy wooden office door and slowly entered the spacious office. Seated behind a desk across the room in a luxurious leather swivel chair was a tall slender man with graying sandy hair in his early 60s. *Rondal McGuire, the King of Cocaine himself.*

"Sit down," McGuire gestured with the small frame long barrel revolver he was holding in his right hand. Sumner and Petersen took a seat in the comfortable leather chairs in front of the desk. "You just couldn't do as you were told, could you?" he asked of Sumner in a calm but firm voice as he pointed the pistol at Sumner's chest.

Sumner heaved a heavy sigh. "Would you let $20,000 of your hard earned money walk away with this?" Sumner nodded toward Peterson.

"You do have a point," McGuire agreed. "But my operations are much more important than your measly $20,000. I am the major supplier of quality cocaine for Santa Clara and Santa Cruz Counties," he boasted. "And I am the only reliable source of heroin for the white community. Fifty grand a day comes through this office, so you see I am not impressed by your money." *That's it big shot. Just keep talking. Buckley and Smythe are recording the entire conversation. You're bragging your way right into prison.*

"I'm not trying to impress you, sir," Sumner explained. "But that money represents every penny my buddies and I earned crawling through those steamy jungles for over a year, living like dinks, eating their disgusting food, and trying to keep from getting our heads blown off. What I am trying to do is establish a mutually profitable business relationship with the most astute businessman around."

McGuire sat up a little taller in his chair at the receipt of the compliment. "You got that right," McGuire continued. "Any drug deals of any consequence in this town go through me."

"So I understand," Sumner agreed. *Did you get that guys?*

McGuire stared across the desk holding the pistol on Sumner as he meticulously contemplated his options. He then spoke slowly, carefully choosing his words. "You know, the only reason I trust you even slightly is because of the way you put that psycho Butch in his place," he allowed himself a contemplative smile. "I would have loved to have been there for that."

Sumner placed the case containing the money on the desk. "So can we do a little business?"

McGuire looked up directly into Sumner's eyes. He then pointed the pistol at the case. "Open it up. Let's see what you got."

Sumner opened the case and turned it to display the cash. McGuire stared at the money for what seemed like several minutes, then slowly closed the case and carried it to a large safe across the room. He opened the safe and deposited the money, closing the heavy door and spinning the dial. He then walked to a door on the other side of the room, which he opened and entered returning with a plastic bag. "This is uncut. You can step on it four or five times to get it street ready," he advised. "This will yield you a about a pound, maybe a little more."

"Excellent," Sumner held out his right hand to shake. "To a mutually profitable relationship."

McGuire looked at Sumner for a moment, then moved the pistol he was still aiming at Sumner to his left hand and shook. Sumner turned to Petersen and nodded toward the door. They both exited.

When they got to the parking garage, Sumner's police radio was still blaring. *Damn that thing. Gotta keep talking, keep her confused, don't let her concentrate.*

"32-18 subjects are leaving the primary target."

"It doesn't sound like the cops are anywhere around here," Sumner started the car. "Can you believe that? He's dealing directly with me. You're safe now, all you have to do is collect your cut," Sumner schmoozed. Sumner pulled onto Los Gatos Blvd. "You feel better now? It couldn't have gone any smoother."

He pulled into the parking lot of Los Gatos GMC and stopped.

"What are you doing?" Petersen demanded.

"I'm just going to take a quick look at the new cars," he replied. "If business is going to be this good, I am going to be in the market for a new ride." Sumner walked toward the showroom as Narcotics Street Enforcement Team Officers Buckley and Smythe approached his vehicle and quickly took Mary Petersen into custody without incident. "Suspect in custody, agent is secure. You have the green light," Smythe announced into his radio.

Sumner returned to his vehicle and started to get in as Officer Buckley grabbed him by the shoulder. "Hold on a minute. The Boss is on his way and he wants to have a word with you."

"Am I in trouble?"

"I'm gonna stick my neck w-a-a-y out here and say...yes," Buckley cackled.

Sergeant Dreyer pulled the unmarked police vehicle up next to Sumner's undercover vehicle. Bertotti exited the car, his jaw set in an obvious state of agitation. He kept himself calm as he approached Sumner but avoided eye contact as Dreyer queried, "What happened?"

"I screwed up and forgot to turn off my police radio after my last transmission. It was blaring traffic," Sumner admitted. "I made up a bullshit story about atmospheric disturbances causing the signal to come over the car radio, but the woman was freaked. She's a mental patient anyway, totally unstable. I had to force McGuire's hand personally."

Bertotti nodded his head as he paced slowly in front of the car. "You forgot to turn your police radio off," he said softly through clinched teeth. "On the biggest undercover operation of the year you forget to turn your radio off," he said to himself as much as Sumner. "We're compromising every undercover in the county and you forgot to turn your radio off." Bertotti walked slowly to the passenger side of the car and climbed in. Dreyer looked at Sumner as if the say "I don't know," then shrugged his shoulders and climbed into the driver seat. They sat for a moment talking and then Dreyer drove off. *Nice job, Chowderhead,* Sumner congratulated himself.

§

Sumner headed back to PAB feeling chasten and humbled. *If anything goes wrong on this bust, it's all going to come down on me. I can't believe I pulled such a rookie stunt leaving the radio on.* But Sumner could not delude himself that he started this operation with every intention of making the direct buy from McGuire if the opportunity presented itself …and he made sure that it did. *Was that consciously or unconsciously? Ahww, what am I doing now. I don't have time for self psychoanalysis.*

He arrived back at the Narcotic Unit where he booked the heroin into the evidence locker and began writing his report. Buckley and Smythe finished processing Petersen and prepared to transport her to the Women's Detention Facility at Elmwood.

"Did you know she's 11550," (under the influence of heroin) Smythe asked Sumner.

"I'm not surprised. She's a stone hype in addition to being a mental case."

"She'll no doubt use that as her defense," Buckley mused.

"Shit, if anything else goes wrong on this operation, everyone will walk anyway and I'll be the one that winds up in jail," Sumner lamented.

Buckley and Smythe looked at each other quizzically and shrugged.

"Well then, justice will finally be done," jabbed Buckley as they both howled with laughter.

Thanks, guys, you two always know how to make me feel so much better.

Sumner went back to his report. *No going home tonight until there is a reckoning with the Boss.*

At 10:35 p.m. Sumner heard "32-12 and 32-16 in route to station with one in custody," over the police communications monitor in the Narcotic Bureau. "32-12, 32-16, 10-4." *Kingsbury and McFarlan transporting McGuire. The Boss won't be far behind. He'll want to take McGuire on personally in the interrogation.*

11:01 p.m. Sumner could hear Ron McFarlan's distinctive laugh as well as the voices of his partner Fred Kingsbury, Lt. Bertotti and Sgt. Dreyer coming down the hallway from the elevator. *Brace yourself, Meathead, this could get ugly.*

They entered the Narcotic Unit, all of them laughing, except for, of course, Rondal McGuire. Kingsbury and McFarlan placed McGuire in a soundproof interrogation room as the Boss headed for his office, removing his jacket and rolling up his sleeves. *That can only mean one thing, McGuire is going to get treated to questioning from the finest interrogator in law enforcement today.*

Dreyer, Kingsbury, and McFarlan continued to joke and laugh as they approached Sumner who was seated at his desk working on the report. Sumner looked up with undisguised curiosity. They stopped their jovial discussion and looked at Sumner questioningly. "What?" Sumner asked.

"What? What?" Dreyer returned as they all shrugged and looked at each other in bewilderment.

"Come on, what did we get?"

"Ohhh, well, it was a complete bust. He was totally dry," Dreyer reported.

Sumner was crestfallen. That on top of everything else that went wrong this night would not only finish his assignments in Narcotics, but make him the laughing stock of not just world of drug enforcement, but of the entire law enforcement community.

"Nothing at all?"

"Not a joint in the joint," they all laughed and shoved each other.

"Wonderful," Sumner stared down at his report.

"What are you numb nuts doing?" yelled Bertotti. "Dreyer, get the recording equipment set up." "Kingsbury, McFarlan, get the Dick Bureau van and get back out there and help those guys. All contraband is to be processed by Bud Byerley. He'll be the case evidence officer."

"Evidence?" Sumner perked up.

"Only one of the largest seizures in the history of this department, not to mention about a quarter million dollars in cash." Bertotti advised. He paused and allowed himself an approving grin. "You did OK, kid."

Sumner looked with undisguised relief at Dreyer and the others. "What? Oh, you think we're buying the drinks tonight. Screw you. You buy your own," said Dreyer as they all laughed and slapped Sumner on the back while they mussed his hair.

CHAPTER 64

3:55 a.m. Sumner finished briefing the MERGE Units that would be serving the grand jury indictments and arrest warrants.

"We're going to need you to guide us in on the Lompico arrest," SWAT Sgt. Mike Van De Vern advised Sumner. Lompico is a small community located off the beaten path amongst the giant redwoods in the mountains that separate San Jose from the Pacific Coast. It is a popular area for drug users and traffickers, due to its remote and difficult location, as well as the extreme shortage of law enforcement personnel in the area. Sumner had made a kilo purchase of hashish from a crook named Patrick Williams several months earlier. Williams was a major supplier, but trafficked only in marijuana and hashish and was not connected to any major criminal organizations. Sumner had made the purchase on an occasion where David Allen had asked for a ride up to Williams place so that he could purchase a kilo of marijuana. Sumner took the opportunity to make a case that would shut that source of illicit drugs down for good.

"Go with Russell and Levy," Van De Vern directed.

Sumner guided SWAT Officers Russell and Levy up Highway 17 and off onto Scotts Valley Road. Then up Mt. Hermon Road and finally off onto a fire road that led to William's cabin. Arriving about thirty minutes before dawn, Sumner banged on the door. A young woman in her early twenties opened the door as smoke from burning marijuana bellowed forth. "Is Patrick home?" Sumner inquired.

"He's in bed."

"Which room," Sumner asked. "I need to talk to him."

The woman pointed to a door across the living room to the right of the fireplace. Sumner opened the door and stepped in observing Williams and another young woman lying in bed.

"What are doing here?" screamed an angry Williams as he leapt naked from the bed. "Get the fuck out of my house."

"Shut up. I'm calling the shots here, and you're under arrest," Sumner commanded. He shoved his badge in Williams's sweaty face just as Officers Russell and Levy entered.

Williams fell to his knees, weeping as he cried "Oh shit."

Russell and Levy took Williams into custody as Sumner photographed and tagged twenty six kilogram bricks of marijuana and seventeen kilogram bricks of hashish. "Do we have enough room in the trunk for all this shit?" Sumner asked.

"Are you taking the women?" asked Levy.

"No. I just ran them through NCIC and neither have warrants. We don't really have anything on them."

"Then we can manage," Levy replied.

§

When they arrived back at PAB it was already a beehive of activity. Over seventy suspects had been apprehended, including Andreas Petersen who had been personally arrested by Sergeant Bercelli. Petersen was sitting in one of the interrogation rooms, whining that Bercelli had grabbed him from his bed and thrown him naked across the garage where he lived, Petersen landing bare assed on the floor and skidding to the feet of newspaper reporters who had accompanied the arrest team. Bercelli, of course, denied that his conduct had been anything short of the highest standards of professionalism and in keeping with the proud traditions of our fine department.

CHAPTER 65

Within forty eight hours, over two hundred of the 223 suspects had been arrested and were in custody. By the end of the week, the number had risen to 221. The remaining two, small time PCP dealers, remained at large for another year before they were finally put behind bars.

Butch Swearengen was picked up on a parole violation. In addition to being a felon in possession of a firearm, he was also found to be in possession of a small amount of cocaine. In a deal worked out with his parole officer, Butch was allowed to remain free for six months, during which time he functioned as a confidential informant for the San Jose Police Narcotic Unit. He was used to bring down two high priority heroin traffickers who were listed as major targets by the SJPD's narcotics unit. Upon completion of those operations, he was to be confined in the state penitentiary for one year, after which he would remain on parole for an additional five years.

Lt. Bertotti suggested that Sumner would be a perfect fit to work Swearengen as they were the same age and looked somewhat alike. However, Sumner refused. He had a strict rule. He would never work undercover with anyone he'd arrested or against whom he had personally made a case. He knew there was always the chance that an informant facing prison time might decide to turn on the primary witness against them. And in Swearengen's case, he knew the man was a sociopath, fully capable of cold blooded murder. It was finally decided that Officer Jones would handle Swearengen.

During a prearranged purchase of heroin by Officer Jones at a Southside shopping center, Butch excused himself and entered a liquor store, ostensibly to purchase a soda. Following the successful purchase of the heroin, Jones and Swearengen entered the undercover vehicle and departed for PAB where Swearengen was to be debriefed. While in route to PAB, Jones noticed several patrol units responding Code 3 toward the location they had just left. After they arrived at PAB, Jones discovered that an armed robbery had just occurred at the liquor store next to the location where he had made the drug purchase. It soon became evident that Butch was the perpetrator. Swearengen's status as a CI was revoked and in a subsequent plea bargain, Butch received a five to fifteen year sentence in the state penitentiary. Jones was ribbed relentlessly for being the wheel man of the getaway car.

Weston Campi's attorney filed numerous motions in an attempt to learn the identity of any informant who might be either conveniently eliminated or perhaps "persuaded" to tailor their testimony in a manner that would be advantageous to Weston. Upon the dismissal of twenty-two motions, Weston pled guilty and received a sentence of seven to ten years in prison.

In a carefully orchestrated conspiracy, Andreas Petersen's attorney requested continuance after continuance of his case until each of Petersen's seventeen sub-dealer's cases had been adjudicated. He then demanded a jury trial. During that trial, each of the sub-dealers testified under oath that Officer Sumner had, in fact, been the supplier of their drugs and that Mr. Petersen had continuously warned them against assisting Officer Sumner in his illegal activities. The three-week trial soon took on the trappings of a circus. The final act culminated with Petersen personally taking the stand, an act that is almost universally discouraged by lawyers. In this case it was a serious tactical blunder. After Peterson presented his carefully rehearsed testimony, he was subjected to a merciless cross-examination by prosecutor Arthur Kendrick. Kendrick was relentless in continually tripping Petersen up. In the end, Kendrick exposed three major contradictions in Petersen's testimony. The jury returned a guilty verdict after eight hours of deliberation. Petersen was given a sentence of fifteen years to life in the state prison.

All of the other suspects were either found guilty by jury or pled guilty in hopes of receiving a lighter sentence. After all the cases had run their course the operation had resulted in a 100 percent conviction rate.

The Chief was ecstatic, the Mayor was overjoyed. Local newspapers and television news covered the arrests and seizures of evidence daily. The operation and the resulting cases made the front page of the *San Jose Mercury News* an unprecedented eight consecutive days. And each and every day Sumner's wife faced her excited coworkers at IBM. They would bring her the newspaper articles describing what her husband had done. Instead of a feeling of pride in what her husband had accomplished, she suffered great distress. Sumner had gone to great lengths to carefully shield her from the details of his work, and these revelations frightened her to her core. Almost immediately, this public disclosure led to a great deal of domestic strife, and Sumner's wife began insisting that he find another line of work. The domestic turmoil added to the already significant pressures of the job. The days became long and the nights became longer. Officer Sumner began to find himself, most mornings, staring at his own reflection in the bathroom mirror. He had come to the bitter realization that, increasingly, life just wasn't any fun.

CHAPTER 66

"Jorge Tenario," Butch bragged. "He's NF. I can take you into him tomorrow."

Sumner and Jones looked at each other curiously. *What the hell is the NF?*

Sumner left the interrogation room and headed for the coffee pot. Jones followed. "Do you what he's talking about?"

"I have never heard of any NF," Sumner replied. "What the hell does it stand for?"

"Let's take a walk down to Intelligence," Jones suggested. "We don't want Swearengen knowing that we don't know."

When they arrived at the Intelligence Unit, they took Officer Mike Mitchell aside and quietly asked him what "NF" stood for. Mitchell looked at each of them, then to the three other Intelligence Officers as the room went silent. "Where did you hear about the NF?" he inquired. Jones filled him in on the source of the information. "You'd better come in here." Mitchell led them to an interrogation room that would serve as a conference room. "I'll be right back."

Mitchell returned with a file the size of a New York City phonebook.

"NF stands for Nuestra Familia," Mitchell explained. "It's Spanish for Our Family. They started out as a prison gang in Folsom, but they've spilled out onto the street. They've become very active in the South Bay Area. They deal primarily in drugs, but also engage in contract killings.

341

Their motto is blood in and blood out. A gangster must take a blood oath to become a member and the only way out of the organization is death. Your guy Jorge Tenario is a principle lieutenant for the general of the organization, Leonard Rezendez."

"Butch Swearengen is going take me in to get me a buy on Tenario tomorrow," explained Jones, "with the intention of getting to Sotello."

"Be careful," advised Mitchell. "Those are some real wildcards. Not the least of whom is Swearengen."

"Thanks, Mike," said Jones as he and Sumner got up to leave.

"No problem."

"Well, you've certainly got the right players lined up to work your way into Simon Sotello," Sumner said. "Good luck."

CHAPTER 67

"They empanelled her as a juror?!" asked new Narcotic
Unit Commander Lt. Don Edwards.

"They did indeed," replied Sumner.

"What the hell is Frank Howard thinking," Edwards wondered
aloud.

Frank Howard was the maverick public defender who was representing Patrick Thornton in his trial. Howard had allowed Edwards's daughter Julie to be selected as a juror in the proceedings.

"Do you think there is any danger?" asked Edwards.

"Naww, there is no upside to messing with the jurors," Sumner explained. "He's going down. He knows it and the Angels know it. They aren't going to expend any resources to help him, he's a lost cause."

"Keep me posted," Edwards ordered.

"Will do."

"Happy Hal, what are you up to?" Sumner inquired of new Narcotic Unit Sergeant Hal Springer.

"Just finished my report. What's up?"

"I want to take a look at Donnie Lamont," Sumner explained. "I got some information that he will be moving a large supply of heroin sometime in the next few days. I'm going to be in court on Thornton the next few weeks, so I'd like to show you the layout."

"Let's go," Springer said, then jumped eagerly to his feet.

§

Springer drove to the location in the East Foothills area of San Jose that Sumner directed. As they pulled onto Hillside Drive, Sumner noticed three Cadillacs parked in front of Lamont's residence.

"It could be ShowTime, Hal," Sumner explained excitedly. "This is how he moves his junk. A caravan. The cops have a one in three chance of catching him holding. He changes up his schedule all the time so nobody, not even the people in his organization, knows when he's going to move."

"Shouldn't we call for assistance?" ask Springer.

"There isn't anyone available. Uniforms would just heat the place up. I can never get any hard intel on this guy to set up a coordinated stop on all vehicles."

Just then, six black men and a young boy about eight or nine years old exited the residence, three of the men carrying briefcases. They entered the vehicles and drove off eastbound on Hillside Drive.

"All we can do is guess," Sumner shrugged. "I think the guy with the kid is Lamont. I say we stick with him."

Springer pulled in behind the trailing Cadillac.

"Now watch this," said Sumner. As they reached the intersection with Mt. Shasta Avenue, the lead vehicle went straight, the last vehicle turned left, but the middle vehicle containing Donnie Lamont turned right. Springer followed. As they reached the stop sign at White Road, Sumner noted that it was 5:18 p.m. The Cadillac suddenly pulled into the flow of traffic, causing vehicles to swerve as it accelerated northbound on White Road.

"He's rabbiting," Sumner yelled to Springer, and the Sergeant hit the gas. *Great, a high speed pursuit in an unmarked vehicle at rush hour.*

Sumner keyed the microphone of the police radio. "Control 32-28 in pursuit," Sumner called.

"All units standby, detective unit in pursuit," came the calm voice of the experienced dispatcher. *Weird Ralph Murphy at the mic. At least we got a cool customer calling this chase.* "32-28, your location."

"Northbound on White Road passing Rocky Mountain," Sumner advised. "We are in an unmarked green Dodge Dart in pursuit of a gold Cadillac. Request marked unit to take over the pursuit."

"6333?" Murphy called.

"6333 standing by at White and Fisher ready to intercept," came the voice of Dan Archie. Archie had become one of Sumner's close friends when they were in the police academy together. They had often played golf until Sumner had been transferred to Narcotics.

"He's turning left onto westbound Warrington," Sumner called as the Cadillac skidded across the intersection and smashed into a parked car. The hood of the Cadillac flew up and the driver was driving blind, as steam and coolant spewed from the engine.

"He's throwing something out the window," Springer noted.

"He's dumping the dope," Sumner yelled. "Control, we need a unit to follow our route, the suspect is jettisoning narcotic evidence."

"10-4, 6331?"

"6331, I'm on it," called Officer Tom Hinton, another academy class-mate of Sumner's. *Old home week.*

The Cadillac T-boned into a parked Chevrolet as the driver attempted to make the turn onto Sundown Lane.

"Control, the vehicle is stopped at Warrington and Sundown," Sumner advised.

Smoke billowed from the rear wheels as the Cadillac pulled back from the parked car and drove up onto the lawn of the residence in front of which the Chevy was parked and lurched across the lawns of the homes in an attempt to escape down the street.

"The pursuit is back on, eastbound on Sundown toward White Road," Sumner advised dispatch.

"6333, I'm in position at White Road and Sundown," Officer Archie radioed calmly.

Suddenly the red lights, spinners, and siren sprang to life from Archie's police car that was strategically positioned in the center of the street. The Cadillac turned violently, smashing sideways into a vehicle parked at the curb as the driver attempted to reverse directions. But his luck had run out as Springer pulled up positioning the Dodge Dart to block any move-ment of the Cadillac.

Sumner ran to the driver's side door and yanked the driver from the vehicle. Archie pulled the passenger from the backseat, handcuffing him before gently removing the child as well.

Officer Hinton pulled up and took custody of Sumner's prisoner to transport to PAB. He then reached into the passenger side of his police vehicle and handed Sumner a package. "I don't know what that stuff it is, but it's got a hell of a strong odor."

Sumner inspected the package. "That is the smell of about $100,000 worth of uncut rock heroin. I'm going to need you to mark this as evidence and cut a Form 3 advising where you recovered it and that you turned it over to me at the scene."

"No problem," advised Hinton. "I'll see you at PAB."

Unit 6332, Officer John Porter, arrived to handle the investigation of the collisions of the suspect's car with the parked vehicles.

"Archie, we'll see you at PAB," Sumner advised. "We're going to make an extensive search of our route to see if there is any evidence that we might have overlooked."

Carefully retracing the route of the pursuit, Sumner and Springer located another package under a parked car on White Road at the intersection with Warrington. "Another pound of uncut rock," Springer beamed reveling in the success of his first major case as a Narcotics Detective.

"Happy Hal, let's head back to Lamont's just in case any of the worker bees returned to the hive," Sumner suggested.

After checking Lamont's residence, they headed to PAB to process the prisoners, write reports, and book evidence. Upon reaching the detective bureau at PAB, the Narcotic Unit was buzzing with activity. The pursuit had been broadcast throughout the bureau over the police communications monitors mounted in each of the units and in the hallways. Detectives from Burglary, Robbery and Homicide were stopping in to congratulate Sumner and Springer on the success of the investigation and their subsequent pursuit and arrest. Springer looked at Sumner shrugging as if to say "we just got lucky man." *Sometimes that's just how it happens.*

"It's Maliene Hazel from the *Merc,*" (Mercury News) Officer Roth held up the phone to Sumner. "She wants to talk to you."

Sumner took the phone and proceeded to give the details of the case to the gifted newspaper reporter.

"Are you certain that you recovered all of the evidence?" Hazel asked.

"I sure hope so. That is uncut 100 percent pure heroin," Sumner reported. "If that fell into the hands of an unsuspecting person and they used any of it, the results could be fatal."

"I think I can get front page coverage with this story," Hazel ruminated. "I'm going to report that anyone in the area of the pursuit who finds anything of a suspicious nature should contact the police immediately."

"Not a bad idea. Lt. Edwards is very concerned and would appreciate your efforts."

"I think I'll let channel 11 News know, so they can run a spot on this during tonight's news."

"Thanks, Maliene, you're priceless."

CHAPTER 68

Sumner picked up the morning paper from the driveway and opened it as he sipped on his coffee. STREETS OF HEROIN was emblazoned across the front page in five inch type. *Well, she got front page coverage all right.* Sumner read the article in which his new commander was quoted three times. *I sure hope Lt. Edwards doesn't mind me speaking on his behalf.*

When Sumner arrived at the Narcotics Unit, he knocked on the Lieutenant's open door. Edwards looked up from the newspaper he was reading and smiled.

"I hope I didn't represent you as saying anything inappropriate," Sumner offered.

"No, not all. This is a great article," gushed Edwards. "I got call from Bob Black early this morning telling me my name was all over the paper." Bob Black was the retired former deputy chief of the Uniformed Division, and Lt. Edwards's former partner and good friend.

"Back in the old days if you were mentioned in the newspaper you had to buy all the other detectives drinks that night," Edwards recalled fondly. "Bob was calling to claim his."

"Well, Maliene, and I agreed that this is a potentially dangerous situation if there is unrecovered evidence, and I felt the admonition to the public would have more horsepower coming from you."

"No problem," said Edwards as he patted Sumner on the back. "How is the trial coming?"

"I'm on my way over to testify this morning," Sumner replied.

§

"Then what happened, Officer?" asked the prosecutor Deputy District Attorney Martin Kenney.

"The door to the apartment opened suddenly and the suspect stepped through the doorway brandishing a long barreled Ruger revolver."

"Then what happened?"

"The suspect aimed the pistol at my head, striking my skull several times with the barrel as he demanded to know if I was armed," Sumner replied

"I should have shot your fucking head off...I will next time!" shouted Patrick Thornton from his seat at the defense bench.

"Order, order in this court!" shouted Judge Sidney Frieberg. "I will not tolerate any disruption of these proceedings!" The judge was visibly shaken by the violent outburst.

Sumner looked over at the jury as their eyes widened with surprise.

"Proceed, counselor," ordered the agitated judge.

"Officer, I was going to ask if that person is in this courtroom today, but I believe that question has been answered," DA Kenney jested and the jurors laughed. "But for the record, do you see that individual in the courtroom?"

Sumner turned slightly, leaned forward and with a pleasant smile, pointed directly at Thornton, "That is the man, the talkative defendant."

Sumner continued with his testimony. As he described the substance that he had purchased, he glanced at Thornton making eye contact. "I'll kill you," hissed Thornton.

"Order, order in the court!" commanded Judge Frieberg as he pounded his gavel. "This court will not tolerate any more such outbursts." The jurors fidgeted in their seats in obvious discomfort. *Frank Howard is losing this jury.*

Sumner finished his testimony on the initial purchase of heroin from

Thornton and went on to describe the subsequent purchases, culminating in the meeting with Officer Jones where Thornton attempted to buy military firearms.

"And what do you think he intended to do with those weapons?" asked the prosecutor.

Sumner shrugged. "Shoot people I suppose."

Thornton lunged to his feet. "You fucking punk, I'll kill you. I'll blow your brains all over the wall. I'll cut your fucking heart out!"

The bailiff, Bob Day, a former Sheriff's Deputy, moved up rapidly behind Thornton and applied a carotid restraint across his neck, quickly rendering him unconscious. He shoved the unconscious defendant down in his seat and applied handcuffs.

"Officer!" the judge ordered Sumner "take custody of the prisoner and confine him to the holding room! Bailiff, remove the jury. This court is in recess!"

Sumner jumped up and out of the witness box and darted across the courtroom leaping up onto and over the defense bench landing behind Thornton as several of the jurors broke into applause. Sumner applied a wrist lock come along, below the cuffs on the groggy Thornton. He then escorted him to the court's holding cells that were located on each floor of the courthouse. There, Sumner, less than gently, locked him up. Sumner then returned to the courtroom where Judge Frieberg was in the process of chastising public defender Frank Howard for not exercising more control over his client. The judge was shaking and in a state of extreme agitation. "What did he want all those guns for?" he demanded of Sumner, who shrugged sheepishly. "I don't like him," groused the judge. "I don't like him at all." DA Marty Kenney smiled coyly at Sumner as if to say "this couldn't be going any better."

"And Officer," the judge called as he paused at the door to his chambers, "next time I order you to take somebody into custody, could you do it without all the acrobatics?"

"Sorry, Your Honor," Sumner replied. "I just got a little excited."

The judge smiled and nodded his head approvingly as he entered his chamber.

CHAPTER 69

"You're back early," Lt. Edwards noticed.

Sumner proceeded to describe for his commander the incidents that had occurred during the morning's testimony.

"You're kidding! And old, Bob Way choked him out?" laughed Edwards.

"Right there in the courtroom in front of god, the jury, and everybody," Sumner allowed himself a laugh.

"Thornton is certainly making Julie's first experience as a juror memorable."

"She hasn't seen anything yet," Sumner replied. "Wait until the jury comes back with a verdict of guilty."

Edwards stiffened. "Are you sure there's no danger?"

"Don't worry, dad. I'll look after your little girl."

Edwards smiled and returned to his office.

"Where is happy Hal?" Sumner asked.

"Code 5," (Stake out) replied Officer Ron McFarlan. "He's monitoring any activity at Lamont's pad."

"I'll drive out and see him. I want to fill him in on who the players are on that case."

§

351

"What are you doing?" Sumner demanded.

Springer's head snapped around in surprise as Sumner opened the passenger door of the Dodge Dart and climbed in.

"Watching to see if there is any activity and see who's coming and going," Springer explained. "I thought you were in court all week."

"Thornton threatened to kill me, the Bailiff choked him out in front of the jury, and the judge recessed for the day."

"Oh, that's too bad; Never a dull moment, huh?"

"You're wasting your time here. Donnie is yesterday's news," Sumner explained. "The other five you saw yesterday were his lieutenants, and they've already taken over and are running the operation. Maybe even killing each other to gain control and become top dog."

"So where does that leave us?"

"Come on back to PAB and I'll fill you in on the other players and where the operation may have moved."

Springer was an intelligent and intuitive officer, but he was new to Narcotics and, though a virtual rookie in the unit, he was, after all, a sergeant and team supervisor and was therefore reluctant to ask for guidance or assistance. And an attitude like that created a great deal of duplication of effort in the world of police investigations.

§

"What did the judge say?" asked Sumner.

"He was plenty pissed about yesterday," explained DA Kenney as he sat next to Sumner at the prosecutor's table. "Look carefully when he comes out of the judge's chambers and you'll notice that Frank Howard doesn't have an ass anymore. That's because the judge chewed it right off his backside."

"All rise," called bailiff Bob Way. "Department 15 of the Superior Court is now in session; the Honorable Judge Sidney Frieberg presiding."

The judge entered and sat at the bench.

"Be seated," called the bailiff.

"The deliberations of this court will not be intimidated or disrupted by anyone," warned the judge. "Any repeat of the behavior of yesterday, and I will have the offending parties shackled and gagged for the remainder of this trial. Is that clear, gentlemen?"

"Yes, Your Honor," came the clear and responsive voices of DA Kenney and Public Defender Howard.

Sumner retook the stand and completed his testimony under direct examination by the District Attorney. He was then subjected to a rigorous cross examination by Public Defender Frank Howard. Disrespectful and condescending, Howard methodically questioned Sumner on the details of his transactions with the defendant.

Upon completion of Sumner's testimony, the entire court was exhausted from the tedious, wearisome and highly repetitive questioning by the public defender. At 5:30 p.m. the court was adjourned with the customary admonitions to the jury not to discuss the case among themselves or with anyone else, "Including police lieutenants," the judge ordered, tossing a good natured jest at Julie Edwards. Julie flashed a dazzling smile at the judge as the jurors laughed while filing out of the courtroom. *Time for a beer.*

§

Sumner sat at his desk reviewing his crime reports on a case involving Jose Merced Luis. He was scheduled to testify that morning on a motion to discover. *They're going to want to know who snitched him off. They're going to be surprised when they discover that no informant was involved.*

"Sumner, would you take this call on line one?" asked Melissa, the receptionist. "It's someone kind of weird."

Aren't they all

"Sure." Sumner picked up the phone. "Narcotics Unit, Officer Sumner."

"Are you a cop?" came the raspy voice.

"Yes, sir, this is Officer Sumner."

"Then listen carefully."

Sumner took notes until the line went dead. He sat quietly for a moment processing the information. He then reviewed what the caller had said, making sure he had it verbatim. *This ought to make Beto's day.* He rose, made his way down the hall, then entered Lt. Edwards's office and sat down pensively.

"What?" the Lieutenant looked up from his paperwork.

"I just took a call," Sumner began. "It was a Hispanic male, mature, in his forties or fifties."

"And..." prodded Edwards.

"And he said that a guy named Danny Sugarboy Lopez had just been given $5000 and a gun to kill a narc named Miguel Alejandro."

"Beto?" asked the Lieutenant.

Sumner nodded, "His full name is Miguel Roberto Alejandro."

Edwards stared at Sumner for moment, "We better get Beto in here right away. And get a hold of Bob Hillburn in Intelligence. We're going to need some hard intel."

A meeting was scheduled in thirty minutes in the office of Chief of Detectives, Ed McKellen. Officer Alejandro arrived last.

"Tell us exactly what the caller said," ordered the Chief.

Sumner went through the details of the call. A male caller, probably in his 40s or early 50s of Hispanic decent. Sumner quoted from his notes, "Danny 'Sugarboy' Lopez was just given $5,000 and a gun to knock off a narc named Miguel Alejandro. That's all."

Edwards, McKellen, Alejandro, and Hillburn questioned Sumner like desperate defense attorneys hoping to turn up an overlooked piece of information that would save their client from the gallows.

"That's all he said," Sumner assured. "Then he hung up."

"Well, here's what we know for sure," Hillburn began. "Lopez is NF, took the blood oath while doing time at Folsom Prison for armed robbery. He's a bad hombre but, other than his association and their reputation, we have no legal information indicating that he's a killer."

"It's probably just a crank call," suggested Alejandro.

"Yeah," challenged Sumner. "They know your first name. That's more than your girlfriend knows."

"Hey, I'm a happily married man," protested Beto.

"And your girlfriend doesn't know that either," Sumner jabbed. "Do you really want to take the chance that it's just a crank call?"

"Maybe we should assign him a bodyguard," suggested Chief McKellen.

"How does an undercover officer function with a bodyguard in tow?" Sumner asked sarcastically.

"We don't know how much information they have. Hell, they might even know where he lives," offered Hillburn. "Lopez took the contract," he explained. "The best thing is, pick up Lopez, but how do we flush him out?"

Sumner thought for a moment then spoke haltingly. "Let me see what I can do."

"What do you have in mind?" Edwards asked.

"I have to testify in a motion to discover this morning," Sumner explained. "They're going to demand that I disclose the informant."

"I don't follow you," said Edwards.

"The defendant is Jose Luis," Sumner continued.

Bob Hillburn's eyebrows raised as he nodded his head knowingly.

"What, what is it?" asked Chief McKellen.

"Jose Luis is an NF soldier," Hillburn began to lay out Sumner's idea for him. "There will no doubt be other NF members in the courtroom hoping to identify the informant and spot an undercover. If Sumner goes in and discloses Lopez as the informant, he will be in some real trouble. The hunter will become the hunted. He'll either have to go on the run, which will disrupt his plan to eliminate Alejandro, or he'll need protective custody from the police."

"Lie in court while under oath?!" asked Edwards.

"Desperate circumstances require desperate measures," Sumner replied.

"I do not condone nor will I authorize such action," admonished the Chief.

"It was just a thought," Sumner shrugged.

"One way or the other, for the time being Roberto will maintain a low profile," ordered the Chief. "No undercover operations. You become a house mouse until we get this sorted out."

"Shit," protested Alejandro.

"I've got to get to court," Sumner excused himself.

§

The courtroom was packed when Sumner arrived. During the hearing of motions, formidable criminal defendants like to have their myrmidons, fierce warriors totally loyal to their leaders, present in order to intimidate and discourage witnesses. Though judges will often react severely to such tactics, many defense attorneys not only tacitly approve, but sometimes even encourage the practice. Today was no exception.

"Raise your right hand," ordered the court clerk. "Do you solemnly swear that the testimony you are about to give is the truth, the whole truth, and nothing but the truth, so help you god?"

"I do," replied Sumner.

Sumner answered the mundane questions put forth by the flamboyant defense attorney Richard Rosa. Finally he launched the keystone question. "And how did you meet my client?"

"I was introduced by a reliable confidential informant," replied Sumner.

"And what is the name of that informant?" asked Rosa.

"Danny Sugarboy Lopez." Sumner felt an icy blast of guilt shoot through his soul as the courtroom began to buzz.

"Order in the court," demanded the judge.

Three heavily tattooed and rough looking Latinos stood up from their seats in the back row and shuffled out of the courtroom. *The genie is out of the bottle.*

CHAPTER 70

"Hello," Sumner sleepily spoke into the phone as he lay in bed.

"Danny Sugarboy Lopez was found dead this morning," Alejandro advised. "A bullet through the head."

"Shit," Sumner sighed.

"Did you out him?"

"Yeah, I sure did." Sumner felt as if someone had stomped on his soul.

After a long silence, Beto spoke. "I don't know what to say, man. Thanks for covering by backside."

"Yeah, yeah, I'm glad it's him and not you." Sumner felt like he was suffocating. *My god, what have I done?*

§

"Where did they find him?" Sumner asked.

"In the trunk of his car at the airport parking lot," replied Homicide Detective Sergeant Conrad; "One bullet right through the forehead, close range."

"How long had he been there?"

"Two days. He was pretty ripe."

"I imagine so in this heat." *So he was executed the same day I testified. They sure didn't waste any time.*

"One of the airport security personnel saw flies all over the rear of the car and decided to investigate," Conrad explained. "He got a real surprise when he forced open the trunk and found the bloated corpse." Conrad displayed a photograph of the body in the trunk of the vehicle. *God, forgive me. But that might have been our officer and my friend.*

"Thanks, Art," Sumner shuffled out of the Homicide Unit.

Sumner returned to his desk where he began to review the file on Weston Campi for the motion to discover that would be heard in court that afternoon. He could not get the bloated image of Lopez's dead body out of his mind. *I don't know how those homicide guys keep their sanity.*

Sergeant Samuel Houston sat down at the desk next to Sumner's. *Sam Houston*, Sumner could never resist allowing himself a chuckle.

"Intelligence has confirmed that Lopez did pick up the contract on Beto," informed Houston in a subdued tone.

"Who is the source of that intel?" Sumner asked.

"A guy named Terrazas. He was in the wrong place at the wrong time and got picked up on your latest round up," Houston explained. "He was in possession of a spoon of junk and a rig." (hypodermic needle) "Jones turned him and he has been a valuable source of intelligence on the NF."

"Anything else?" asked Sumner, sensing there was more.

"There was a matchbook with Beto's home address written on the cover found on Lopez's body."

Sumner dropped his head into his open hands as he wept like a baby. Houston stood, placed his hand on Sumner's shoulder and patted him gently. "Feel better, kid," he said graciously. "You saved a good man's life."

§

"And exactly when did you first meet my client?" asked the overweight, bloviating attorney in a vociferate bark.

Sumner answered the question, speaking softly, but directly to the judge.

Henry Belvoir, the attorney for Weston Campi, a San Francisco scumbag, was well known for his loud, theatrical, and offensive courtroom behavior.

"Speak up!" shouted Mr. Belvoir, gesturing with a wild upswing of his arms.

Sumner repeated his answer, leaning toward the judge and speaking even more softly.

"I can't hear you!" screamed Belvoir, spittle flying from his mouth, his red face, made so by generous daily consumption of alcoholic beverages, becoming even redder.

"I can hear the officer fine," interrupted Judge Nakahara in a stern voice. "Perhaps if you would pay more attention to his answers rather than your own cacophonous bellowing, you might be able to hear." This was not a request.

Showboating in front of a jury might get you somewhere, but in front of a judge during motions it will just get you roasted.

Mr. Belvoir continued his questioning. Sumner glanced at his watch… *An hour and fifteen minutes on a motion to discover?*

"I believe the officer has answered your question several times," scolded His Honor. "There was no informant involved in the introduction of the officer to your client."

"Well, Your Honor, we believe that there was and that the officer is being untruthful in an attempt to protect the identity of a paid police informant," Belvoir pleaded.

Judge Nakahara, a veteran of the World War II relocation camps and Professor Emiratis at the University of Santa Clara Law School, was in no mood for grandstanding by this vulgar, boisterous, egomaniacal gasbag, particularly in his attempts to besmirch the integrity of a police officer.

"Your questions have been asked and answered," the judged admonished, "by a respected officer of unimpeachable integrity."

Sumner was deflated… *"unimpeachable integrity?" I didn't think I could feel any lower. Your Honor, if you only knew.*

"The court rules that full disclosure has been made," the judge ordered. "Clerk of the court, the next matter please."

§

Sumner exited the courtroom and walked slowly back to the Narcotic Unit. A police motorcycle roared up in front of him. Sumner looked up into the broadly smiling face of Officer Dennis Dawkins. Dawkins was also the owner of the "Fitness Center Health Club" where Sumner trained. Dawkins's face went gloomy with concern as he noticed Sumner's expression.

"You OK, buddy?"

"Yeah, I just need a drink."

"You don't need a drink, you need a workout," encouraged Dawkins, an avid bodybuilder and exercise enthusiast of the first magnitude. "I'm off duty. Meet me at the Fitness Center."

"Yeah, yeah, that might just do it," Sumner replied, feeling somewhat better already. "I'm heading out right now."

§

Sumner was feeling in great shape as they completed their workout and entered the sauna. "So what's got you down, pal?" asked Dawkins.

Sumner agonized. Should he confess his transgression to his friend? Dennis was a good man, loyal, honest, and a devout Christian. *Perhaps unburdening my guilty conscience would give me some peace. No!* Sumner grabbed hold of his emotions and clearly realized that by off loading his guilt feelings he would be placing his friend in jeopardy. *I will confess this sin to God Almighty, repent, ask forgiveness and then bury it so deep in my soul it will never come out.*

"Oh, that execution style homicide at the airport was a guy I was working. Looking at the body and smelling it just left me a little unsettled."

"Nobody important I hope."

"Just a doper crook."

"The same thing happens to me at the scene of fatal traffic accidents," consoled Dawkins. "The mangled bodies of little kids and innocent people—that image takes a long time to fade."

Yeah, but you didn't cause the traffic accidents, my friend.

§

"And were you wearing a wire during your conversation with Mr. McGuire?" asked the prosecutor, Deputy District Attorney Kevin Barnett. After four months of motions to dismiss, motions to discover, motions to suppress, Mr. Rondal McGuire had finally come to trial for the first time in his long and storied criminal career.

"Yes, sir."

"And was that conversation recorded?"

"Yes, sir," replied Sumner.

"And is this the tape of that conversation?" asked Barnett, handing a cassette cartridge to Sumner who examined it carefully. "Yes, sir, it is."

"And how do you know that it is the same cartridge that recorded your conversation with the defendant?"

"It is marked in my handwriting with the date of the incident, case number and my initials and badge number. It is also marked with the initials and badge number of Officer Smith, who was assigned to operate the receiver/recorder."

"Your Honor, I ask that this cartridge be admitted as people's exhibit number one," said Barnett, taking the cartridge and handing it to the court clerk.

"The tape will be admitted and so marked," ruled Judge Judith Zachary.

Deputy DA Barnett then received the marked evidence from the court clerk and inserted it into a cassette player and turned it to play. The voices of Sumner and McGuire poured forth clearly from the player. Then McGuire's unmistakable voice cracked from the tape player through the silence of courtroom.

"I am the major supplier of quality cocaine for Santa Clara and Santa Cruz Counties," he boasted. "And I am the only reliable source of heroin for the white community. Fifty grand a day comes through this office."

Barnett pressed the stop button, glaring at McGuire and then turning slowly and circumspectly to the jury, smiling as if to ask "have you had enough?" all the while holding on to the silent tension in the courtroom like a long bowman straining to hold his bow drawn just before unleashing the bolt that brings all hell down on his foe. "Your witness," he offered to Spencer Houseman, a former United States public defender and defense council for the socially connected Rondal McGuire.

Houseman was intelligent, articulate, and dapper; a Stanford University graduate, Harvard Law School, editor of the *Harvard Law Review* and well connected to the San Francisco Bay Area power brokers. The gifted defense lawyer stood at the defense table silent, sinking like a drowning man who had just been handed an anvil. Barnett had masterfully woven a prosecutorial web that nothing, not even a spider like McGuire, could escape. Houseman jousted with Sumner in an attempt to create contradiction in his testimony and, if possible, plant seeds of doubt with the jury about his honesty, integrity, or ability to recall. The more he questioned Sumner, the more information Sumner offered, extemporizing with details about McGuire's past criminal activities and even editorializing as to his prominent position as the "King of Cocaine." Frustrated, Houseman turned to the judge and pleaded "Will the court please direct the witness to answer the questions and not elaborate beyond the scope of the questions intent?"

"Counselor, you are asking the questions. Perhaps you should frame your questions more narrowly," advised Judge Zachary.

"But he runs for daylight every time I ask anything!" protested Houseman red faced with frustration.

The judge looked down at the defense counselor from the bench with a measure of sympathy for what he was going through. Defense counsel had the impossible job of attempting to defend an obviously guilty client against a flawlessly constructed case, masterfully prosecuted by a gifted young lawyer. Added to that was the tremendous respect that the jury held for Sumner. During direct examination, Deputy DA Barnett had skillfully presented Sumner's credibility as an experienced undercover officer by questioning him as to many of the details of some of his more famous cases that had been extensively featured in the media. During the testimony, the jurors had leaned forward in their seats in rapt fascination as if listening to the reading of an adventure novel. They were enthralled with Sumner's experiences in particular and police work in general. This time, McGuire was not going to escape retribution through the legal sleight of hand of his brilliant attorney. He was going down big time. His attorney knew it and there was nothing he could do but grandstand a little.

"Officer, please confine your responses as much as possible to yes or no," directed the judge.

"Yes, Your Honor."

But the damage was done. Houseman was frustrated with what had become an untenable position. He had uncharacteristically left the pro-verbial barn door open with his questions; and now the jury knew far more about McGuire's criminal activities than he had intended.

Houseman wrapped up his cross examination and sat down brooding about this latest turn in the case.

"This court is adjourned until 9:00 a.m. tomorrow," the judge ordered.

Barnett clapped Sumner on the back. "We make a hell of a team."

"All I did was answer the questions."

"Yeah, uh huh, that's all you did," smiled Barnett, who then clapped Sumner on the back once again for good measure. "He just answered the questions," Barnett called to the departing Houseman, who scowled back in angry contempt as he exited the courtroom. Barnett laughed out loud.

§

"The jury is back," Kenney announced. "You coming over?"

"I'll be right there," Sumner said and hung up the phone.

§

The jury filed in and took their seats.

"Have you reached a decision," asked Judge Frieberg.

"We have," answered the jury foreman, handing the bailiff a piece of paper, which the bailiff took to the judge. The judge opened the paper and read the contents.

"The defendant will stand and face the jury," ordered the judge.

Patrick Thornton stood up. He was shackled with handcuffs and chains that hobbled his feet and kept his hands on his lap. He glared hatefully at Sumner, then at the judge, and finally at the jury.

"How say you?" asked the judge.

"We the jury find the defendant guilty on all cou..."

"YOU'RE DEAD!" screamed Thornton. "All you mutherfuckers, you're dead!" he shouted at the jury. "You're dead, you lying fuck!" he yelled at Sumner. "I'll break out and I'll kill all..." his threat was choked off by the application of the court security officer's carotid restraint hold around his neck. Nervous about Thornton's violent tendencies as well as his circle of friends, the judge had requested additional security from the sheriff. The request had been honored in the persons of two strapping deputies.

"Get him out of here," ordered the judge as the security officers dragged the unconscious Thornton from the courtroom.

"Ladies and Gentlemen of the jury, you are discharged," said the judge. "Thank you for your exemplary service in the face of very difficult circumstances."

The judge looked sullenly at Sumner as the courtroom emptied. "I don't like him," groused the judge. Sumner laughed.

CHAPTER 71

"He threatened the jury?" asked an astonished Lt. Edwards.

"The jury, the judge, and me," Sumner explained. "I think he was about to include the DA when the deputies choked him out."

"Do you think there is any chance of danger to anyone? My daughter was on that jury."

"None. Jones is fully inserted and has been keeping company with several of the Angel's bosses. They've written Thornton off and now consider him a liability. They won't do squat for him."

Edwards shook his head in parental concern.

Sumner pointed out, "Sheriff Winter responded with two young torpedoes when the Judge requested more security. I'm telling you, those deputies were both built like Tarzan."

"Her roommate Brandy is dating Roger Simpson. He's working swing patrol," Edwards mused. "I'll make sure he and his partner security check their apartment regularly."

"Simpson's partner is Bluto Baxter," chimed in Officer Glazer looking up from his report writing. "With that horn dogger, I think she would be safer with the Hell's Angels hanging around." The room erupted in laughter. Officer Gerald "Bluto" Baxter had a reputation around the department for regarding women as little more than sex objects.

Sumner crossed the hall and entered the offices of the Major Violators Team. Sumner caught Sergeant Bill Byerley exiting an interrogation room where he had been questioning a hype brought in by a Patrol Unit.

"What did you guys work out with Charlie James?" Sumner inquired.

"The DA agreed to a negotiated plea based upon the cooperation of his wife Sherry. He'll do one year in county, and she'll work Garza through the sublevels to Sotello."

"Do you think she can get him all the way to Sotello?"

"I hope so. If not, at least close enough for us to build a case that's strong enough to close him down on conspiracy and racketeering."

Lt. Edwards entered the room. "Excuse me, but Judge Zachery just called." Sumner stiffened. She was the presiding judge in the McGuire case. *What the hell could be going wrong?* "She would like to see you in her chambers."

"When?"

"Right now."

What could she possibly want? This was a textbook case and the trial couldn't be going any better. Sumner's mind went into overdrive. This was a very unusual course of action for the judge; and given the recent events that had occurred, relative to Sumner's court testimonies, anything was possible. *Hell,* Sumner thought, *I may wind up in jail tonight.*

Sumner arrived at Superior Court Department #17. The doors were locked. He knocked firmly. The bailiff opened the door and smiled.

"Come on in," he swung the door wide. "Her Honor is expecting you."

Sumner proceeded to the door leading to the judge's chambers and knocked. "Come in."

Sumner entered to find the judge standing at the credenza at the side of her grand walnut desk preparing a cup of coffee. "Sit down, officer. Can I offer you a cup of coffee?" *At least she's cordial. Maybe this won't be catastrophic.*

"Thank you," it had been a long day and Sumner needed a pick me up. "A little cream please."

The judge handed Sumner his coffee then sat down in her elegant wing back leather chair behind her desk. "You seemed very comfortable during your testimony the other day."

"I just answered the questions. Barnett is doing an incredible job."

"Officer, you are a very composed, articulate, and credible witness with great jury appeal. This jury has really warmed to you." *But? Sumner thought.*

"Is that why you wanted to see me Your Honor? Did I in any way behave inappropriately before the jury?" Sumner's mouth dried as he swallowed hard. His guilt over his testimony still weighed heavily on him.

"Not at all," assured the judge. "This case has been a pleasure to hear...professionally constructed and brilliantly prosecuted. I have enjoyed having you in my courtroom." *Buuutttt?*

"Thank you, Your Honor, but like I said, I just answer the questions honestly."

"And thoroughly," the judge chided. "You really had Houseman chasing his tail, and that's not easy to do."

"I apologize if my elaborated responses were in any way inappropriate, but he has slid McGuire out from under the hammer of justice several times, and I just thought that a little light shed on the extent of his criminal activities might help."

"Noble...and selfless," came the mildly sarcastic reply. "You were flirting with a motion for mistrial by enhancing the scope of your responses, but fortunately he made no such request."

"And that would have been bad..."

"After two weeks of testimony, if you had lost this to mistrial because of your exaggerate aggrandizement...I would have had you skinned!" the judge replied in almost evil delight.

"I will keep that in mind, Your Honor. Is that all?"

"No, I want to talk to you about sentencing," she began. "I have been sending black and Hispanic drug dealers to prison for extended terms only to have well-to-do white criminals negotiate light sentences through their high priced attorneys. When the jury comes back with a guilty verdict, and they will, I intend to impose an extended sentence on Mr. McGuire."

"That's a good thing," Sumner assured. "He should have gone to prison several years ago, but Houseman got the search warrants suppressed in both cases."

"What I need from you is a meticulously detailed probation report to justify my sentence," the judge revealed. "I want you to dig out every piece of evidence, intelligence, and verifiable information that has been compiled on this man over the years."

"You can count on me."

"Anything that occurred during your case that was maybe left out of the reports that speaks to the extent of his culpability as a major drug trafficker."

"I will get you everything."

"And I do not care if it is as long as a phonebook, just be thorough and verifiable."

"Absolutely."

The judge stood and walked Sumner to the door. "This really was a masterful investigation," commented the judge as she opened the door. "My compliments." Sumner slipped sheepishly out the door red faced and humbled by the commendation. *Whew!*

§

Sumner arrived at the Fog Horn Restaurant and Bar about 7:30 p.m. As he entered the darkened tavern he observed his fellow narcotics officers seated in the booth in the far corner. As he approached his eyes adjusted to the darkness and he noticed the officers as well as the lieutenant staring as if to ask "what the hell happened?"

Sumner took a seat at the end of the booth and ordered a beer. As he sat there innocently, with his hand wrapped around the cool glass, he began to notice the furtive glances thrown his way. It became clear that the assembled officers were openly staring at him with an apprehension that bordered on fear. Sumner took a sip of his draft beer, sighed, and began staring thoughtfully into the distance.

"Long day," Sumner said to himself in a barely audible mummer. He lifted his beer and took another long draw. Sumner looked casually over at the eight officers openly staring at him. "What?!"

"What the fuck did the judge want?" demanded Sgt. Byerley.

"Ohhh," Sumner answered conspiratorially; "She wanted to know about you."

Sumner took another long draw on his beer and indicated to the nearby waitress that he was ready for another.

"ME?!" Byerley exploded.

"Yeah you,...a-a-a-n-n-d you and you and you," said Sumner with roguish innocence pointing to each of the officers present, as each in turn, reacted with bewilderment. As they looked at each other in baffled confusion, Sumner took another draw on his newly delivered beer.

"What the fuck did I do?" asked several of the officers in astonishment at being indicted by Sumner. "I've never even testified in her courtroom," bemoaned Officer Winter, who was intending to enter law school the next year.

"Ahh, but your name has been on evidence and reports that have figured prominently in several cases that have been tried in her court," Sumner pointed out as he took another swallow of beer. "You are much more high profile than you think...all of you," Sumner admonished.

He took another long sip as he began to feel the effects of the alcohol. He smirked, and then barely stifled a laugh.

"What...?" came the collective inquiry.

"He's fucking with you," chuckled Lt. Edwards who sat, amused, in the corner. Unnoticed by the group, he had been watching Sumner's increasingly prankish behavior which he apparently found mildly entertaining.

"No, this is serious," insisted the now mildly impaired Sumner. "She thinks you guys are a bunch of fuck-ups." Sumner laughed with a bellow. "She really feels that it's you assholes who belong in jail, not the crooks." He howled in growing, pain free merriment.

"Asshole," sneered Byerley.

"I'm serious. You dumb asses better clean up your act before you enter her courtroom."

"Before you get any more shitfaced...what did she want?" demanded Lt. Edwards.

OK, enough screwing around with these numb nuts. The Boss wants the poop.

"Well, Boss" *naw, this is too funny and we need a few more laughs.* "She wanted to know if you were single and if you would interested in a bi-sexual three way with her and Bluto Baxter," Sumner guffawed uncontrollably and beer spouted from his nose. He continued to laugh uncontrollably.

"You little prick," shot Farnsworth with undisguised scorn.

"Leave him alone," ordered Lt. Edwards. "He's had a tough couple of months. It wasn't anything too important or he wouldn't be screwing around like this. Sumner, my office, tomorrow, 8:00 a.m."

"Sir," replied Sumner. "Who's buying the next round?"

"You are, asshole," was the collective response.

About midnight Farnsworth looked over at Sumner, who was now flowing in his cups. "Hey, Red Skelton, give me your keys." Sumner handed over the keys to his undercover vehicle to Farnsworth who tossed them to Officer Vincent. "You guys drop his car off at the annex. I'll take his drunken ass home."

Farnsworth dropped Sumner off in front of his house in the early morning hours. "Eight a.m. in the boss's office...and don't be late!" Sumner made his way to the bedroom where he undressed. As he had been in court that day he was wearing a suit and tie. He then flopped into bed, still sniggering to himself and fell fast asleep.

§

Sumner awoke at 6:00 a.m. with a slight headache. He made his way to the kitchen where he poured a cup of coffee, then downed some Tylenol. *Back to court today.* Ted reminded himself, *Motions on the Mark Stithe case today. Nice clean cases, but he has high powered legal representation and they will try anything. Damn, I wish this headache would go away.*

§

Sumner arrived at the Narcotic Bureau at 7:57 a.m. He proceeded to the Crime Scene Unit where he poured a cup of coffee, then headed to the Boss's office. Lt. Edwards sat at his desk smirking knowingly.

"How's the head?"

"A little rough. I had a lot of steam to blow off."

"I understand," said the Lieutenant sympathetically. "Here's your car keys. It's parked over at the annex."

"Thanks. That was probably a good call not letting me drive."

Sumner proceeded to brief the Lieutenant as to the details of his meeting with Judge Zachery.

"Very unusual," mused Edwards. "She may become a very influential ally of this unit."

"Well, if she is half as cooperative as Judge Markham in approving search warrants, she could become indispensable to us."

"Make sure you give her everything she needs...then dig out a little more," ordered Edwards. "And make this one of your Hemingway reports." Sumner's penchant for imitating the prose of the great American author Ernest Hemingway that he developed as an English minor in college had earned him the nickname "Hemingway" among the probation department and courthouse personnel.

"It'll be another Old Man and the Sea. I gotta get to court."

Sumner arrived at Judge Wright's courtroom at 9:00 a.m. Deputy District Attorney David Goldstein was waiting anxiously.

"We have a motion to disclose any informants," Goldstein advised.

"There was no paid informant," Sumner advised. "I was introduced by another crook who was trying to make a little money off a drug transaction."

"This should be pretty straightforward," commented Goldstein. "Is there anything else I should know?" he asked pensively.

"Not that I can think of," replied Sumner, somewhat confused by the DA's consternation.

"OK."

The judge entered the courtroom and called the matter of the motion to disclose. Sumner took the stand and was sworn in. The flamboyant and eloquent Dennis Harrington, counsel for the defense, asked the usual questions relative to who had introduced him to the suspect and what that person's status was relative to the defendant, as well as his relationship with the police.

"I was introduced to the defendant by David Allen, whom I had met by chance that day at the Race Street Fish and Poultry," Sumner advised.

"Was he in any way compensated by either you or the San Jose Police Department for his services?"

"Allen is a drug dealer who was looking to make a commission by arranging a purchase of LSD."

"And is it not true that immediately upon receiving the alleged drugs from my client that you immediately sold half of the contents of the bag to David Allen?"

"No, sir, it is not."

"Are you claiming that David Allen was in no way compensated for his service?"

"Not by me."

"Did David Allen come into possession of any drugs during this transaction?"

"Yes, sir, he did."

"So you supplied him with drugs for his services?"

"No, sir, I did not."

"Then how is it that Mr. Allen came to into possession of drugs you had just purchased?"

"When the defendant produced the drugs, they were received by Mr. Allen who then removed fifty tablets as his commission, for introducing me to a supplier of LSD."

"And this was his payment by the police department?"

"No, sir."

"Payment by you then?"

"No, sir."

"How then would you characterize this indemnification?"

"The seizure of property by Mr. Allen for what he perceived as the performance of a valuable service to someone he believed to be of a criminal persuasion."

The judge snickered.

"Officer Sumner, is the San Jose Police Department in the business of allowing criminals to seize, at will, property of evidentiary value?"

"No, sir."

"Then why did you allow this action to occur?"

"Because it is very common practice amongst drug users to acquire part of the merchandise for which they have arranged the purchase," Sumner replied. "As I had not taken possession of the evidence at that time, to object to Mr. Allen's actions would have been considered suspicious behavior by the suspects and might have resulted in me getting my head shot off."

"And the San Jose Police Department is in the habit of purchasing the safety of its officers by supplying drugs to dangerous criminals?"

"Objection, Your Honor," interjected DA Goldstein.

"Sustained," replied the judge. "The officer does not relinquish his right to self defense or good judgment while in the conduct of an undercover investigation."

"Your Honor, at this time the defense would like to move for dismissal of all charges against my client in light of the blatantly illegal actions of Officer Sumner in supplying dangerous criminals with powerful hallucinogenic drugs," requested Harrington.

"I have not heard that the officer supplied anyone with anything," replied the judge. "Part of the evidence was taken before it came into his custody. Motion denied."

"But, Your Honor…"

"Motion denied," repeated the judge. "Madame Clerk, next matter."

§

"The defendant will rise and face the jury," ordered Judge Judith Zachery.

Rondal McGuire stood slowly, haltingly, and turned, slightly stooping to face the jury foreman. *Damn, he has aged in the last six month.*

"How say you?" asked the judge.

"We find the defendant guilty on all counts," replied the jury foreman.

McGuire let out a quick gasp, then a quiet whimper that slowly cascaded into open weeping. Rondal McGuire, the King of Cocaine, stood before his judge and jury bawling like a child, a totally defeated and broken man. *Pitiable. One could almost feel sorry for the man…but only if they were unaware of how many lives he had ruthlessly destroyed.*

"Sentencing is set for one month from today," ordered the judge. "Ladies and gentlemen of the jury, you are discharged. Thank you for your service. The defendant is remanded into custody. Bailiff, take custody of the defendant."

"Your Honor," protested defense counsel Houseman, "my client has been at large on bail for the last six months and has posed no threats."

"Given the nature of the crimes, the defendant's age, and financial situation, it is the determination of the court that the defendant now poses a flight risk. The defendant will remain in custody until sentencing." The judge pounded her gavel, thereby signifying that court was adjourned.

Barnett stood and patted Sumner on the shoulder. "Superb job."

"No, you're the one who conducted this prosecution," Sumner protested.

"Well, the fact is, Mr. Rondal McGuire will never get out of prison. He'll die in there, and society will be better for it."

"No question," agreed Sumner. "The book is finally closed on his long and sordid career."

§

When Sumner returned to the Narcotic Bureau, he was greeted by Street Enforcement Team Officer Moran. "Hey, we need some help. We've got an old friend of yours here."

"What's up?"

"We picked up a hype you went to school with— a guy named Greg Brewster."

"No kidding…old 'Baro-o-ouster,'" Sumner reflected on Greg's high school nickname. "You know he was a hell of an athlete until he got involved with drugs."

"His connection is holding big right now," explained Moran. "He's willing to take you in and we'll bust behind the buy."

"Who's the connection?"

"A guy named Johnny Griljava."

"Why don't you use Beto or Melendez or Joe T?" Sumner asked. "I've been in court all morning and these are the only clothes I have," indicating the blue navy blue pin strip suit, white button down shirt, and silk tie he had worn for his appearance in court.

"They're not around and Brewster is spooky. He said he only wants to work with you." "Besides, you guys can pass for brothers."

"You told him I work here?"

"I'm afraid he already knew," explained Moran. "Apparently your reputation precedes you."

That's not good, Sumner thought in passing.

"Oh, what the hell, let me debrief Brewster."

§

Sumner entered the interrogation room where Brewster was being confined. At first glance Sumner was able to determine that he was under the influence of heroin. After the customary pleasantries associated with a reunion of old friends, Sumner learned that Griljava was a mid level dealer supplying street level dealer-users. Griljava required that everyone who made a purchase was to shoot dope in the house before leaving with any narcotics. At the moment he was in possession of several ounces of heroin.

"This is going to be difficult," Sumner explained to Moran and his partner Bill Parks. "He requires everyone to shoot dope before he will allow them to leave with any contraband."

"What do you want to do?"

"We'll go in and I'll attempt to make a purchase," Sumner explained. "I'll make up some bullshit story about why I can't shoot the dope right now and see if he will cooperate. If not, I'll do the best I can to make observations of criminal activity and the presence of illicit property sufficient to justify the bust...then we take the place down. Don't be disappointed if this all gets dismissed."

Sumner walked down the hall to the Crime Scene Investigations Unit where he was fitted with a body transmitter. He then enlisted Narcotics Officer James Kaiser and his partner "Wild Bill" Hofsler to operate the monitor recorder.

"You're going in wearing a suit and tie?" asked Kaiser.

"It's that or my knickers, and if I do that, the guy's wife will want me to come back every day." Kaiser and Hofsler snickered.

§

An unmarked MERGE Team Unit that Officer Moran had requested to assist was already in position down the street from the target's residence when they arrived. Sumner and Brewster proceeded toward the residence. *Goats, the guy has goats grazing in his front yard.*

"What's with the goats?" asked Sumner.

"I guess it's easier than mowing the lawn," replied Brewster. *Some lawn, looks like all weeds.*

The door was answered by a slender Hispanic man in his mid-twenties.

"You back already?" he asked Brewster in surprise.

"This is my buddy Les," explained Brewster. "He's in a pinch and wants to know if you can help him out."

"Come on in." Griljava swung the door open.

Just then an idea began to germinate in Sumner's mind. He untied the rope holding one of the goats and walked the goat into the house like a dog on a leash.

"What's with goat?" asked Griljava.

"I like animals," replied Sumner. "I lived on a ranch when I was a kid and we had goats."

Griljava looked at Brewster with a measure of curiosity.

"He's a little screwy," said Brewster gesturing with his index finger in circles around his ear. "The war messed up his head."

"Why are you all dressed up?" asked Griljava.

"I have to go to court this afternoon."

Griljava stiffened noticeably. "What's the beef?"

"Assault and battery," Sumner explained. "When I got home from Nam, my old lady was shacking up with some punk...I had to beat the shit out of both of them."

Griljava relaxed in the assurance that it was not a drug violation for which he might be snitching for the police in return for a reduced sentence.

"What do you need?"

"I'm going to be coming down at about 3:00," Sumner explained. "I need a couple bags to get well as soon as I get out of court."

"You'll have to shoot the dope here...nothing leaves unless it's in your body."

"Hey...I'm crazy, I'm not stupid. Do you really think I'm going to waltz into a courtroom filled with cops while I'm loaded?"

"Sorry, man, I don't let anything leave this house unless I see you shoot some dope first."

"I can't shoot now."

"Well, come back when you get out of court."

Sumner sat on the sofa petting the goat. "You really want me coming back here in full withdrawal, snot running out of my nose and puking my guts out...the cops with never suspect anything there, will they?"

The goat started biting the corner of the sofa cushion, tearing away the fabric and proceeding to eat the stuffing.

"I'm sorry, man, but I don't know you and...hey be cool, man, your goat is eating my sofa!"

"It's your goat. I'm just visiting with him."

"Shit, man, that's not cool. My old lady is going to be pissed."

"Look, man, I gotta get to court." Sumner laid two $20 bills on the coffee table. "Just give me the junk."

"Man, look at my sofa," lamented Griljava as Sumner pulled the goat away from its meal. The goat then turned and bit onto the money Sumner had placed on the coffee table. Griljava grabbed the money from the goat's mouth.

"Get that fucking goat out of here," he ordered. "My old lady is going to go ballistic."

Sumner stood and pulled the goat toward the front door as he held out his hand to receive the heroin. Griljava stood, nodding his head as he assessed the damage to his furniture.

"Hey, man, I gotta go," called Sumner gesturing with left hand for Griljava to hand him the dope.

Griljava stood with his left hand on his forehead murmuring in Spanish as he handed Sumner two rolled balloons containing heroin. Brewster exited as Sumner stepped from the living room to the porch whispering "Banzai" into the microphone of the body transmitter. "Banzai" was the prearranged signal for the bust team to take down the residence. Sumner then tied the rope holding the goat to the faucet at the edge of the porch as the bust team deployed at the two entrances to the house.

"Police, you're under arrest. Come out with your hands up!" called Officer Moran in compliance with sections 844 and 1531 of the California Penal Code, the so called "knock and notice" requirement.

Sumner gently patted the goat on the head. "Banzai, that's going to be your new name," said Sumner to the goat. "And thanks for the help, little buddy."

"He's headed for the toilet," yelled Officer Kaiser from the backyard, a sure indication that the suspect intended to dispose of evidence.

Kaboom! The front door exploded off its hinges in response to a kick from the size twelve boot of the MERGE Team Officer Glen Harris. The Narcotics Officers and uniformed MERGE Officers stormed the residence as Sumner stood in the sunshine outside petting his newest friend "Banzai."

Brewster was frantic running back and forth in front of the house yelling "What the hell is going on?"

Sumner stood at the edge of the porch, petting the goat as the uniformed MERGE Officers exited with a handcuffed and terrified Johnny Griljava.

"I named him Banzai," said Sumner as the officer and suspect passed. "He's my new best friend." *That ought to verify that I'm nuts.*

Sumner entered the residence. "What did you come up with?"

"About two ounces and a lot of paraphernalia, scales, measuring spoons, balloons," advised Moran.

"Wow, certainly looks like possession for sale…oh, yeah, and, uh, sales of heroin," replied Sumner displaying the two balloons. "I'm going to take Brewster back to PAB before he pisses his pants."

CHAPTER 72

Sumner returned to the Narcotic Unit where he deposited Brewster in an interrogation room then proceeded to book the evidence and began writing his report.

"You bought dope dressed like that?" asked Sergeant Springer.

"I felt it was time to begin upgrading the image of undercover narcotic officers," cracked Sumner.

"I'm beginning to think that he could buy dope in uniform," replied Lt. Edwards.

"What do you think about adopting a goat as our unit mascot?" asked Sumner. "I'm thinking that navy blue Brooks Brother's pin stripe suits, silk neckties, and a goat should be the new undercover narc dress."

"You really are losing it. Aren't you due back in court?" scoffed Edwards as he walked to his office, shaking his head.

§

"What are you working on?" inquired Sergeant Jansen, the new buy team supervisor.

"Probation reports," replied Sumner. "I have about fifty to write. You know, somebody ought to create a form that addresses the essential issues that should be covered in these reports."

"Why don't you do that."

"Maybe I will…when I get some free time."

"What's the status?" inquired Lt. Edwards.

"Most of the crooks have pled. The probation department is waiting for my reports to make their recommendations to the judges for sentencing," Sumner replied. "Have you given anymore thought to my idea of buying a goat?"

"You've been out in the sun too long. Your brain is starting to fry."

"That goat was the indispensible element that led to success in the Griljava case. With that goat I could get in anywhere, buy from anyone."

"I know you like screwing with people's heads, but the administration is not buying you a goat," replied Edwards. "Now get those probation reports finished up."

Nobody gets it. Maybe I should get a three legged dog. That would mess with everyone's mind. Awww, nobody is going to take this seriously.

§

"Sumner!" Lt. Edwards bellowed. "Judge Zachery's clerk just called. McGuire is going to be sentenced at 1:30…she wants you there."

"Really? I've never been requested at a sentencing before."

"Well, let's get going. I'm coming with you."

"Why?"

"I want you to introduce me to Judge Zachery."

"OK, let's go."

§

Sumner and Edwards drove downtown to the Superior Court's courthouse. When they arrived, Kevin Barnett and Spencer Houseman were sitting in the empty courtroom, waiting for the sentencing to begin. Barnett looked up and smiled, obviously delighted to have an ally to talk with rather than sitting in silence with glowering Houseman. The bailiff entered the courtroom and picked up the telephone. "Bring up the defendant."

The court clerk and stenographer entered the courtroom as the sheriff's deputies brought in McGuire. McGuire was clothed in the standard inmate's orange jumpsuit and was handcuffed and shackled. He was seated next to his attorney.

"We're ready, Your Honor," the bailiff spoke into the phone. "All rise. Department 17 of the Superior Court of Santa Clara County is now in session, the Honorable Judge Judith Zachery presiding."

The judge entered and took her seat on the bench. The clerk read the matter before the court. The judge looked down at McGuire.

"The defendant will rise," she ordered.

McGuire and Houseman stood facing the judge.

"It is the ruling of this court that the defendant will be imprisoned in the state penitentiary for a period of not less than twenty-five years and not more than his natural life."

McGuire dropped to his knees as he let out a mournful moan, then began to cry unashamedly, tears pouring from his eyes. The two deputies stepped to either side of him and lifted him to his feet, but he collapsed in their arms as they walked him from the courtroom.

Edwards and Barnett looked at Sumner in astonishment. While the sentence was not excessive for the nature of the crime, it was extremely unusual for someone so socially and politically connected to receive such a sentence. *Good for you, judge. That's showing a pair.*

The judge stood.

"All rise," called the bailiff. "This court stands adjourned."

The judge stopped at the door to her chambers. "Would the district attorney and the investigating officer please join me in my chambers."

"Come on, Boss," said Sumner as they headed for the door.

"Your Honor, I would like to introduce my supervisor, Lt. Don Edwards, commander of the San Jose Police Narcotic Unit." They shook hands. "I have been raving about the no-nonsense efficiency of your court so much that the Lieutenant wanted very much to meet you."

"Well, the pleasure is all mine," smiled the judge. "You have excellent people, Lieutenant."

"He is one of my best."

"Mr. Barnett, Officer Sumner, you gentlemen conducted a remarkable investigation and prosecution of someone whom I believe, after reading Officer Sumner's report to the probation department and their report to court, has been a frightful bane upon society for quite some time. You gentlemen did your part to remove this affliction, and today the court did our part." "Congratulations, gentlemen, on a noble service to your community."

"It might have all been for nothing without your steady hand throughout the trial and your fearless sentencing," pointed out Barnett.

"Indeed," agreed Sumner and Edwards.

"Well, I know there will be some backlash. He has friends in high places, but this man has to go away," mused the judge. "Thank you, gentlemen, for an expertly conducted prosecution."

"Lieutenant, may I have a word with you?" requested the judge.

Sumner and Barnett exited to the elevator to head back to the office.

"Have you ever had anything like that occur?" asked Sumner.

"Never; I've never had a judge thank me for doing my job," replied Barnett. "I've never even heard of it ever happening."

"Well, we've got a lot to live up to in the future."

"I'm up to it," replied Barnett. "It's been a pleasure. I look forward to working with you a great deal in the future." The two men shook hands. Sumner took a seat on a park bench outside the courthouse to wait for Lt. Edwards.

§

The last of the trials of the Dillingham/Swearengen operation were now completed. With the exception of four suspects, minor players, who had as yet to be apprehended, Sumner had achieved a 100 percent conviction rate. *All I have to do is complete all those other probation reports and I can get back out on the street.* Sumner heaved a huge sigh, happy to be done with this operation.

RETROSPECT:

Ted Sumner ultimately took an early retirement from the San Jose Police Department. At that point, a full account of his exploits would fill volumes. But he is anything but a man of leisure. He has remained active teaching Kenpo Karate and has achieved the honored rank of Ninth Degree Black. His domineering father would have been pleased to learn that he has also become a successful businessman and author. But there seemed to be no rest from the activities of criminals for former Officer Sumner.

CHAPTER 73

Technically, no peace officer is ever totally "off duty." They can be off duty (out of service) as far as the department is concerned but their responsibility to the public never sleeps. That's why they are required to go armed even when they are not officially on duty. As a result of years on the street they become defensive predators, ever alert, constantly assessing potential threats and evaluating people and situations even when on vacation. It becomes part of their thought process and it affects the way they interact with people, park their cars and even their choice of seating when dining out. Some might consider this mind set to be obsessive; but to those whose lives depend on being constantly vigilant, it is the difference between the quick and the dead.

Ted Sumner had become a finely honed weapon. It was not just his street smarts and years on the force, though those were considerable; it was that in concert with his decades of martial arts training that had molded him into what Ed Parker (Creator of American Kenpo Karate) called a "thinking warrior." Ted had developed that quiet confidence that allowed him to handle intense and stressful situations with a minimum display of trauma or outward show of force. Nevertheless, when occasion called for it, he could unleash the Tasmanian devil hidden within the blue uniform.

Even the most battle tested veterans have to take R&R from time to time; and so it was that Sumner and his wife chose to take a vacation. Suzanne Francois, who had recently become Mrs. Suzanne Sumner is one of those rare women who have extraordinary beauty, natural charm and the patience to be a wife and companion to, not just a dedicated police officer, but even more trying, a fanatical martial artist. Her friends were convinced that at some point she would be nominated for Sainthood for being able to live harmoniously with Sumner. To him she was the reason for his existence.

The Sumners were staying with close friends, the Williams, at their vacation condominium in Lake Tahoe that winter. Sumner had known Bill and Kelly Williams from high school days, years before they had become husband and wife. Kelly was a stunning blonde and, like Suzanne, she had both the charm and the patience to be married to a policeman.

Bill Williams had been Sumner's Sergeant and handler during many of his undercover assignments at San Jose Police Narcotics. Bill had retired from SJPD as a Captain and was currently working as the Chief of the Palo Alto Police Department near Stanford University. This was an opportunity for good friends to relax and get away from the pressures of the job.

The snow was deep and Bill and Ted had kicked off their boots and were sprawled in the living room in front of the fire when their wives returned from the grocery store. The ladies were planning a Chateaubriand for dinner.

The split level condo featured bedrooms and a guest room down stairs, just past the front door. Upstairs was the living room and kitchen with a loft sleeping area directly above the kitchen. Ted and Suzanne Sumner occupied the guest room.

A couple of doors over from the Williams's condo, there arose the typical weekend renter racket created by a group of six or seven inebriated men in their early to mid twenties. They had arrived for a weekend of snow boarding and "fun" and were noisily unpacking without thought or concern for their neighbors. The young men had paid close attention when the two women had arrived back at the condo, however. They watched them carry in the groceries by themselves and assumed they were alone.

Later in the evening Sumner went downstairs to the guest room get a pair of dry socks for Suzanne. As he approached the landing he was

surprised to see front door slowly opening. Instantly he became the predator. In the gathering darkness he crouched and watched with anticipation as the shadow of a young man crept stealthily in the posture of a
prowler entering the doorway. Sumner was hidden by the darkness. He
took a breath, let it half way out and suddenly slammed his flattened right
hand into the intruder's upper chest, with his middle finger positioned just
over the bronchial nerve. The man let out an, "u-fff" as the breath was
knocked out of his chest. He staggered back a step and with wide eyes reflecting the yard light he stammered, "…wrong house." Sumner drove his
finger into the intruder's throat cavity applying sharp pressure onto the
bronchial nerve. The young man gagged and choked as he reeled back-
ward out the door flipping over the porch railing and landing face down
in four feet of snow. The stunned young man got up, took a panicky look
at Sumner standing in the doorway like a vengeful wraith and ran back to
the security of his friends.

§

The very next night was Monday Night Football and, as was their
custom, the two couples dressed for a casual evening out. Sumner wore
his favorite Tommy Bahama, Tropical Traveler shirt—mostly white with
subtle blossoms on the left shoulder and right side at the waist, tan Dock-
ers and as a concession to the cold, his well worn leather bomber jacket.
He and Suzanne piled into the back seat of the William's SUV and they
drove to a local sports bar to enjoy the game over dinner. They were discussing a spectacular pass play that had just occurred when they noticed a
group of men enter the sports bar as if they owned the place.

Bill recognized them as the crowd staying in their complex. He looked
at Sumner in the subtle communicative mode that soldier and police officers under duress so understand and cocked his head as if to say, *look who
just walked in.* Sumner nodded imperceptibly and followed the group with
his eyes like a lion watching a gazelle.

While the prowler would not look Sumner in the eye, the other five
stared at him with undisguised contempt. The women were not concerned and as police officers one learns to ignore such things so Ted and
Bill turned back to the game.

At half time Sumner excused himself and headed for the comfort of the men's room. As he approached the table occupied by the young men he observed the larger of the men move his chair. He positioned it directly in Sumner's path. Ignoring the obvious belligerence, Sumner started to walk around the chair when the seated man thrust out his arm, grabbing Sumner's right wrist in a vise like grasp. Without hesitation Sumner countered the attack with a Kenpo self defense technique known as "Crossing Talon". He instantly leveraged a reversal of the grab and holding the man's right wrist, with great force drove the blade of his own left forearm into the nerve cavity just above the back of his attacker's elbow, commonly known as the "crazy bone". This attack on the nerve had the effect of causing the muscles in the man's right arm to fail and his elbow to hyper extend, assisted, of course, by pressure from Sumner's left arm. The man screamed in reaction to the excruciating pain as his buddies jumped to their feet intent on assisting their friend.

"One more step and I'll break this assholes arm" Sumner snarled. The expression on his face was that of a feral animal protecting its kill. Williams moved instantly to cover his friend, his hand on his concealed 9MM pistol. Sumner shook his head "no" and Williams removed his hand from the pistol.

The bouncer shoved his way through the curious onlookers and demanded that Sumner release the individual that he perceived as the victim of the altercation. "Just a moment" Sumner said quietly to the bouncer. Then turning to his captive he said through bared teeth, "You just had to be a little asshole, didn't you?" "Your buddy got his pride ruffled and you just had to show you were a bigger asshole." Then, he applied a little more pressure to the nerve cavity which elicited a yelp of pain. "Well you really showed everyone didn't you". At that point Sumner realized that when he had applied, "Crossing Talon," he had moved so quickly that it had lifted the attacker and his chair off the floor and that, now, the leg of the man's chair was directly on the top of Sumner's left foot. As the adrenalin rush wore off the pain was excruciating, but he dare not let on that he was in more pain than the asshole.

Sumner applied another slight burst of pressure to the elbow warning, "I ought to break this so you will have something to remember what a little asshole you are." At that point the worried bouncer, concerned that the situation was about to escalate, moved a little closer and warned, "Don't do that, let him go" to which Sumner replied "just a second". Then to the attacker he spoke very softly, "you are such a little asshole you just aren't worth it". Inwardly Sumner felt like an idiot. He had to get the chair off his foot but he did not want to loose the painful psychological victory he had just won, with any show of weakness. His final statement was punctuated with action. He released the asshole by tossing over the chair and the jerk into a heap on the floor saying, as he turned toward the men's room, "grow up, asshole".

The bouncer was an off duty Oakland Police Officer and ski enthusiast. He had recognized Chief Williams and approached him asking, "What the hell's going on here?" Williams had informed him who Sumner was and of what he was capable. The bouncer smiled thinly and then politely but firmly escorted the "neighbors" out the building with the parting warning "you dumb asses have no idea how lucky you are."

Sumner had a little reminder of his own errors in that encounter. His left foot was black and blue from his ankle to his toes as a result of the chair landing on his foot. It took over a month for the bruising to clear up, but fortunately he had no broken bones. Lesson learned. "Off duty?"... yeah, right!

CHAPTER 74

Ted Sumner sat in the office of his 5,500 square foot martial arts dojo on Malone Road in San Jose's Willow Glen area. He shifted his position uncomfortably in response to the nagging pain in his hip. He was just six months post surgery from having his left hip replaced.

Pain is your friend, he thought. *Pain is your teacher...* he continued the Mantra. He was no masochist. He just didn't like drugs. Through his decades in the martial arts, he had spent countless hours studying the healing arts and he had come to realize that western pain medicine too often blurred the senses and dulled the mind. They had their uses, but his choice was to discontinue their use as soon as the pain became tolerable. After six months he still struggled with the after effects of major surgery.

His school was a 5500 square foot tribute to eastern taste and western efficiency. In addition to a large matted area there was a locker room with showers... immaculate, of course. The strength center boasted a fully equipped weight room, and he had added an 800 square foot treatment room where the healing arts were taught and practiced. Finally there was his large office where he sat brooding over an assortment of bills and statements that represented the schools previous month's overhead. Carefully he entered them into Quick Books—not his favorite task.

Along the wall of the treatment room were three doors covering the electrical panels. Whenever someone opened the front door of the school, the electrical panel doors would rattle, letting Ted know he had visitors.

The doors rattled. Sumner glanced at the clock; it read 3:00 p.m. *No students due,* he thought, *It must be the UPS driver…a little early, but it's about his scheduled time.* With that assumption, he turned back to his computer and finished the Quick Books entries before heading for the dojo area.

As he walked out of his office, through the treatment room and into the dojo, he noticed a young man in his late twenties exiting the front door with two of the samurai swords that had been on display on the wall below his diplomas and awards. Sumner yelled "Hold it" and started toward the thief. His surgical wounds slowed his gait to more of a shuffle.

The young thief stopped in his tracks, saw the shuffling old guy coming at him and hesitated for a moment between fight and flight. He made his decision and began to draw the katana (the longer of the two swords), which was razor sharp. Sumner had a split second to decide whether to veer off and arm himself with the remaining samurai sword on the wall or increase his speed to close the distance and engage the thief before he fully drew the sword. He made the tactical decision. If he chose the sword, there was a chance that one or both would be severely injured or killed. Ignoring the burning pain in his hip, he put on a burst of speed and closed with the suspect while the katana's blade was still ten inches into the scabbard.

The world shifted into slow motion as Sumner engaged his opponent. Mere feet from contact, Sumner had time to mentally dissect his opponent. *Twenty-eight or twenty-nine years old, six foot one or two and around 195 pounds, no need to hold back.* Sumner's hand covered the final six inches and his right hand clamped onto the thief's throat in what is known in Kenpo as a tiger jaw. Simultaneously his left hand grabbed the burglar's right hand in which he was holding the sword. The move neutralized the man's attempt to draw the weapon and left him at Sumner's mercy, of which little remained. Sumner dropped his weight, pulled the opponent toward him, and pivoted sharply, sweeping the thief off his feet and slamming him to the hard floor of the school's foyer. In the following move, he slammed his right knee into the man's ribs, released the tiger jaw and, though the assailant appeared unconscious, threw two sharp punches into his face.

Sumner recovered his swords, took a deep breath, and carefully assessed the situation. The surge of adrenaline still coursed through his veins. He became enraged that this person had intended to remove his Sumner's head from his shoulders with Sumner's own weapon. He wasn't just a thief; he was also a would be assassin.

Still under the overpowering influence of adrenaline, Sumner grabbed the thief and applied a resuscitation technique of the healing arts. It had been taught to him by the great Professor Sig Kufferath who counseled, "You have mastered the techniques by which life can be taken; now you must master the techniques by which life can be saved." Once the man had been restored to consciousness, Sumner beat him unconscious again, an act which he later regretted, but left him in awe of the overwhelming and inexorable power of adrenaline.

Sumner then dragged the unconscious thief to his office and dumped him in a corner like a rag doll. He was still in a rage when he dialed the number for police dispatch, bypassing the normal complaint desk. His anger began to cool as dispatch answered. At that moment, the thief came to and sat hunched in a ball in the corner of Sumner's office crying and sobbing "Don't hit me anymore, please don't hit me anymore."

The panel doors rattled. That unmistakable sound indicated that someone had entered the school. Sumner started toward the front when a familiar voice called out "Hey, Ted, I have a report of a theft. Where are all the body parts?" Into the office strode Sumner's longtime friend Jim Palmentier. They had gone through the academy together thirty years earlier.

Sumner looked at his friend with a mixture of relief and disbelief. "I don't believe it," he said, "you're still in harness" (still working in uniform).

"Just a few more years," Jim replied, then he turned his attention to the shivering, sobbing suspect. "You idiot!" he spat. "You're lucky you're alive...And quit whining."

Without ceremony, Jim grabbed the office phone and dialed the station. After a quick background check, he hung up the phone, shook his head, and looked at the suspect. "You didn't waste any time, did you?" Jim then turned to Ted, pensively shook his head and said "This clown just got out of San Quentin this morning…Did five years for burglary. His parole officer wants him booked."

As Jim handcuffed the suspect, Ted folded his arms in mock casualness. It was an attempt to cover the aftereffects of the adrenaline high that was rapidly fading. The residual dose caused a slight tremor in Ted's hands. He cleared his throat and asked "How's is Bonnie?"

Bonnie Palmentier, Jim's beautiful wife, was a former classmate of Ted's. Her maiden name was Bonnie Budrose. She and Ted had attended grade school, junior high, and high school together. Jim smiled broadly.

"She's doing great. I'll tell her I ran into you. How is your family?"

"My wife left me twenty years ago. But both my kids are doing great. My son is on the PD and my daughter is an executive with Dolby Labs in San Francisco."

"Sorry to hear that. Did you ever remarry?"

"As a matter of fact, I have been dating a fabulous woman for the last ten years. We're getting married at the end of August".

"Ten years? She stuck around for ten years?"

"Jim, I resolved when my divorce was final that I would not remarry, regardless of the woman, until my kids were grown, educated, employed and out of the house. I would not allow any relationship to distract me from my job as a father. Suzanne Francois never gave me any trouble about it. She is an outstanding woman."

"Suzanne Francois…that's a beautiful name."

"And she is a stunningly beautiful woman."

"You're lucky a lucky guy. I don't know too many women who would stick around for ten years without some promise of marriage."

"You're right. I got the right woman this time."

Jim grunted as he lifted the prisoner to his feet. "Looks like you're going to do the rest of that ten year's sentence inside the joint." With that, Jim walked his prisoner to the patrol car parked outside. Ted followed them to the door. Jim carefully deposited the unrepentant felon in the backseat, taking care that the battered thief didn't bump his head. Jim climbed into the driver's seat, rolled down his window and yelled, "See you around" and sped off.

Just then, the diminutive Vietnamese proprietor of the small grocery store next door appeared and cautiously inquired, "What'd he do?" Ted explained that the thief had tried to steal Ted's prized swords. He added that the would-be repeat thief had just been released from prison and would be going back. The proprietor nodded knowingly. Then he volunteered that the suspect had come into his store asking where he could find a pay phone. He had directed the man to an improvised phone booth he had constructed that had an exterior door that opened next to the front door of Sumner's school. The grocer then added "When I see him sneak in you door, I know there be trouble."

Sumner stared at the man in disbelief. He didn't dare respond to his commercial neighbor. Fighting another adrenaline surge, Ted turned and walked away. As he reentered the dojo he said to himself "Thanks for the help, dumbass."

Sumner eased into his office chair to continue his paperwork before his students began arriving. As the adrenaline subsided, the pain in his hip began to amplify. *Damn...I've been off the department for years and I still have to deal with crooks and assholes.*

Epilogue

"IT NEVER STOPS"

CHAPTER 75

The members of the force change from time to time, like interchangeable pieces on a chessboard. They put in their time, work hard, and either move on to another profession or eventually retire; but it never stops. The constant grind of the street, the relentless, never ending flood of nefarious crooks, the reprobate enterprise masquerading as "business" and casually referred to by the great uninitiated majority of society as mere criminal activity never quits.

Geoff Sumner grew to be a man, and followed after his father in a variety of ways. For example, he has his own record of bizarre cases. Though his dad was a mere 5'10" and 190 pounds, his mother was from sturdy Irish stock, and that combination produced a son of 6'3" and 210 pounds. Geoff was an athlete who won a bronze medal in the Triathlon and silver in the Toughest Cop Alive (ten events, much like a decathlon) events at the International Police Olympics. In addition, he studied Kenpo from his dad since adolescence. He was blessed with all the physical gifts that God dare endow a mere human. Like his father, Ted, Geoff was a fearless man of action. There was the time he was working patrol in the downtown area:

Geoff responded to a call involving a possible robbery at a pawnshop in the downtown area. When he arrived, he observed two small police officers, of Vietnamese extraction, clinging to a large black suspect as they exit the pawnshop. The suspect effortlessly scraped the two diminutive officers off his arms and turned to face 6'3" of Celtic fury exiting the police car. The suspect realized this new threat was substantial. He fled down and across the street into St. Joseph's Cathedral, the Catholic Archdiocese of San Jose, with Geoff Sumner in hot pursuit. The suspect crashed into the church where 300 guests were attending a wedding, bolted past the bride, groom, and priest who were in the midst of matrimonial vows, vaulted up onto the alter where he grabbed a candlestick holder and turned menacingly toward the onrushing officer and shouted, "Come on, muther fucker." Without breaking stride, Geoff Sumner mounted the alter and broke his nightstick over the suspect's head. At that point the battle began in earnest and escalated to a level of unremitting fury. The spectators watched with mouths agape. They had come prepared to watch the Sacrament of Marriage, but now were witness to a gladiatorial spectacle worthy of the Roman Coliseum.

In the process of subduing the suspect, the combatants managed to destroy virtually everything on the altar. During the struggle, the adrenaline rush got the best of Geoff, and while in the heat of battle he used several less than proper comments yelling "Stay down, you stupid son of a bitch." Finally, he brought the suspect into submission, handcuffed the man, and stood him on his feet.

At that point, he looked out into the church and, for the first time, saw 300 guests, the wedding party, and the attending priest all looking on in shocked fascination. Sumner feared the worst. He quickly replayed the recent events in his mind. Did he use profanity? Probably. Did he make racial slurs? Possibly. Was his job in danger? Most assuredly.

Adrenalin still raging, he stepped up to the priest and whispered "I'm sorry about all this Father," to which the priest replied in a heavy Irish brogue and gesturing with a right cross punch "That's ok, son, sometimes they go down hard."

At this point, the groom stepped up and asked Geoff "Could my wife and I possibly get a picture of you and the crook with the wedding party?" Incredulous, Geoff meekly posed for pictures with this pummeled crook and the bride and groom as well as the entire wedding party. He later speculated that the newlyweds dined out on that story for months.

Later that same evening, Geoff telephoned his father. In a voice heavy with trepidation, he retold the story. At the point where the groom asked for pictures, Ted Sumner broke into bellicose peels of uncontrollable laughter.

When he could finally speak he said "Geoff, I do not miss all the BS of police work, but I do miss nights like you just had."

That didn't allay all of Geoff's concerns about his conduct, but at least he managed a chuckle. All police officers face physical combat at one time or another, but there is no record of any other police officer who has gone into battle with a crook in front of 300 wedding guests on the altar of a Catholic cathedral. This was definitely one for the books.

§

Like his father, Geoff Sumner did not go into law enforcement to stand by and watch. He is generally in the middle of whatever might be going on. Partly, Ted Sumner and his second wife Suzanne were enjoying a relaxing evening at home when, at about six p.m. Ted received a call from his good friend Mike LaMarca.

"Hey, Ted, there are something like fifteen or twenty police cars all around the Almaden Villas. What the hell is going on?"

"And a pleasant good evening to you, too, Mike. How're the wife and kids? Gee, Mike, it looks like the chief, once again, has neglected to call and ask my advice, seeing that I'm RETIRED. Tell you what I'll do though, I'll make some calls, see what I can learn, and if I find out anything significant, I'll call you back and fill you in, OK?"

"Uh, yeah. Thanks, buddy...appreciate it."

"My pleasure, Mike, talk at you later."

Sumner lived in the upscale Almaden Valley area of San Jose. The Villas are a complex of multi-million dollar townhomes built on what is basically a giant rock situated at the entrance to the valley. *Why the hell would there be a bunch of cop cars at the Villas. Nothing there but a bunch of millionaires.* Though he'd never admit it to his friend Mike, Sumner was now quite curious about what was going on with the SJPD in his neighborhood.

Sumner knew his son Geoff was working swing shift that night, so he picked up the phone and tried to contact Geoff on his cell phone. Geoff had followed in his father's footsteps. He not only had become a San Jose police officer, but excelled in every aspect of the job. Moreover, he had become a Kenpo Black Belt of surpassing skill. Geoff was bigger than his father at 6'3" and his rugged good looks have managed to land him several parts in Hollywood feature films and on television.

No answer. Sumner left a message and headed for the next door neighbor's house where Ted and his wife had been invited for poolside cocktails.

§

At about 6:45 p.m. as he was enjoying his second Bombay Sapphire martini while sitting around his neighbor's swimming pool, Geoff called back.

"Hey, Dad, what's up?"

"I understand there's been some activity in our neighborhood. What can you tell me about it?"

Geoff chuckled at what he seemed to feel was an inside joke. "Yeah, sure. You know that Rite Aid Pharmacy about a half mile from your place?"

"Yeah?"

"Well, about five o'clock this afternoon a young punk, ex con entered the pharmacy and pulled a 211." (Armed robbery) What this loser didn't realize was that two of our officers were enjoying a cup of coffee, sitting outside in the front of the Almaden Roasting Company at the other end of the center. They heard the alarm sound as the crook bolted from the pharmacy and the chase was on."

Sumner could picture the scene in his mind and silently shook his head.

"I was the only officer on duty with tactical experience, so dispatch summoned me from the downtown area, ten minutes away." Geoff had served tours of duty in both the rugged METRO Special Operations unit and as a member of the brutally efficient SJPD SWAT Team. "As the only officer with SWAT experience, I knew the routine and ordered the area cordoned off and locked down, then ordered in K-9 Units. When Mark Johnson and his dog Will Rogers arrived, we began a methodical search of the area, including Mike LaMarca's yard. Mike's next door neighbor is a racing enthusiast and has a race car parked in a trailer in his driveway. I searched under the trailer and was ready to move on, but when Mark tried to get the dog to move on, he refused. So Mark began a search of the underneath of the trailer. I felt like an idiot. I had just searched in and under the trailer and if the now the K-9 Officer found something I missed, I'd lose all credibility as a tactical officer. Mark also searched under the trailer and he couldn't find anything either and was ready to move on...but the dog still wouldn't budge," he explained. "We looked at each other, and Mark shrugged his shoulders and unleashed his beast. Will Rogers went under the trailer and actually climbed up over the axel. We could see that the dog was engaged and growling viscously. Then the dog dragged a 125 pound asshole down and out from under the trailer. Mark let his puppy chew on the robber for a few seconds before calling him off. Case closed."

"It sounds like justice has been served," said Sumner. "Thanks for the report."

"No problem. See you in Kenpo class on Tuesday."

RETROSPECT

The K-9 Unit commended Geoff with an honorary K-9 Unit coin, much like our Special Forces coins, for directing 12 operations over the last year in which all eight K-9s got a "bite." The K-9 guys really appreciate a case in which their dogs get to bite a bad guy and the animals are ecstatic that they get to play with a new "toy."

All this happened within a half mile from Ted Sumner's home, coordinated by his son, while Ted was enjoying a martini with his neighbors. Then there was the time... but that's a story for another day. It never stops